The Makers of
Hebrew Books in Italy

THE HOLLAND PRESS LIMITED LONDON MCMLXIII

The Holland Press Ltd
37 Connaught Street
London W2 2AZ

© Holland Press Ltd, London 1963

This edition printed in 1988

ISBN 0 900470 46 1

Printed and bound in Great Britain
by Bookcraft (Bath) Ltd

INSCRIBED

TO

LEWIS W. STEINBACH

WISE AND SKILFUL PHYSICIAN

LOYAL AND DEVOTED FRIEND

LOVER OF HIS PEOPLE AND THEIR INHERITANCE

WORTHY SUCCESSOR TO THE LONG LINE OF THOSE WHO IN ALL THE GENERATIONS OF ISRAEL NOT ONLY FULFILLED THE EXACTING DUTIES OF THEIR NOBLE PROFESSION BUT FOUND TIME FOR THE CULTIVATION OF THE BEAUTIES OF THEIR RELIGION AND ITS LITERATURE; NOT LEAST AMONG WHOM WERE THOSE WHO STOOD AT THE CRADLE OF THE HEBREW PRESS

PREFACE

SOME of the chapters of this book originally appeared as a series of articles entitled "Hebrew Printers and Printing in Italy" published in the Jewish Exponent of Philadelphia in 1906–1907. These have been revised and enlarged.

In preparing the work I had the use of the splendid library of Dr. Julius H. Greenstone, rich in examples of nearly every Hebrew press in the world and containing many incunabula and other rarities. Many of the illustrations in this book are made from his collection.

My manuscript was revised by my wife, and many of her valuable suggestions have found a place in these pages.

TABLE OF CONTENTS

CHAPTER VII.

Daniel Bomberg (1515–1522).

CHAPTER VIII.

Daniel Bomberg (1523–1536).

CHAPTER IX.

Daniel Bomberg (1537–1549).

CHAPTER X.

SOME MINOR PRESSES.

CHAPTER XI.

THE QUARREL OF GIUSTINIANI AND BRAGADINI AND THE CONDEMNATION OF THE TALMUD.

LIST OF ILLUSTRATIONS

LIST OF ILLUSTRATIONS

LIST OF ILLUSTRATIONS

[xvii]

ERRATA

Page 29, line 20,		read	"was" for "were."
" 29, " 24,		"	"among" for "between."
" 30, " 24,		"	"last" for "latter."
" 68, " 8,		"	"had" for "has."
" 159, " 5,		"	"knew" for "know."
" 240, " 23,		"	"1467" for "1407."
" 297, " 4,		"	"Latin" for "Hebrew."
" 319 " 22,		"	"Zeri hayagon."
" 343, " 21,		"	"Zahab."
" 346, " 15, notes,		"	"Abkat."
" 350, " last, "		"	"hashpaat tub" "hamuskalot."
" 354, " "		"	"biur" for "bine."
" 397, " 20, "		"	"Omer Naka."

Indulgence is asked for other typographical errors in transliterating Hebrew titles.

Printer s mark of Gerson Soncino, Rimini

CHAPTER I.

INTRODUCTORY.

Jewish Historiography—Jews of Italy—History of Hebrew Typography—The "Holy Work" of Printing—Gutenberg and the Jews—Legendary Antiquity of Printing—Hebrew Types at Avignon, 1444—Schweinheim and Pannartz at Subiaco—The Benedictines.

THE history of the Jews has not yet been adequately presented, for the sources whence alone sound information is obtainable have been made accessible only in recent times. Modern Christian scholarship has scarcely touched upon the history of the Jews of the Christian Era and it is only within the last century that Jewish scholars have turned their attention to an historical consideration of their people. Before the nineteenth century neither Jewish nor Christian scholarship could do justice to the subject for in addition to lack of sufficient knowledge, scholars were influenced by conceptions which, though different in origin and theory, led to the same paradoxical conclusion, namely, that since the destruction of the temple at Jerusalem the Jews had no history. Jewish scholars conceived the life of the Jews in their dispersion throughout the nations of the world as a punishment for "on account of our sins have we been exiled from our country and taken far away from our land."* Christian scholarship

* From the Mussaf prayer on New Year's Day, see Dembitz "Jewish Services in Synagogue and Home", Phila. 1898, p. 150, where the author says that this prayer "is one of the first banished wherever men deal boldly with the liturgy."

went a step further and considered the dispersion as a punishment visited on the Jews because of their rejection of Jesus and explained their partial preservation by the legend of the Wandering Jew, which, translated into the language of theology, signified that the Jew was preserved as a wanderer on the face of the earth as a living witness to the truth of Christianity.

When the discoveries of the great explorers, the Renaissance of letters and art and the Protestant Reformation broadened the outlook of men, a new conception of Jewish history was made possible. Scepticism and heresy made great breaches in the old entrenchments of religion and as soon as the new invading forces found themselves securely established they subjected the entire wealth of ideas of the olden time to re-examination and revision. The literary remains of annalists and chroniclers were studied anew from a point of view that represented the interest of men in the real things of life rather than in those alleged truths that had so long been considered as alone worthy of acquisition. Preceded by some minor attempts Jacob Christian Basnage, a French Protestant, produced the first history of the Jews during the Christian Era, a work that remained the best of its kind until Jewish historiography of the nineteenth century began.

One of the results of the political emancipation of the Jews at the end of the eighteenth century was the development of their historic consciousness. True, they had never lacked the strongest feeling of solidarity, which had led to organized resistance against attempts made to surpress their nationality, but these sentiments of national and racial solidarity served only to stimulate their religious faith and keep alive their love of Zion. The scant chronicles of the middle ages were mere genealogies, martyrologies and records of persecutions;* the loftier sentiments of the literati in the philosophical, theological and poetic literature expressed on the one hand the contrition of a broken people who believed themselves punished for their sins by their Father in Heaven, on the other their longing for a return to the Promised Land, if only to rest in its sacred soil.†

Political emancipation, with its gift of civil rights, transmuted into an intellectual concept the emotional sentiment that had inspired and sus-

---

*Such as Abraham ibn Daud's "Book of Tradition" (Sefer Hakabbalah), Abraham Zacuto's "Book of Genealogies" (Sefer Yuhasin), Joseph Hacohen's "Chronicles of the Kings of France and Turkey" (Sefer Dibre Hayamim lemalkhe Zarfat umalkhe bet Ottoman Hatogar) and "Vale of Tears" (Emek Habakha), David Gans' "Branch of David" (Zemah David), Gedaliah ibn Yahya's "Chain of Tradition" (Shalshelet Hakabbalah) and Judah ibn Verga's "Rod of Judah" (Shebet Yehudah).

† "How can Judah forget Judah?
    All is emptiness compared with my love for thee,
    Until I enter thy gates with thanksgiving,
    Where I long to abide, . . .
    That I may prepare my grave in thy land."
From a poem of Judah Halevi, quoted by Edelman and Dukes "Treasures of Oxford" London 1851, p. 51.

tained the Jewish nation throughout the centuries of its dispersion. The Jew released from the Ghetto and made a part of the state became susceptible to the influences that were awake in Europe. While the tendency of the newly released Jew was to disregard his national heritage and with ardent patriotism to identify himself with his new-found mother country, he was likewise strongly influenced by the wave of nationalism that broke over Europe with the fall of Napoleon. For the first time since their dispersion the Jewish people became conscious of the fact that their records and institutions, preserved for centuries, formed a substantial basis for an account of their history, and we find the great pioneers of Jewish historiography contemporaries of the leaders of the political movements that unified Italy and Germany and established the independence of Greece. The histories of Jost, Graetz and Cassel are monuments of vast learning and splendid plan, but their achievement is insufficient, for they attempted nothing less comprehensive than a history of the Jews from the beginnings to their own times. Their great contemporaries Zunz, Rapaport, Steinschneider and others devoted themselves on the other hand to the more fruitful work of discovering and presenting the sources of history. In this field an ever increasing number of scholars are preparing the ground for histories of the Jews in the lands of their dispersion from which there shall ultimately be written a great universal history wherein the last two thousand years of the life of this people may find adequate expression.

The story of the Jews of Italy has never even been attempted. The Jews of Spain have had their Amador de los Rios, the Jews of Portugal their Kayserling; the Jews of Italy still await their historian. We have such medieval chronicles as Abraham Zacuto's "Book of Genealogies", and Joseph Ha-Cohen's "Vale of Tears"; but no Vasari has recounted the lives of Jewish literary artists, no Guicciardini has unravelled the threads of ghetto histories, no Machiavelli has analyzed the motives of their leaders. Even the chroniclers are far too few, the biographers entirely lacking, for Jewish writers were concerned with matters of the spirit rather than of the body; they recorded the ideas rather than the lives of men. Their writings contain none of those detailed descriptions and personal touches that make the heroes of Plutarch and Suetonius live again for us, the looks of the man, his habits, his way of speech, his experiences and opinions; all those details that give living interest to the flitting shade of his memory. By the flickering rush light of a stray reference, through a title page or colophon, an approbation or introduction, we may catch a glimpse of the man himself, but the real records, if any there be, from which his personal history might be constructed, lie hidden away in the dusty nooks of unvisited libraries. If this be true even of many of the great men of Italian Jewry, how much more so of the humbler craftsmen whose lives are less heroic in outline, less picturesque in achievement.

The impression seems to prevail that the Italian Jews were an insignificant factor in European Jewish life, an impression due, no doubt, to the fact that modern historical scholarship found its greatest development among the Jews of central Europe, and occupied itself, most naturally, with the history of its own communities. Within the last twenty-five years the lamp of historical scholarship has commenced to illumine the darkness of forgotten corners of libraries and archives, of synagogues and cloisters, of ducal and episcopal palaces, where the records of the trials and wanderings of the Jews of Italy have lain in an obscurity no less profound than that which conceals the mortal remains of the heroes of these Odyssies.*

The instinct for culture and classical tradition never died out among the Jews of Italy. They cultivated the Hebrew, Italian and Latin literatures, and their thirst for knowledge was turned into every channel open to them. They mingled in the learned and polite society of the Courts and participated in the highest culture of the times as

* It is significant that when some of the monasteries were secularized in Naples in 1860, the government of Italy came into the possession of books and manuscripts, said to be of great value, relating to Hebrew antiquities. (Hebraische Bibliographie 4 : 70). The Jewish Chronicle of London, quoting the 'Educatore Israelitico', states that a congregational library was discovered in the town of Pitiliano, an obscure place in Tuscany. (Heb. Bib. 4 : 119).

long as they could elude the jealous eye of the Church. Since the fourteenth century they had attempted to establish congregational libraries, but the constant persecution to which they were subjected, and the ever grasping hand of the Inquisitor, made it impossible to maintain such collections until 1767, when Mantua appears as the first of the Italian cities to establish a permanent communal library.

From these record rooms and libraries preserved by Christian and Jew, lips long silent in the dust may speak again to tell us the story of sorrows and tribulations withstood and outlived, of ambitions vaulting to the skies but thwarted by the bounds of intolerance, of thoughts surpressed that might have leavened the life of a generation, of impulses seeking to do the work of the world but forced to expend themselves within the narrow limits of the ghetto. In a certain sense it is true that the history of the Jews of the dispersion is a history of arrested growth, of dwarfed development. Although their power and skill were used by princes and ecclesiastics, no decent public acknowledgment could be made of it. The Church took away from the Jews what individual churchmen often gladly gave them, honor, wealth and station. To-day the instinctive liberality of the Italian character, nurtured by a most ancient and unbroken tradition of culture, has given to the Jews, freed from ecclesiastical restrictions, an equal station as citizens. It is sufficient to say that the

Jew in Italy, without being obliged to give up his affiliation with the synagogue, participates in the highest councils of state, presides at its great universities, serves as commander-in-chief of all of the armies of the nation, and sits in the chair of the chief magistracy of the Eternal City.

The history of Hebrew typography is an important auxiliary to the study of Jewish history* for it reflects the degree of culture, the scope of interest and the physical and intellectual activities of the people. The mere outward form of the book will often give significant hints to the student. In the books issued by the early Italian Hebrew presses the quality of the paper, the shining lustre of the ink, the artistic form of the letters, the broad spacing and margins, reflect a life of comparative ease and security in the most cultured of all modern lands. In the later books we may read the vicissitudes of life in the gradual degeneration of the art of Hebrew printing, as well as in the change in the character of the works produced, for trials and tribulations soon cut a people off from the need and enjoyment of the higher and more varied forms of literature and throw them back to the prayer book, where their sorrows may find expression and consolation. Following a period of peace came a time of despair when the Jews of Italy felt the unrestrained fury of mobs, drank the insidious poison distilled by clerical fanaticism, and were ground under the heels of the soldiers of

* Ersch & Gruber 28: 21.

Emperor and Pope. Now and then they enjoyed a temporary respite through the kindly influence of cultured friends of learning and humanity, but on the whole their lives were tragic with a woe unutterable.

In the Scriptorium

All this appears when we review the productions of the Italian presses from the day when in the reign of Pope Sixtus IV the first Hebrew books saw the light, to the day when in the reign of Pope Pius VII, Napoleon's cannon tore wide breaches in the walls of obscurantism and blew the freshening blasts of new thought into the moldy retreats of moribund intolerance. The old Christian and Jewish printers called their art a "holy work."* We moderns are apt to smile at the application of the word "holy" to the productions of the press, for apart from the nature of many modern books, scarcely to be denominated holy by even the most careless critic, holy things, as a rule, do not exist for us at all. We are rapidly losing the Anglo-Saxon concept of *halig*,—perfect; complete; free from blemish; as well as the Roman concept of *sacer*, something apart or hallowed. The levelling tendencies of our day, one of the results of a too generous application of the evolutionary philosophy, assume on the one hand that nothing is perfect, and on the other, that nothing is privileged. Holy things are confused with religious charlatanism and the narrowness of outworn creeds, and therefore held in contempt. It is only in the cemeteries that we find a survival of the old notion in the inscription: "Sacred to the memory of", and even this hallowed ground which of old was under the protection of spirits and gods, is now cut up into public highways at the command of traffic. For our fathers literature was a holy thing, and the writer a man inspired; nor was every one permitted to desecrate the sacred art of writing by using it to set down his own unworthy thoughts; and they called printing a "holy work" for its mission, like that of the pen, was to teach both old and new knowledge. "With-

* Ersch & Gruber 28: 22.

out the press," said Joseph Teomim, "the law would have been forgotten." *

The manner in which the old books were produced, the infinite care devoted to the perfection of details, and the loving interest with which the work was brought ever nearer to perfection, contrast broadly with modern methods, which, always excepting books specially prepared for booklovers, produce great masses of material inferior in style, contemptible in thought, bearing the signs of crudeness and haste and the desire for a speedy monetary equivalent. Considering this contrast we have another point of view from which to understand the use of the phrase "holy work" by the old printers; it was the medieval equivalent of "the old article of Jewish faith, that things done delightfully and rightly were always done by the help and in the spirit of God."†

* Ersch & Gruber 28 : 22 n. 13.

† Ruskin : Praeterita III. 1. "But now that I had a missal of my own and could touch its leaves and turn, and even here and there understand the Latin of it, no girl of seven years old with a new doll is prouder or happier; but the feeling was something between the girl's with the doll and Aladdin's in a new spirit-slave to build palaces for him with jewel windows. For truly a well illuminated missal is a fairy cathedral full of painted windows, bound together to carry in one's pocket, with the music and the blessing of all its prayers besides. And then followed, of course, the discovery that all beautiful prayers were Catholic, all wise interpretations of the Bible, Catholic; and every manner of Protestant written service whatsoever, either insolently altered corruptions, or washed-out and ground-down rags and debris of the great Catholic collects, litanies and songs of praise." A comparison of the old Hebrew prayer book with its modern substitute, tempts me to cite this opinion of Ruskin with much approval.

Different from their conception, yet equally noble, was that of a later generation, which looking back at the work of the press, judged it by what it had accomplished. How it flooded the lowlands of ignorance with the waters of knowledge; how it slowly and surely raised the level of enlightenment and morality in Europe; how it destroyed the foundations of that paternal form of government, which while in theory not different from modern socialistic propaganda, seeking to do all things for the good of all men, was in fact suppressing the will of the many and holding them in subjection and ignorance in order that the few might prosper and rule.

As to the inventor of the art of printing, the contending claims of Gutenberg, Koster and others have not yet been finally adjudicated. David Gans, whose statement on the origin of Hebrew printing in Venice led many into error as to the actual date of the first Hebrew press in Italy, gives credit to Johannes Gutenberg of Strasburg as the inventor of printing at Mainz, in the year 1440, "in the first year of the reign of the pious Emperor Frederick." In a humble way the Jews were connected with the beginnings of the art for they helped Gutenberg to finance his enterprise.

The Jews played a very important part in the finances of the middle ages. Cut off in most cases from other avenues of enterprise, they were obliged to resort to finance for their livelihood, and their wealth made them useful to prince and pope as bankers and collectors of taxes. The Canonical law having high regard for the salvation of Christian souls would not permit interest to be taken for loans of money, a restriction that of course did not apply to Jews who were without the pale of the Church. In order to prevent the money thus accumulated by Jews from remaining in infidel hands, the Church from time to time confiscated their means and by this indirect method, which commended itself to the moral sense of the time, brought back good Christian money into the treasury of the Church for the purpose of promoting God's kingdom on earth in the various ways well known to the ecclesiastical masters of Europe.*

When Gutenberg needed money, he applied to his former associate in Strasburg, Andrea Dmitzehen, who negotiated a loan from the Jews of Ehnheim, an insignificant village in Alsace, and his associate, John Fust, another candidate for the honors of the invention of printing, likewise borrowed money from the Jews, and advanced it to Gutenberg.†

After the art had been once established, contemporary scholars sought to find a most ancient origin for it, in recognition of its high value and in profound reverence for its accomplishments.‡ For, as it was a noble and most excellent thing, it

* Jew. Enc. 12 : 390.

† Loew "Graphische Requisiten" Leipzig 1870, 1 : 189.

‡ Ersch & Gruber 28 : 22.

must necessarily, according to the workings of the medieval mind, have been known to the best and most excellent men who lived in ancient times. In the 19th chapter of the Book of Job, the martyred patriarch says, "Oh, that my words were now written. Oh, that they were printed in a book; that they were graven with an iron pen and lead in the rock forever." What could this possibly have meant, except that the Patriarch Job knew all about the art of printing, and Dr. Abraham Portaleone, distinguished equally as physician and scholar, in his book entitled "Shields of the Mighty" (p. 183 b.) expresses his contempt for the ignorance of his contemporaries in ascribing a modern origin to this ancient art.* "I, indeed," he says, "am not able to restrain myself from accusing all the sages of our time of error for it is true that they believe the art of printing to be a new thing, unknown in former ages, and discovered only one hundred years ago, as they say; and they neither know nor understand that printing has been known to us for hundred and thousands of years, almost back to the time of the creation."

Leaving the realm of fancy and taking our stand upon the ascertained facts, we find the beginning of Hebrew printing in Italy, where the first dated Hebrew books appear in 1475, about thirty-five years after the invention of the art and ten years after its introduction into Italy. Further research

* De Rossi "Annales Hebraeo-typographici Sec. XV." Parma 1795, p. VII.

and discovery may establish an earlier beginning for Hebrew printing for as early as 1444 we hear of Hebrew types in Avignon, and there is some record of a transaction between Procop Waldvogel of Prague, and a Jew named Davin of Caderousse, whereby Waldvogel taught Davin the science and art of printing, and bound himself to give him twenty-seven matrices for Hebrew letters; in return for instruction in the art of dyeing. Davin broke his contract, and he was compelled to re-deliver the matrices and to agree to keep the art of printing secret within a radius of thirty miles.* Quite recently the suggestion has been made that Spain may contest the primacy of Italy in Hebrew typography,† but it is very doubtful whether such theses will ever be supported by indisputable and unambiguous facts.

While Thomas de Torquemada, in an odor of sanctity, was glooming in the Dominican monastery of Segovia, preparing himself for that high office of Inquisitor General of Castile and Leon, through which he became the incarnation of hell on earth for thousands of so-called heretics, his kinsman, Johannes de Turrecremata, was called from his priory at Toledo to become Abbot of Santa Scholastica at Subiaco, in the hills, forty miles from Rome. Even after he was elevated to the cardinalate by Pope Eugenius IV, Turrecremata preferred to spend most of his time amidst the

* Z. H. B. 8 : 46.
† R. E. J. 1907 p. 246; J. Q. R. 20 : 527.

precious treasures of learning of his monastery and in the company of his monks, among whom were some Germans who had seen or heard of the work of the men of Mainz, Frankfurt, and Strasburg, whose new art was slowly making itself felt among the learned.

Among the Christian printers driven from the City of Mainz after its capture by the warrior Archbishop Adolph of Nassau in 1462 were Conrad Schweinheim and Arnold Pannartz, who in the year 1464 knocked at the friendly gates of the monastery of Santa Scholastica, and were received with open arms by the abbot and his monks, and thus began the "holy work" in Italy.

The real meaning of the press was little seen by the church whose rule it was destined to overthrow. The Cardinal-abbot gladly opened the doors of his monastery to the printers, and later took them to the Pope under whose most holy patronage they continued their work.*

In time the eyes of the churchmen were opened, and it was seen that this instrument, which they fondly hoped had been fashioned for further promoting their rule on earth, had become the weapon of the devil and was spreading heresy among the faithful, and with the thunders of excommunication, the fires of autosdafe, the scissors and ink of the censors, they vainly strove to undo the work of the press and to put men back into intellectual

* Putnam "Books and their makers during the Middle Ages" N. Y. and London 1897, 1 : 404.

leading strings. That time had gone by forever. The new thought was given wide expression by the press and the fairy tale popular literature of the Middle Ages was supplanted by matter better adapted to the needs of men. For the Jew, however, there was no Renaissance—no new birth

The pioneer press

with its implication of death and resurrection. Jewish literary tradition had never died but was flourishing vigorously in the times of the greatest intellectual darkness of all Europe. The Christian printer who published Greek classics was introducing a new element into the intellectual life of his time; the Jewish printer who reprinted the philosophy of Albo, Maimonides or Gersonides was merely enabling what was already well known to be circulated more freely and at less expense. The Christian printers gradually introduced a non-Christian literature very different from the martyrologies and saintly biographies dear to the Middle Ages; the Jewish printers made no breach in the tradition of Jewish learning, but merely made accessible books studied by generations of scholars.

Subiaco is one of the delights of the dilettante. Lying on a lovely hillside, surmounted by one of the castellated summer residences of the Pope, surrounded by ancient forests and overlooking a sparkling waterfall, it has long been the gathering place for artists and idlers. Its real significance, however, lies in the monastery of Santa Scholastica, founded by the Benedictines and named in honor of the sister of their patron saint. In this monastery, so appropriately named, peaceful monks dwelt for centuries, disturbed at times by the soldiery of Emperor and Pope, who used Italy as a playground for their bloody games of war, but devoted always to prayer, labor and learning, copying and recopying thousands of precious manuscripts of classical antiquity, until the darkness of military barbarism and religious decadence should vanish before the dawn of a new day for literature and learning in Italy. In this place St. Benedict began his monastic career at the beginning of the seventh century, and stamped it with the characteristic that it shares with the famous monastery of Monte Cassino as the home of learning in Italy; most appropriately, therefore, in the whirlgig of time, eight hundred and fifty years later it witnessed the establishment of the printing press in Italy.

A word about these Benedictine monks, who saved Italy from intellectual barbarism—the Christian Scribes who wrote and copied the books in which was deposited the precious residuum of the slow process of the thoughts of the generations. Remembering the opinion held by the early Christians of the Jewish Scribes, the recorders and expounders of law and tradition,* an opinion reflecting the hatred of the ignorant zealot for the accumulated wisdom of the learned, we shall not fail to appreciate the service of the Christian Scribes in saving literature from the hands of their more zealous and ignorant fellows. The tradition of the Benedictines permeated all the monasteries of Europe. In northern Europe the monks preserved chiefly the religious literature, but in Italy the traditions of Roman and Greek culture had never quite died out, and in the monasteries many a high-strung soul found rest and happiness in preserving this classical tradition by copying with loving care the best works of antiquity.† Thus the pure fount of Castalia was kept fresh from generation to generation until its waters flowed out of the narrow confines of the monastery into

* Matt. XXIII passim.
† Putnam 1 : 25.

the broad river of the general life and helped to restore to men that freedom of thought and dignity of intellect which were the heritage of the Renaissance from Ancient Greece. "To take an illustration from St. Benedict's own beloved Subiaco, the work of his disciples has been like one of the great aqueducts of the valley of the Arno—sometimes carried underground for centuries through the obscurity of unremembered existence, sometimes emerging to the daylight and borne high upon the arcade of noble lives, but equally through all its course bearing the precious stream of ancient thought from the far-off hills of time into the humming and crowded cities of modern civilization." *

* Hodgkin 4 : 497–8.

CHAPTER II.

THE PIONEERS (1475–1482).

Origin of the Hebrew Press—The Work of De Rossi—Abraham b. Garton of Reggio di Calabria—Dr. Meshullam Cusi of Pieve di Sacco—The Garden of Pico della Mirandola—Dr. Abraham Conat of Mantua—Estellina Conat—The Scribe and the Printer—Abraham the Dyer of Pesaro—Duke Ercole of Ferrara—The Hebrew Press at Ferrara—The Press of Caravita at Bologna—Jewish Booksellers at the Universities.

WHENCE came the first Hebrew printed books? Not from proud Rome or Venice, where Jews were many and strong, not from renowned Lisbon, whose public squares were as yet undefiled by the smoking embers of the autodafe, not from castellated Prague, metropolis of the north, nor from Ferrara or Mantua prospering in the south. The Hebrew press was born in a marshy hamlet among the Venetian lagoons or in an earthquake-torn city by the Straits in farthest Calabria. It was in Italy that Hebrew printing first began, in Italy where European science found its new birth and where Jewish learning and Jewish men so often found a refuge from persecution. And here, where the cradle of the Hebrew press stood, it attained its fullest and most perfect maturity. Although Germany may rightly claim the honor of this great invention, it was at that time, by reason of its coarse manners, unfit to cultivate and develop this or any other art and to create an atmosphere in which they could flourish and come to perfection. Italy, like Germany, saw her cities sacked and given over to murder, rapine and pillage, but her condottieri graced their leisure hours with the beauties of literature, painting and architecture. The quickening interest in culture for its own sake that characterized the fifteenth century in Italy combined with the Italian decorative instinct and skill in all kinds of artistic handicraft, made Italy the land of all lands where the new art could yield its richest fruits. In Spain and Portugal Hebrew typography was throttled in its cradle by the hand of ecclesiastical bigotry. In Turkey it flourished though in less perfect form under the benevolent protection of the Crescent. Rapidly the new art spread through Germany and the Slavic lands, through Holland France and England, in all the great cities of the world, even in old time-worn Jerusalem;* but for beauty and artistic perfection we must always go back to the productions of the early Italian printers.

Of the men that saw the first cradle books, precious incunabula, fresh and new from the press, we know the names and after that, nothing. Abraham ben Garton ben Isaac of Reggio di Calabria, and Meshullam Cusi of Pieve di Sacco, have inscribed their names in the single book that each of them has left us. Who were they, of what family, what led them to engage in the "holy work,"

* Ersch & Gruber 28 : 23.

who were their patrons and what their success? Perhaps the Inquisition has forever buried the answer in the ashes of its fires, perhaps there lies some sybilline leaf in the darkness of an archive from which some future searcher may yet wrest its secret.

Giambernardo de Rossi of Parma, learned professor of Oriental languages at its university, is to be reckoned among those righteous strangers within the gates whom the Jews should hold in affectionate remembrance. While others pursued gaberdined Jews through hooting mobs, and exacted a golden tribute in return for scant mercy, while others preached from pulpit and rostrum against the perfidious tribe of Israel, de Rossi sat in his library and with loving care, as though himself of the seed of Abraham, studied the words of the sages of Israel. With scholar's care and lover's patience, this noble Christian sought the cradle books of the Hebrew presses, and he has left a lasting memorial in the splendid books, wherein he has deposited the result of his research in the history of the incunabula from 1475 to 1540 and the annals of the Hebrew presses of Ferrara, Sabbioneta and Cremona. Dying, he bequeathed his collection of books to the Grand Ducal Library at Parma, where among his rare and beautiful Hebraica there lies a time-stained, tear-stained and much mutilated volume,* whose one hundred and sixteen pages can tell a tale much sadder than

* Jew. Enc. 6: 575, Fürst, Bibl. Jud. 11: 80.

stands printed there in the clear type which Abraham ben Garton ben Isaac set in Reggio di Calabria in 1475.* Alone of all its brethren this precious book survives. A kind fate sent it into de Rossi's loving hand; with him it lay in safety until it found its last resting place under the jealous guardian eye of the librarian of the Grand Duke of Parma. Time alone would not have destroyed its fellows, but man, enthroned in papal chair, or cowled in monkish habit reached forth his destroying hand and they have all disappeared. The flames of funeral pyres whose victims were the books of Israel, blazing in all the market places of Italy, left, of the all too small edition of this precious commentary on the Pentateuch, first written by Rashi seven hundred years ago, this single copy to help us remember that there was once a man named Abraham ben Garton and that he was a printer in Reggio.†

While Abraham ben Garton was showing his wealthy Jewish patrons, the silk merchants of Reggio, the first of all books printed in their city another printer was pulling the sheets from a press in the village of Pieve di Sacco. Separated by the whole length of Italy they stood, the one at the Straits of Messina, the other almost within sight of the Campanile of St. Mark, equally zealous

---

*10 Adar 5235—17 February 1475   Ersch & Gruber 28 : 34. Jew. Enc. article "Incunabula" gives the date as February 5th.

† He probably lived in the Jewish quarter of the town, which gave its name to the nearest city gate, the Porta della Judeca. Fumagalli 323.

to spread and multiply knowledge among Israel, by that new process whereby the immemorial impulse "to make books, many, without end, of the books of the law of God" should find a new and better method of expression. While the Jews of Trent were passing days and nights of terror, facing the blind fury of the Franciscan monk Bernardino da Feltre, whose insane fanaticism made a saint of a drowned peasant child; while Bishop Hindernach was forging the evidence which was to prove that Jews had killed the boy at Passover, and that as Saint Simon his poor little body would do miracles and be forever thereafter held in holy reverence; not a hundred miles away, one hot summer day, Meshullam Cusi ben Moses Jacob thanked God that he had been permitted to finish part of the printing of the four sections of the great code of law "the pillars" which upheld the fallen hut of David in the land of the stranger.*

In the press the enthusiastic printer, his senses not yet dulled by familiarity with its simple mechanism, perceived a new revelation, and in the colophon of his work he tells us what the press said to him:—

> Wisdom am I, and crown of all science,
> Hidden am I, a mystery to all.
> Without pen stroke, my imprint stands patent,

* "The Four Pillars," by Jacob b. Asher; small folio; 28 Tammuz 5235,—3 July 1475. Ersch & Gruber 28 : 34. Asulai "Shem Hagedolim" 2 : 48.

Without scribe, lo! a volume appears.
One instant, and ink o'er me flowing,
Without guide lines, straight stands every word.
Do you wonder at Deborah, the mighty,
Who ruled with the pen of the scribes?
Had she seen me displaying my power,
She had taken me, a crown for her head.

The zealous craftsman did not live to see his work completed, but died after the third part was finished, leaving his sons to piously complete the work.* Why did Meshullam Cusi ben Moses Jacob, physician as well as printer, print his books in Pieve? Was he one of the many learned and distinguished alumni of the great University of Padua, which reared its walls scarcely ten miles away, and did he seek seclusion here to practice medicine and printing, undisturbed by the life of the greater city. Was he driven into exile by Christian persecution, professional rivalry, or personal misfortune? Did the prohibition of 1455, by which Paduan Jewish bankers were deprived of their business, send him to Pieve, with others who there transacted the affairs forbidden within the walls of Padua?† Was he among those who were left in Pieve after the Jewish money brokers had been expelled?‡ We may stand on the high road that passes through the village of Pieve and look wonderingly toward Padua or toward the sea. There is no answer to our questioning and

* Berliner, "Einfluss," 2.
† Jew. Enc. 10: 56.
‡ Ibid.

beyond these few simple recorded facts the life of Meshullam Cusi passes from the narrow realms of history into the limitless domain of imagination.

Unconscious of their own importance, these ancient pioneer scholar-printers neglected, as unworthy of record, mere narrative, chronicle or gossip, which to us, bred in the atmosphere of historical research, would have proved of supreme importance. As expressed by a writer of the eighteenth century, "The reader will find just cause of wonder that this art, which has been styled the nurse and preserver of arts and science, should (if I may use the expression) be so forgetful of itself, as not to leave us the least sketch of its own history, the inventors being more ambitious of deserving than of purchasing praise."* A notable exception is found in the dedication of the works of St. Thomas Aquinas, published in 1480, where the famed Nicolas Jensen of Venice thus speaks of himself:—

> Nicholas Jensen gallicus vir
> imprimis catholicus: erga
> omnes gratus: beneficus:
> liberalis: verax: constans;
> pulcritudine: magnitudine:
> fidelitateque impremendi:
> in toto terrarum orbe:
> pace omnium dixerim:
> primus.†

* S. Palmer "A General History of Printing" London 1733, p. 3.
† Brown, "The Venetian Printing Press" N. Y. and London 1891, p. 18.

Had the Jewish printers left us some memorial of their lives we should not now be guessing as to who was the first of them and in which city the art was first applied to Hebrew books. There are those who begin to think that perhaps Spain may yet be entitled to first place; there is the story of Davin of Caderousse as far back as 1444; there is the book of Peter Schwarz, of Eslingen,* printed in 1475 and containing Hebrew words.† These data give us a sense of doubt as to the finality of our verdict. But until this doubt is resolved we shall be content to remember Abraham ben Garton of Reggio, and Meshullam Cusi of Pieve as the first of the Hebrew printers.

We leave the lowlands and pass over the mountains to Florence, the Florence of Lorenzo di Medici, of Poliziano and Ficino, of Michelangelo and Machiavelli, of Savonarola and Pico della Mirandola. The mere recital of these names calls to mind a period unsurpassed in splendor and interest. Count Giovanni Pico della Mirandola that handsome youth the Renaissance incarnate with its love of culture, of refinement, of beauty, was the centre of a radiant circle which attracted many a wandering Jewish scholar.‡ In his palace

* "Contra Perfidis Judaeos de conditionibus veri Messiae." B. H. 2 : 941. Schwarz is supposed to have been a Jewish apostate. Stobbe "Die Juden in Deutschland während des Mittelalters" Braunschweig 1866 p. 77.

† Loew 1 : 190.

‡ Pico was a student of the Cabbala and maintained that this esoteric Jewish discipline proved the divinity of Jesus. He collected

Jew and Christian, Moslem and Heathen met and discoursed, united by the common bond of culture and philosophy. Here the man of intellect found an always open door and here, nothing that was human was foreign. In the salons and gardens of Italian gentlemen the two great cultural elements the Hellenic and the Hebraic were united,* when the minds of men sought stimulus and refreshment beyond the narrow limits of medieval scholasticism. This union is typified in the Moses of Michelangelo. The great protagonist of the Jewish race, who according to Jewish tradition wore the triple crown of wisdom, of sovereignty and of priesthood, sits majestic in deathless marble carved by the greatest artist of the Renaissance, thrice crowned in painting, in architecture and in sculpture.

In the garden of the Count, one summer evening, three Jewish physicians were the centre of interest, brilliantly debating some abstruse, philosophic theme. Among the scholars present were Marsilio Ficino, who fortunately for us did not fail to make mention in a gossipy letter to his friend Domenico Beniveni, that he heard this debate between the Jewish physicians, Elias, Abra-

Hebrew manuscripts. Zunz "Zur Gesch. u. Lit." Berlin 1845 p. 523. He was a disciple of Elijah del Medigo who taught philosophy at Padua and Florence and violently opposed Cabbalism and of Yohanan Alemanno who as strongly supported it. Graetz 8 : 243.

* Pico tried to harmonize the philosophy of Plato and Aristotle with the Cabbala and Neo-Platonism. Jew. Enc. 10 : 32. Messer Leon of Naples was the first to compare the language of Cicero and that of the Prophets and Psalmists. Graetz 8 : 240.

ham and Guglielmo.* Jewish physicians were to
be found in the house of every nobleman, many
a good Christian household was entrusted solely
to their ministrations, and Pope, Cardinal and
Prince received their potions only from a Jewish
hand, from which they need not fear the poison
which passed so often among Christian gentlemen.† Often indeed did the word of the Jewish
physicians turn aside the wrath of prince or
pontiff from some hapless ghetto, for they possessed
"the key to the hearts of the great upon whom
the fate of the Jews depends." So spake Don
Isaac Abrabanel out of the fullness of his life of
bitter experience.‡

Of these three debaters in the garden of Pico
we know Elijah del Medigo, physician scholar
and writer, and Guglielmo of Moncada a baptized
Jew who translated the Koran for the Duke of
Urbino.¶ And the third? Which of the three
Abrahams who graced that circle, Abraham Farissol
a favorite at the Courts of Ferrara and Florence,
Abraham de Balmes one time physician to Cardinal
Domenico Grimani or Abraham Conat of Mantua?
We like to believe that it was the latter, a man
who added to his professional eminence and philoso-
phic mind the practical skill of the craftsman.
For he was the founder of the Hebrew press at
Mantua, and unique among all the printers he

* R. E. J. 12 : 251.
† Graetz 4: 407.
‡ Graetz 4: 287.
¶ H. B. 20: 124.

associated with him in his work, his wife Estellina. A mere recital of the six books known to have been produced by his press from 1476 to 1480, with care and skill and grace, leads us into the heart of the man, to whom law travel history and exegesis, astronomy and rhetoric were equally dear: The legal code "Path of Life" * the traveler's tales of Eldad the Danite, the popular version of Josephus,† Rabbi Levi ben Gerson's commentary on the Pentateuch,‡ an astronomical table by Mordecai Finzi and "The Drippings of the Honeycomb," by Rabbi Judah ben Yehiel, the first Hebrew book published in the lifetime of its author.¶

In 1471 Duke Lodovico had invited the learned and noble Doctor of Laws, Messer Pietro Adam de

---

* 6 June 1476. He also printed about one-third of the "Yore Deah," completed in the following year at Ferrara by Abraham the Dyer. Ersch & Gruber 38 : 34.

† Yosippon.

‡ Assisted by Abraham Jedidiah of Cologna (Cologne?).

¶ Alas, for the author of the "Drippings of the Honeycomb." He attempted to apply to Scripture the rules and terminology of classical rhetoric as found in the writings of Cicero and Quintilian. How could such heresy be countenanced? Rabbi Joseph Kolon, staunch pillar of traditionalism, soon took up the cudgels against the innovator. (Bacher "Hebr. Sprachwissenschaft" 101.) Hardly was the book finished when a quarrel with Kolon compelled the Duke of Mantua, Lodovico Gonzaga II., not Francesco (Jost 3 : 107) nor Joseph (Graetz 8 : 252) to save himself from the importunities of the wrangling theologians, (Heilprin "Seder Hadorot" 235,) by exiling them both. Their quarrel was inevitable for Joseph Kolon represented the narrow dogmatism and pious zeal that characterized most of the scholars who had been trained on the inhospitable soil of Germany, whereas Judah ben Yehiel, better known as Messer Leon, born and bred in Southern Italy, expressed the culture, the philosophy, the classical taste and the free spirit of inquiry that flourished in the warmer and freer air of the South.

Micheli, to establish a press in Mantua. He called in German workmen, probably from neighboring Ferrara, where a press had just been established by Belfort, and soon the Mantuan presses were at work under the charge of Pietro Adamo, as well as of the printers George and Paul Putzbach of Mainz, Thomas von Siebenburger of Hermanstadt and Johann Wurster of Kempten.* At one of these presses Conat caught the inspiration to print Hebrew books, and communicated it to his worthy help-meet, Estellina. She was no weak woman who left her husband to his labors and enjoyed the fruits of idleness; nor did she believe that woman's share in the labors of men exempted her from the duties of motherhood. She printed a book on her own account, no less important a work than the "Investigation of the World," by Jedaiah Bedersi and in the colophon she writes, "I, Estellina, wife of my master my husband the honored Rabbi Abraham Conat, may he be blessed with children and may his days be prolonged, Amen! wrote this book 'Investigation of the World' with the aid of the youth Jacob Levi of Provence of Tarascon, may he live."† She "wrote" the book, as her husband said, "with many pens without the aid of miracle," for the

---

* Fumagalli 200.

† Women were employed as copyists of manuscripts. Dr. Schechter reports the following postscript in a manuscript or catalogue seen by him. "I beseech the reader not to judge me very harshly when he finds that mistakes have crept into this work; for when I was engaged in copying it God blessed me with a son, and thus I could not attend to my business properly." Schechter "Studies in Judaism" p. 264.

וּבָא אַהֲרֹן אֶל אֹהֶל מוֹעֵד

וְהִנִּיחָם שָׁם

וְרָחַץ אֶת בְּשָׂרוֹ בַמַּיִם בְּמָקוֹם

קָדוֹשׁ

A page of Gersonides' Commentary on the Pentateuch

Conat, Mantua, before 1480

art had not yet invented the word "printing" by which to define itself.* Abraham the Dyer was the first to use the term in 1477 at Ferrara.†

The printed book was still a mere copy of the manuscript ‡ an imitation of the slower process of the scribe, which roused the ire of the book-lovers, who saw in its cheaper and more numerous products a vitiating influence on the penman's art. "What hired amanuensis can be equal to the scribe who loves the words that grow under his hand, and to whom an error or indistinctness in the text is more painful than a sudden darkness or an obstacle across his path? And even these

* According to ancient tradition, the correction of a single error in a book justified the corrector in saying that he wrote it. Blau "Althebr. Bucherwesen" p. 187.

† In the very first decades of Jewish typography Hebrew terminology had already been perfected in the form in which it has remained to the present day. The word "defus" from the Greek "tupos" was used as early as the year 1477 by Abraham the Dyer. This word was already known in Mishnic Hebrew in a modified form, and its verbal forms, the obsolete "dafas" and the common "hidfis" meaning respectively "to print" and "to have printed", first appeared in the sixteenth century. In the edition of the Psalms 1477 this word appears to have still retained its old meaning of "form" or "shape". The verse in which it appears, "bidfuse haotiot" should be translated "through the form of letters". (See also Talmud Pesahim 37 a.) Another Hebraized form of the Greek word "tupos" is the word "tofes" which also appears in the Mishna, meaning "formula". This as used in the terminology of typography probably means "proofs". The word "madfis" meaning "printer" is still found to-day as the family name of many Jews whose ancestors were among the pioneers of the art. The early printers used the word "katab" "to write", as in the non-Jewish books the word "scribere" was used for to "print". They also used the verb "hakak", "to engrave", which subsequently became obsolete. (Ersch & Gruber 28 : 23; see also Berliner "Einfluss" p. 3.)

‡ Putnam 1: 365.

mechanical printers who threaten to make learning a base and vulgar thing even they must depend on the manuscript over which we scholars have bent with that insight into the poet's meaning which is closely akin to the mens divinior of the poet himself; unless they would flood the world with grammatical falsities and inexplicable anomalies that would turn the very fountain of Parnassus into a deluge of poisonous mud."* The blind Bardo well expressed the sentiment of the literati of his day. But there was no need of such fear for Hebrew literature. No one studied manuscripts with greater care than the Hebrew printer, who was engaged in a "holy work," whose duty it was to transmit the words of the sages unchanged by a single letter; who prepared his book with extraordinary care from old and valuable manuscripts, corrected by learned scholars and inspired by the desire to leave nothing undone that makes for perfection.† Still more vigorous was the resentment of the monkish scribes, who foresaw the doom of their art through the competition of the new machine.‡ The wail of Abbot Trithemius of Spanheim may serve as a type of the complaints of the booklovers. Writing to the Abbot Gerlach of Dentz ¶ he says:—"A work written on

* George Eliot: Romola Chap. V.

† Depping, " Die Juden im Mittelalter " Stuttgart 1834, p. 382.

‡ Chwolson " Reshith maase hadefus beyisrael " Warsaw 1897 p. 6.

¶ In a letter printed in 1494 in Mainz, under the title "de laude scriptorum manualium" Putnam 1 : 366–367.

parchment could be preserved for a thousand years, while it is probable that no volume printed on paper will last for more than two centuries. Many important works have not been printed, and the copies required of these must be prepared by scribes. The scribe who ceases his work because of the invention of the printing-press can be no true lover of books, in that, regarding only the present he gives no due thought to the intellectual cultivation of his successors. The printer has no care for the beauty and the artistic form of books, while with the scribe this is a labour of love."

The Jewish copyists likewise soon felt the pressure of this new competition,* and their natural outcry against those who were taking away their bread brought out the stern warning of one of the Neapolitan printers, "let those who speak ill of this art bear their sin." † With the exception of an occasional protesting voice, a chorus of praise arose for the new art. No religious community made so widespread a use of the press as the Jews, who saw in it a perpetual guarantee against monopoly of knowledge by the rich, who alone could afford to buy manuscripts. In the mechanical process of printing they had an assurance that after careful editing and correction of proofs the correctness of texts would no longer be dependent on the skill, knowledge and scholarly accuracy of the copyist; and literature was saved

* Berliner "Einfluss," p. 6.
† Ersch & Gruber 28: 22.

from the danger of fire and water and secure against destruction by fanaticism and ignorance.*   While the older scholars and booklovers naturally continued to prefer manuscripts † and manuscript copies were still required for certain ritualistic books‡ the printed book supplanted the manuscript and the traditional reverence paid by the "people of the writing" to the written word was transferred to the printed page.¶   The form of the manuscript letters and page was long retained, even to the omission of a few letters or words to be filled in by hand and the printing of the colophon in lines of diminishing size when the text was not sufficient to fill the last page.**   But beyond these natural and sentimental tributes to the older art it was with a sense of relief that the printers compared their presses with the slow and tiresome pen of the scribe.   The old scribe often groaned at his labor, "For he that knows not how to write thinks this no labor. O, how hard is writing! It tires the eyes, saps the vitality and depresses every organ of the body. Three fingers write; the whole body labors." And the printer's antiphonal exultation responds: "I advise the once weary hand and pen to rest, For labor is ended by art and skill."††

* Jost 3: 257, 258.

† Putnam 1: 243

‡ Scrolls of the law to be used in the synagogue, phylacteries, doorpost amulets, bills of divorce, etc.

¶ Berliner " Einfluss " p. 9.

** Berliner " Einfluss " 7.

†† Brown 23.

Among the earliest craftsmen who took up the work was Abraham ben Hayyim, "one of the inhabitants and dyers * (dei Tintori) of Pesaro," whose name first appears in a book published by him at Ferrara in 1477; but who is supposed by some† to have been the first to establish a Hebrew press and to cut Hebrew type in 1473.‡

Not far to the north of Pesaro lay the territory of the Dukes of Este, who had ruled from their capital Ferrara from the beginning of the twelfth century, when Obizzo d'Este swooped down upon it from his Paduan hills, until 1597 when, at the death of Alfonso d'Este II, it was annexed by Pope Clement VIII to the States of the Church. Ferrara first enters into the history of the Hebrew press in the days of Duke Ercole I, best known and most distinguished of his race. His court was a gathering place for the most brilliant spirits of the age, of all those peripatetic scholars, philosophers, artists, poets and musicians who were welcomed in all the courts of Italy, from Milan and Venice to Naples. Ercole, like so many of his contemporaries, Christian in faith but heathen in

*Dyeing was largely in the hands of Jews. Güdemann, "Geschichte des Erziehungswesens und der Cultur der Juden in Italien " p. 69, ventures to say that they controlled this industry which was during the Middle Ages the chief industry of Italy.

† Jew. Enc. Art. "Bible editions."

‡ As we now have several candidates presented by different scholars for the distinction of typographical primacy, we shall reserve judgment until the evidence is more convincing and in the meantime accept as the pioneers those whose names are connected with earliest dated books.

culture, was concerned rather with the things of this world of beauty of intellect and of power, than of that mysterious and pale region beyond the grave which constituted the realm of the Church.

The dukes of the House of Este harbored the plan of rivalling the commercial importance of the Queen of the Adriatic, and where such a magnificent enterprise was conceived the pettiness of theological hair-splitting might amuse an idle hour, but could not seriously affect the policy of the State. The Jews, trained by long continued persecution to recognize from afar signs of danger or of safety, did not fail to observe that wherever there was commercial prosperity the influence of the Church spirit was weak, and a place of safety might be found for those who stood without the pale. Therefore they flocked to Ferrara and prospered and were treated by the duke with the consideration that their services deserved. The decree of the duke published in 1473, relieving the Jews of all exceptional taxation, was testimony of his practical sagacity and an act of far-reaching importance, for it was a blow to the revenues of the Church, which were in part maintained by a special scheme of taxation levied by the Pope's legate. The Church was of course always in need of funds and a very important part of its administration consisted in devising ways and means for raising revenue. A favorite expedient was the levying of special taxes on the Jews, a plan devised at Rome and ingeniously worked out in detail, which went so far as to compel the Jews to pay the expenses to which the Church was put in attempting their own conversion, and likewise to pay for the maintenance of those apostate Jews who yielded to its threats or blandishments.

In 1624, after Ferrara had been absorbed into the States of the Church, a ghetto was established from Via della Scienze, where stood its famous university, to the Piazza del Mercato, flanked by the cathedral and facing the ducal palace. In this section of the city, the very heart of Ferrara, the Jews had lived since time immemorial, topographically as well as intellectually and financially in closest touch with the ruling powers. To this place they came from other cities of Italy, even from Venice, at the direct invitation of Duke Ercole, and finally in 1492 in great numbers from the inhospitable shores of Spain and Portugal.* When the citizens of Ferrara complained to the Duke that the incoming Jews were overcrowding their quarter and discommoding their neighbors, he was not guilty of the folly of restricting immigration, but doubled the size of his city by commencing those great building operations north of what is now the Via Cavour and the Strada della Giovecca. When the duchy was made part of the States of the Church, this part of the city became forlorn and deserted, and until the days of Victor Emanuel II lay neglected and forgotten in grass-grown obscurity, a monument to the

* Kayserling "Sephardim" p. 138 etc.

ruinous inefficiency of the administration of the Church.

To the Ferrara of Ercole came Abraham the Dyer of Pesaro. Why he left his native city and found his way to Ferrara we do not know. Perhaps, as de Rossi surmises, he was attracted to Ferrara by "the number of its Jews, the splendor of its Jewish academies and the fame of its rabbinical doctors," or, what is more likely, by the less lofty motive of getting a better living at his trade than in his native Pesaro. Andre of Belfort, the Frenchman, had established the first press at Ferrara in 1471, and other printers, mostly Frenchmen, soon followed him.* It may be that the healthy curiosity of the dyer was attracted by the new method of perpetuating literature, and that he entered the shop of one of these craftsmen as a journeyman apprentice. He soon became a master, for in 1477 he set up his own press and printed two books, both of them favorites with the early printers, and therefore most probably in good demand among Jewish readers; the first one, a commentary on the Book of Job,† one of the many commentaries of the popular Rabbi Levi ben Gerson, whose books written some one hundred and fifty years before this time, were issued from nearly all of the presses in Italy, and the second, "He shall Teach Knowledge" (Yoreh

* Fumagalli 126.

† Schwab "les incunables etc." p. 30, finished Friday 16 May 1477; corrected by Nathan of Salo. Ersch & Gruber 28 : 34.

De'ah),* begun at Mantua by Dr. Conat and finished by the Dyer, within a month of his first book.

Although after 1477 the activity of Abraham the Dyer is unrecorded, it is not likely that his press was idle, at a time so favorable for the publication of Hebrew works. After five years Abraham the Dyer suddenly appears in the city of Bologna in company with one of the German printers of the family of Strassburg, whom we shall meet again at Naples, Venice and elsewhere, working at the press of a rich patron Joseph ben Abraham Caravita.† Joseph Hayyim of Strassburg expressed his appreciation of Abraham the Dyer in the epigraph wherein Abraham is called "a workman whose equal in Hebrew typography does not exist in the whole world, a man celebrated everywhere"—rather exaggerated praise, seeing that there were at that time perhaps not half a dozen Jewish master-printers in the world. Its extravagance is somewhat modified by the fact that Abraham was a pioneer of the art, one of

* One of the four sections of the great code of the law, The Turim, a book in universal use as a guide in all matters, legal, ritualistic and religious, and printed by the pioneers at Pieve, Mantua, Ferrara and Soncino as well as at Ixar, Lisbon and Guadalaxara. Berliner "Aus meiner Bibliothek" p. 30; Zunz "Zur Geschichte etc." p. 219.

† Caravita defrayed the cost of publishing the Pentateuch printed by Abraham the Dyer and Joseph Hayyim ben Aaron, of Strassburg, who also acted as corrector, at Bologna, on January 26, 1482. Ersch & Gruber 28 : 34. It is supposed that the edition of Megillot with Rashi and commentary of Ibn Ezra on Esther came from Caravita's press in the same year. R. Gottheil in Jew. Enc. 3 : 299.

Duke Ercole I of Ferrara

those early printers who reached perfection in their work almost at the very outset. Their clear types, rich black inks and clean strong press work are not excelled by the best productions of the modern press, and their successors of the sixteenth century did little to improve upon their work. Later printers, feeling the goad of competition and vying with each other to supply the demand for cheap books, hurried their work and in their haste sacrificed their art to the gods of the market place.*

About the middle of the fifteenth century Bologna became the storm centre of Jewish life in Italy, as the meeting place of a great congress of rabbis. The times were out of joint and the wise men met to consult upon the public weal, for bitter and relentless persecution threatened the House of Israel. Nor did the rabbis meet in vain, for when in 1473 Bernardino da Feltre preached at

---

* Brown pp. 50–51. Some of the peculiarities, we can hardly call them imperfections, of the early editions may be noted. The first types showed too great a similarity between certain letters, such as "he" and "het", "daled" and "resh", "kaf" and "bet". In the older books empty spaces at the end of lines were filled up by two strokes, or by the first or first and second letters of the first word on the following line. This was the custom in manuscripts and copied by the first printers, but was soon discontinued. The first words of chapters were often omitted, in order to be filled in afterward in writing or with wood cut ornaments. This was often forgotten. Signatures and pagination are wanting in the earliest books, and when they first appear they are very irregular. The pagination is usually in Hebrew, rarely in Arabic figures, and is used to number the leaves and not the pages. Vowel points and accents are found in the earlier Bibles and prayer books; but they are likewise irregularly and unskillfully introduced, and it is very difficult to distinguish between "patah" and "kamez". (Ersch & Gruber 28: 23.)

Bologna, his furious ranting fell upon deaf ears. The influence of the humanistic movement had made it difficult to stir up the rulers of the people to religious crusades, and the stern but wise Giovanni Bentivoglio checked the preaching friar and compelled him to seek more sympathetic auditors elsewhere. Nevertheless, the curse of bigotry rested on the world, and men were judged not by what they did, but by what they believed. The Jews were still debarred by the statutes of the great university from direct participation in its literary life and had only their own intellectual predilections to stimulate their interest in non-Jewish learning. In one respect, however, they may be said to have directly promoted the interest of the universities, for as book sellers they wandered far and wide, collecting manuscripts from all corners of the world, and turning their immemorial love for books into humble but useful service to the great movement for the revival of learning, which was to shake the old world from its lethargy of centuries. Of course, in those sad days, as soon as the Jew prospered in any undertaking, the Church authorities felt obliged, upon the complaint of Christian competitors, to put an end to a material success that seemed incompatible with infidelity. When Jewish book sellers at the beginning of the fourteenth century began to deal in Latin, Greek and other manuscripts, the heavy hand of the Church fell upon them and they were prohibited, under severe penalties, from selling

books to Christians or from buying from them.*
However, Church regulations, that in earlier centuries would have been implicitly obeyed, had now lost some of their force.   Monasteries and churches in need of money sold or pledged their books to Jews, and as these were mostly religious works, the Jews presumably did not purchase them for home consumption.†   At the universities of Padua and Bologna, the necessities of the students forced the authorities to permit the Jewish book trade to be openly carried on.   Through the dimness of the centuries we may still see one Jacob of Padua, in high-peaked cap and pleated gown, hurrying across the Foro dei Mercanti on his way to the university, with a dozen precious parchment scrolls under his arm; ‡ and at an earlier date, another, named Moses, from whom, in defiance of Church regulations, some unknown scholar purchased a valuable code, recording the transaction in this inscription: "Emi hunc Anno Domini MCCCC die XXI mensis Novembris a Moysi Judeo pro VIII florenes."¶

We naturally look to Bologna, the university town, for early recognition of the press, and we

---

* If Jews had manuscripts to dispose of, it was necessary to place them in the hands of the stationarii, who sold them on commission. Putnam 1 : 185.

† Putnam 1 : 231, 232.

‡ He carried on his business of selling manuscripts between 1455–1460. His inscription occurs in many classical codices. In a manuscript of Horace of the twelfth century the owner notes that he bought it in 1458 from Jacob the Hebrew librarius. Putnam 1 : 249.

¶ Putnam 1 : 246.

find that at the invitation of the prince Giovanni
Bentivoglio a press was established there in 1471
by Baldasarre Azzoguidi, who proudly calls himself "first employer of the art of printing in his
city for the benefit of the human race,"* in sharp
contrast to the modesty of the Hebrew craftsman
Gerson Soncino, who calls himself "least of all
the printers", though in fact he was among the
first. A few years after Azzoguidi's advent,
"Meister" Joseph (probably Joseph Hayyim of
Strassburg) and two associates, one unidentified
and the other Hezekiah of Ventura † published
on August 29, 1477 ‡ an edition of three hundred
copies of a commentary to the Psalms by Rabbi
David Kimhi, most illustrious bearer of his great
family name, a luminous and erudite commentator
grammarian and lexicographer, whose works had

* Fumagalli p. 37.

† Richard Gottheil (Jew. Enc. 3 : 299) gives but two names,
Joseph Hayyim Mordecai and Hezekiah da Ventura; Steinschneider
gives three, Meister Joseph, Nerijah Hayyim Mordecai and Hezekiah
of Ventura. (Ersch & Gruber 28 : 35.) De Rossi, who cites the
colophon of the Kimhi to Psalms, seems to justify Steinschneider's
reading. But the "Ve-Nerijah" of the second name is by no means
clear. That Joseph was a German is suggested by the form of his
title "Meister" instead of "Messer". De Rossi cites Tychsen as first
to suggest this. (De Rossi ann. XV 19.) I have ventured to suggest
his identity with Joseph of Strassburg, who printed with Abraham the
Dyer in 1482. Apropos of this suggestion, Chwolson (p. 21) calls
attention to the fact that the types of the Kimhi of 1477 are similar
to those of the Rashi text in the Pentateuch of 1482, of which Joseph
of Strassburg was corrector and associate printer. This type is the
so-called "Weiberteutsch" used in later times only for Judaeo-German
books. (Ersch & Gruber 28 : 23.)

‡ Schwab "les incunables etc." p. 29.

the distinction of being ten times printed at six different presses before the year 1500.

After Abraham the Dyer left Bologna, he again disappears for a time, until we catch one last glimpse of him working at the press of the most renowned of the craft in the city of Soncino, in 1488, and with his departure from Bologna that ancient and famous city passes out of the history of the Hebrew press until after half a century, a loyal company of Jewish silk weavers again engage for a little while in the "holy work" of printing.

It was not only the physicians and men of science who were devoted to the new art. Scholarship and knowledge were not the exclusive possession of professional men. Artisans and craftsmen had always partaken freely of the "Prepared Table", * as Joseph Caro so significantly called it, and, in conformity with the immemorial practice of Israel not to use scholarship as a spade to dig with, had devoted their leisure to its cultivation and dissemination. Therefore it was no strange sight in the days of old to see Rabbi Joshua, the needle maker, and Rabbi Yohanan, the sandal maker, sitting in the highest places of the great academies of learning to learn and to teach, or at a later time to see the dyer of Pesaro, the butchers of Padua,† or the silk weavers of Bologna engage

---

* The "Shulhan Arukh" the great code of the law compiled by Caro, finished 1555, first printed at Venice 1565.

† They helped to establish the Hebrew press at Rome in 1518 and one of them printed at Trino 1525.

in the "holy work."   For it was not greed or even
the hope of adequate pecuniary reward that
prompted most of the pioneers to engage in the
hazardous business of printing. They seem to
have had some of the feeling that stimulates explorers, who are willing to risk the dangers and
terrors of unknown lands for the sake of the joy
of discovery and the thrill of adventure. And like
the explorers of the wilds, many of them have
fallen leaving no record of their existence. It is
not unlikely that there were books printed in
Bologna between 1477 and 1482* and that there
were presses established in other cities of Italy
besides those of which we have knowledge, but no
trace of them exists to-day. When we see that, in
some instances, but a single copy of a book remains to indicate the existence of the printer, we
may reasonably believe that the fierce persecution
that followed Jewish books as well as Jewish men
in the sixteenth and seventeenth centuries, destroyed all traces of many books and all records of
many lives.†

* Chwolson p. 21.

† Chwolson p. 22.   One can appreciate the rarity of Hebrew incunabula by noting that of the 100 books printed before 1500, about
20 are now known only through a single copy. Freimann p. 4. Christian incunabula are usually in fine condition, Hebrew ones exceptionally
so.

CHAPTER III.

THE SONS OF SONCINO.

Moses Mentzlan and Giovanni di Capistrano—Samuel b. Moses at Soncino—Dr. Israel Nathan Soncino—Joshua Solomon Soncino—The First Talmudic Treatise—The First Mahzor—At Casalmaggiore—The First Bible—Joshua Solomon Soncino at Naples—The Neapolitan Printers—The Ashkenazi—Katorzi—The Canon and the Agur.

THE family of Soncino traces its origin to one Moses of the City of Speyer in Alsace, who lived about the middle of the thirteenth century.* Its history like that of most other families is obscure, for although everybody has ancestors they are not all recorded in the College of Heralds. From the middle of the thirteenth to the middle of the fifteenth century the family continued to live in Speyer, and they were probably among the Jews who were expelled from that city by a general edict of expulsion in 1435.† The forefathers of the Soncinati like the other tribes of the wandering foot and weary breast found no permanent resting place in Germany, and later on we find one of them in the city of Furth in Bavaria—a spirited somewhat obstinate man who fought for his people with whole-souled and self-sacrificing devotion.‡ Moses Mentzlan (Menschlein, manikin) so called

---

* Sacchi "I tipografi ebrei di Soncino" Cremona 1877 p. 13.

† Rothschild "Die Judengemeinden Mainz, Speyer and Worms" p. 165.

‡ Sacchi p. 46.

perhaps because of his insignificant stature, or through the contempt of his Christian fellows is made visible to us for a moment in the chaos of time when he vainly appealed to the scholars and princes of Furth to save his coreligionists from the fanatical hatred aroused by the fulminations of the crusading Franciscan Giovanni di Capistrano. Of his fate we know nothing, whether he found his grave in his native land or went into exile with his brethren. Samuel his son fled from Bavaria, crossed the mountains and settled in the little village of Orzinovi in what is now the district of Brescia, at that time under the dominion of the Republic of Venice. But Samuel's abilities did not permit him to remain long in Orzinovi; and on May 9, 1454, Francesco Sforza Duke of Milan issued to him letters patent, permitting him to settle with his family in the fortified city of Soncino.*

To-day the traveler in Northern Italy would hardly know where to look for the city of Soncino, for it is merely a prosperous market town † in the District of Cremona on the high road from Brescia to Pavia, about thirty-five miles east of Milan. In the fifteenth century, however, it was a commercial centre, a flourishing city well forti-fied and containing many men-at-arms. Its importance was first established under Gian Galeazzo Visconti the most notorious of the line of Dukes

* Sacchi, p. 47, where the document is quoted in full.
† Grosso e bellissimo borgo. Soave, p. 5.

of Milan bearing that name, and continued under Francesco Sforza who drove out the Visconti and made himself Duke of Milan. The new Duke being a wise statesman recognized the need of commercial and financial talent in his Duchy, for then as now the strength of princes depended upon their treasury. It was therefore good policy on the part of the Duke to induce useful citizens from the neighboring principalities to settle in his dominion, strengthening his power at the expense of his powerful and dangerous rival, the great flourishing Republic of Venice who had extended her influence far to the west, and had absorbed several principalities that lay between her and Milan. Samuel and his family the only Jews at that time in Soncino were permitted by the Duke to open a bank and lend money, and out of gratitude to his patron and to the country of his adoption where for the first time the "manikin" had become a "man", Samuel discarded his contemptuous German surname and adopted that of the city of his residence.

It is characteristic of many of the old Jewish families in Italy as elsewhere that they united great practical ability and sagacity with idealistic devotion to scholarship and science. Bankers and craftsmen devoted their leisure to the cultivation of medicine, natural science, literature, law and poetry. Like so many of his distinguished contemporaries Israel Nathan Soncino, the son of Samuel Mentzlan practiced that profession of medicine which has the peculiar attraction of combining love of science with practical helpfulness at the same time that he continued the banking business of his father. In the year 1478 the establishment of the public loan office or Monte di Pieta in Soncino compelled him to abandon the business * and in 1480 he turned his attention to the new art of printing, which was exercising its fascination over so many of the brightest minds of the time. Israel Nathan Soncino, reared in almost princely fashion and educated in the disciplines of the Jews and the Gentiles, became the founder of the great Hebrew press that bears the name of Soncino.†

The Soncino family presents a typical medieval picture of an entire family at work at the same press, one of the sons in general charge the other son and the grandson among the workmen and all under the supervision of the grandfather "the learned Rabbi Israel Nathan, father of all the sons of Soncino."‡ The aged founder of the house was permitted to enjoy the first and most splendid fruits of this press, the several Talmudical Treatises, the great Mahzor containing the entire ritual for the year the first complete Bible printed with

---

* Sacchi p. 14.

† The productions of this press have been studied by several Christian scholars, Bartolocci, Wolf, De Rossi, Sacchi, Manzoni and others.

‡ So notable were the productions of their press that for a long time bibliographers forgot the existence of earlier printers and thought the Soncinati the first Hebrew printers in Italy. Wolf Bib. Heb. 4 : 941.

FRANCESCO SFORZA I
DVCA DI MILANO

the help of Abraham the Dyer* and other books on ethics exegesis and philosophy. In 1489, Israel Nathan Soncino was gathered to his fathers, and within a year his son Moses followed him into eternity.† With their deaths the press of the sons of Soncino practically came to an end and the fortunes of the family followed the two survivors, Joshua Solomon and Gerson into other cities and lands.

Let us go back to the beginning of the press at Soncino in the early part of the eighth decade. Under the direction of his father, Joshua Solomon Soncino provided the material and the men, and laid the foundations for this notable undertaking. All was new to these pioneers; presses had to be provided, types cut, inks made and tested, paper supplied and manuscripts examined and approved for publication. Not that they were obliged to study the contending claims of living authors, who sought to immortalize their lucubrations through the press; to this fate a later generation of craftsmen was doomed. The pioneers were concerned with the publication of works of the recognized masters of Jewish literature; they were troubled

* Of this notable work a modern bibliographer says: "The first Hebrew Bible printed in Europe was issued at Soncino in 1488 from the press of Abraham Colonto." Putnam 1 : 459. This citation illustrates the manner in which Jewish historical facts are treated by many non-Jewish scholars. Abraham Colonto may have been intended for Abraham the Dyer, or Abraham Conat of Mantua. Whatever it may have been, it is quite wrong.

† Sacchi p. 15. The date there given 1480 is evidently a typographical error.

only by the question of the accuracy of manuscripts that had come down to them from former ages. The work of revision and correction was done by scholars of approved ability, who carefully studied the manuscripts and followed the sheets through the press. Among the proofreaders of the old printers we find some of the greatest names of the time, for eminent scholars considered it a pious duty to assist in the work of perpetuating some ancient authority through the thousand impressions of the press.

Having gathered his force and his appliances, Joshua Solomon selected as the first publication of his press the first treatise of the most important Jewish book since the completion of the Biblical canon, the treatise "Blessings" (Berakhot) of the Babylonian Talmud. Carefully and patiently the sons of Soncino labored at their first book under the guidance of Gabriel ben Aaron of Strassburg, whose brother Joseph Hayyim ben Aaron of Strassburg had assisted Abraham the Dyer at the press of Caravita, in Bologna. At last it was finished, and December 19, 1483, when the complete treatise Berakhot was laid before the aged Israel Nathan, was a day of jubilee in the house of the ci-devant banker. On the same day there was completed another Talmudical treatise, "An Egg" (Bezah) so called from the first word of the text of the Mishnah with which it begins, which had been run through the press at the same time as the treatise "Blessings." The British Museum the

Bodleian Library at Oxford the Stadt-Bibliothek of Frankfurt am Main have a copy of each, the Biblioteca Palatina at Parma has the "Berakhot" and the Vaticana has the "Bezah." The Talmud has been many times reprinted since the days of the sons of Soncino, in Venice Lublin Salonica Constantinople Basel Cracow Amsterdam and many other cities of Germany Austria and Poland.* But the Soncino treatises are inferior to none in press work and paper, and equalled only by the Bomberg editions in the correctness of texts, especially those texts that were subsequently mutilated and altered through fear of the censors.†

From the solid substance of these two Talmudical treatises the printers of Soncino turned to lighter work and within a month (January 14, 1484) they finished the "Choice of Pearls" (Mibhar Hapeninim)‡ written by "the Jewish Plato" poet philosopher and moralist the far-famed Solomon Ibn Gabirol.

> "Den Gebirol, diesen treuen
> Gottgeweihten Minnesaenger
> Diese fromme Nachtigall
> Deren Rose Gott gewesen—
> Diese Nachtigall, die zaertlich
> Ihre Liebeslieder sang
> In der Dunkelheit der Gotisch
> Mittelalterlichen Nacht!"

* Rabbinovicz "Maamar al hadefasat ha Talmud."

† S. D. Luzzato in H. B. 1 : 86.

‡ Corrected by Solomon ben Perez Bonfoi, who subsequently worked at Naples.

This string of pearls of wisdom and ethics first presented to the world about the middle of the eleventh century, in what Heine has called "the darkness of the Gothic-medieval night" of Europe, was translated from the original Arabic into Hebrew by the Spanish Jewish scholar Judah Ibn Tibbon, and for several centuries was cherished as a fountain of wisdom. The "Choice of Pearls" was quickly followed at Soncino by the "Investigation of the World" (Behinat Olam) by Jedaiah Bedersi, first printed by Estellina Conat at Mantua, and the "Chapters of the Fathers" (Pirke Aboth) with the commentary of Maimonides. Thus the printers of Soncino gave up the entire year 1484 to works of moral philosophy.

In the following year after having printed another Talmudic treatise, "The Scroll" (Megillah) they completed one of the most important of their publications the first part of the Mahzor,* containing the complete ritual for the Jewish year according to the Roman rite, and known as the ritual according to the custom of Italy (Mahzor Minhag Italiani). Under the name of Mahzor Romaniya this ritual the oldest in Europe had come from far Byzantium to Southern Italy, where it was transformed by the Congregation of Rome into the standard ritual for Italy.† A bulky vol-

---

* The term Mahzor is applied by the Sephardim to all the prayers of the year, by the Ashkenazim only to the prayers for the festivals.

† Benjacob, Ozar Hasepharim, title "Mahzor." This Mahzor was republished twice by Soncino, again by the silk weavers of Bologna in 1540, and several Italian translations have been published. In the Mantua (1560) edition it is called Mahzor Itali.

ume is this first Soncino edition; found entire only when pieced together from stray fragments and pages by the care and knowledge of the booklover. It seems especially to have roused the ire of the Inquisitors, for its destruction is almost complete; of the copies extant all bear traces of the hand of its foes, and torn pages still further defaced by the ink scrawl of censors are eloquent in their silence.* This great Mahzor which Israel Nathan Soncino likened to a "ladder set up on the earth whose top reaches into heaven upon which we may ascend to supplicate our Maker, may He be blessed," was commenced "by us the sons of Sonzin in the City of Sonzin on the New Moon of Tishri in the year 246 of the Sixth Millennium, and completed here in Casal Maiore (Casal Maggiore) on the second day of the week the twentieth day of the month Ellul in the year 5246 of the creation of the world." The family had evidently taken hasty flight from Soncino to Casalmaggiore, a little town about twenty-two miles east of Cremona, a flight which marks the beginning of their wanderings from city to city until Gerson Soncino's final exodus from Italy in 1527.

In 1485, before their flight to Casalmaggiore, they printed their first Biblical text the "Earlier

---

* In the Alenu prayer of this edition Joshua Solomon Soncino censored the text for fear of offending the ecclesiastics. In the passage " they worship vanity and emptiness and make supplication to a god who cannot save " the words "vanity and emptiness" and "to a god who cannot save" are omitted and a staring blank indicates to the knowing reader that words are here to be introduced which may be spoken but not written.

Prophets," * followed by the famous philosophical work on the fundamentals of the Jewish religion "The Book of Roots" (Ikkarim) by Joseph Albo, a contemporary of Israel Nathan Soncino, who died while the latter was still a young man. His book essays to develop the religious philosophy of Judaism along the lines laid down by Maimonides in his thirteen articles, and although scholars are divided as to its originality, it is admittedly one of the most influential books of religious philosophy.†

At the completion of the edition of the Ikkarim, the printers at Soncino in the justifiable pride of accomplishment wrote, playing on the well-known text of Isaiah, "From Zion shall go forth the law and the word of God from Soncino." We do not know whether their interpretation of the "word of God" included all the splendid works in Jewish literature that they had already published, or whether the phrase used in its narrower sense as referring to the Bible alone was intended to fore-

---

* The importance of this edition is shown by the variae lectiones found in it by Tychsen, De Rossi and Baer. Berliner "Aus Meiner Bibliothek", p. 25.

† A later commentator, one Gedalyah ben Solomon of Poland, published a commentary which he called "The Tree Planted" a title taken from the verse of the first Psalm, "And he shall be like a tree planted by the rivers of water that bringeth forth his fruit in his season; his leaf also shall not wither," and playing upon the title of Albo's book of "Roots" he divided his commentary into portions called "trunks" "branches" and "leaves" all of them based upon the "roots" of the Master.

In 1486 the "Later Prophets" and the first printed prayer book 'Sidorello', whose title is a quaint union of Hebrew and Italian, were printed before the flight to Casal Maggiore.

cast their great undertaking the complete text of the Bible. For this great work they had the expert assistance of the Dyer of Pesaro the skilled Abraham ben Hayyim, who came to Soncino from Bologna where he had been working at the press of Caravita, and together they produced the first edition of the most important book in the Hebrew language and in the literatures of the world the complete edition of the Bible with accents and vowel points* finished at Soncino on Tuesday the second day of Iyyar 5284 corresponding to February 23, 1488.† In the same year after the completion of this work Joshua Solomon issued the "Supplication of the M's"‡ of Bedersi and Kimhi's grammar "Walk through the pathways of knowledge"¶ and his nephew Gerson the most renowned of the family, appears as the publisher of the code of Moses of Coucy the "Semag."** After having issued in 1489 a number of Talmudic treatises, Joshua Solomon determined to leave Soncino probably moved by the death of his father and brother and the turbulent conditions in the principalities of Northern Italy which interfered with all peaceful pursuits. There was renewed persecution of the

---

* In 1492 Reuchlin paid 6 gold florins at Rome for a copy of this book. Freimann, Ueber heb. Ink. p. 4.

† Before this publication they issued the "Tahanunim" and Rashi to the Pentateuch in 1487.

‡ So called because M is the initial letter of the whole supplication.

¶ Mahalah Shebile Hadaat.

** "Semag" is a word formed of the initial letters of Sefer Mizvot Gadol, the Great Book of the Commandments, a code of law compiled in the 13th century.

Jews throughout the Duchy of Milan, and to use the words of the chronicler Joseph Hacohen* "Lodovico Il Moro the regent of Milan again falsely accused the Jews cast them into prison and exiled them from his land, after having extorted much money from them."

Looking about him for a new home Joshua Solomon decided to follow his workmen Solomon ben Perez Bonfoi to Naples where King Ferrante I, under the influence of his Jewish physician Guglielmo di Portaleone, showed the large and prosperous Jewish community many marks of his favor.

One of the first books of Jewish interest published at Naples issued from the press of Francesco di Dino a Florentine residing at Naples near the monastery of Fuligno.† It was an alleged epistle of Rabbi Samuel a Moroccan Jew ‡ but was one of the many infamous books written against Jews by their bitterest foes the apostates who were anxious to prove the completeness of their Christianity by the most inhuman and barbarous attacks on their former brethren in faith. The first Hebrew press at Naples was founded in 1486 by Germans—witness their Hebrew name Ashkenazi and their surname probably taken from their native town Gunzenhauser.¶

* Emek Habacha, ed. Letteris, p. 83.

† Fumagalli, p. 138.

‡ Berliner "Aus Meiner Bibliothek", p. 56; Schwab, "les incunables", p. 10.

¶ The first book of their press published by Hayyim the Levite the German (Ashkenazi) is the "Proverbs" of Immanuel of Rome,

About the same time that Joshua Solomon Soncino came to Naples we hear of another printer Isaac ben Judah Ibn Katorzi of Aragon, whose name indicates that his family had lived in the Iberian peninsula during the days of the Moor and who had probably learned his trade from one of the masters of the press who flourished there before the general expulsion in 1492.* Four of

then followed Hagiographa 1486; Psalms 1487; Ibn Ezra's commentary on the Pentateuch 1488; the "Makre Dardeke" or Instructor of boys, issued in this year is a Hebrew, Italian, Arabic and French lexicon; printer unknown. In 1489, the year in which Joshua Solomon Soncino probably left his native city, the presses of Ashkenazi under the direction of Joseph ben Jacob Gunzenhauser produced several philosophic works, among them the "Tried Stone" (Eben Bohan) of Kalonymos ben Kalonymos of the Provence, the "Duties of the Heart" (Hobot Halebabot) by Bahya ben Joseph ibn Pakuda, and the "Gate of Reward" (Shaar Hagemul) the eschatological conclusion of a larger book dealing with mourning and burial ceremonies written by Nahmanides about the middle of the thirteenth century. Some of these books were corrected for the press of the Ashkenazi by the brothers Yomtob and Solomon ben Perez Bonfoi the latter of whom had been employed at the press of Soncino. The cosmopolitanism of the Hebrew workshop is shown by the names of the printers of Naples, among whom we find Germans, Frenchmen, Italians, Portuguese and Spaniards. Ersch & Gruber 28 : 36.

* Only two of his publications are known, Nahmanides' commentary on the Pentateuch which immediately preceded, and Rabbi David Kimhi's "Book of Roots" which immediately followed Joshua Solomon Soncino's first publication in that city in 1490. Katorzi recommends the "Book of Roots" in the epigraph as a book in which the reader will find no end of information, and which differs from all other books of the kind which by comparison are insipid without salt. This may have been an attack on the edition of the "Book of Roots" issued by Joseph Gunzenhauser in August 1490 edited by Samuel ben Meir Latif, perhaps the same Samuel Latif who printed at Mantua in 1513 and an attempt to divert book buyers from the shop of the older printer.

Soncino's publications are known,* most important among them a fine edition of the Pentateuch. No doubt he as well as his fellow-craftsmen in Naples would have continued to produce good books had not the world politics of the year 1492 and the problems of the Jewish community arising out of the expulsion of the Jews from Spain put an end forever to the activity of the Neapolitan Hebrew presses.

Two of the last books published at Naples were the "Agur" of Jacob Landau, and the "Canon" of Avicenna. Abu Ali ben Abdallah Ibn Sina or as he is known by the Latinized corruption of his name Avicenna about the beginning of the eleventh century wrote a medical encyclopedia, which for five hundred years was a recognized authority at the European universities. The Jews' knowledge of Arabic gave them the key to this great storehouse of medical knowledge, to which they were devoted *par excellence* throughout the Middle Ages.†   In the middle of the thirteenth century it was translated into Hebrew by Nathan of Cento, and one of the distinctions of Dr. Israel Nathan Soncino was his index to this great work, never printed but seen in manuscript by De Rossi,‡ and now in the Royal Library at Parma.¶ In 1491

* Psalms, Proverbs and Job, 1490; Bible, 1491; Pentateuch with accents, 1491; Mishnah, 1492. He probably printed others not now identified.

† Depping, p. 386.

‡ Sacchi, p. 48.

¶ Hebr. Codex 927 ; Soave p. 6.

the press of Ashkenazi this time presided over by Azriel ben Joseph Gunzenhauser, undertook the publication of this immense work in five parts. Among the compositors was Abraham ben Jacob Landau a kinsman of Jacob Baruh ben Judah Landau who after having corrected the edition of the Psalms with the commentary of Kimhi published by the Ashkenazi in 1487, prepared for publication his own work the "Agur" probably the last work printed in Naples and the second Hebrew book published during the lifetime of the author.* It is further distinguished in Hebrew book-making as the first book containing a rabbinical approbation† by the same Messer Leon, who no doubt met the author while he was living in Northern Italy. These are the words with which Messer Leon introduced the work of his contemporary to the reading public:

"Behold I have seen that which our distinguished master and teacher Jacob Landau has wrought, who has compiled a valuable book called "Agur" wherein he has gathered and collected the laws of the daily service and of the festivals and all that is forbidden and allowed, and all matters thereunto appertaining. And it is a work that

---

* The first having been the "Drippings of the Honeycomb" (Nofet Zufim) by Messer Leon, published at Mantua.

† In fact it contains eight approbations by Messer Leon, Jacob ben David Provencal, of Marseilles, Benzion ben Raphael Danuit(?), Isaac ben Samuel, Moses ben Shemtob Ibn Habib, Solomon Hayyim ben Yehiel, Raphael Cohen, Nathanel ben Levi of Jerusalem, and David ben Judah Messer Leon.

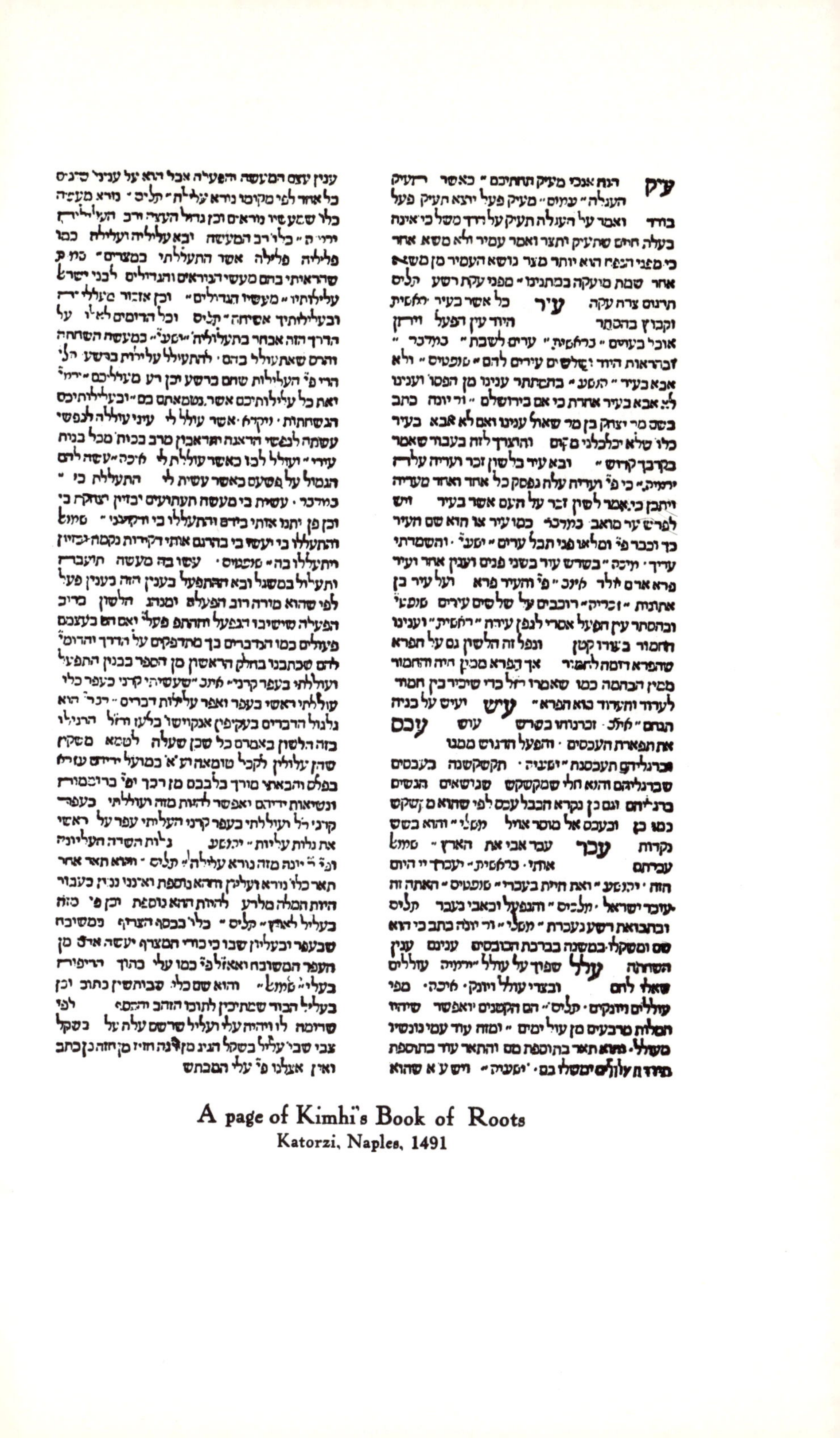

A page of Kimhi's Book of Roots

Katorzi, Naples, 1491

giveth goodly words concerning customs and important decisions. Therefore have I set my hand to these drippings of the honeycomb, these words of pleasantness."*

The press of Naples was silenced by the momentous events of the year 1492. When the Jews of Spain had landed at Naples a plague broke out among them; this has scarcely abated when Charles VIII. of France entered Naples and put it to the sword. In this misery and tumult the entire Jewish community of Naples was dissolved and the fate of its printers is sealed in eternal darkness. Whether Joshua Solomon Soncino died in Naples, or fleeing survived these fearsome events is unknown. Probably he met his death; otherwise he must have taken refuge at Brescia with his nephew Gerson, in whose books his name would have appeared. In 1520 there were no Hebrew types left in Naples, for in the book of Benedicto de Falco published in that year on the Hebrew Latin and Greek alphabets, the names of Hebrew letters are given in Latin.† Soon after this the Jews were expelled from Naples by royal decree and for nearly three hundred years Naples lay outside the pale of Jewish history. It was not

---

* Approbations were unknown during the Middle Ages and books passed on their merits. The approbation was an invention of Christian clergy, intended to guarantee the orthodoxy of the work; the Hebrew approbation or Haskamah followed. Perles "Beiträge" p. 202 states that the approbation to Elijah Levita's "Bahur" Rome, 1518 is the first. This is an error.

† Schwab, p. 84.

until the settlement there of five or six Jews in the
early part of the nineteenth century that the
foundations were laid for a new congregation of
Israel in this beautiful but unfortunate city.

CHAPTER IV.

GERSON SONCINO (1488–1497).

Milan and Venice—The Name of Gerson—His Biographers—His Character and Achievements—The First Illustrated Book—At Brescia—War and Persecution—At Barco—Expurgation—Gerson the Wanderer—At Venice—Padre Georgi.

THE Jews who entered the Duchy of Milan after the valiant soldier and wise administrator Francesco Sforza had permitted Samuel Mentzlan to settle at Soncino, were sent forth into exile through the unwisdom of his son the usurping Lodovico Il Moro.* Among the wanderers from this land of persecution two figures attract our attention, Joshua Solomon Soncino bidding farewell to his nephew and fellow-craftsman Gerson, and journeying to far Naples—Gerson, after a short struggle to retain a hold in his native city, also grasping the wanderer's staff, turning his back on Soncino forever to find a temporary home in Brescia under the protection of the winged lion of St. Mark. We have followed Joshua Solomon to Naples, where he had hoped to escape persecution and find a peaceful home, and we know how the events of the year 1492 and the wars following the invasion of Charles VIII shattered his dreams, how in the final capture of Naples the Jewish community was broken and scattered and the devoted printer probably laid

* Sacchi, p. 51.

among the unknown dead whose unmarked graves
were the only relics of the once flourishing community of Jews in that fateful city.

What of the other survivor of the house of
Soncino? Lodovico Sforza, though wise and skillful enough to wrest the throne of Milan from its
lawful possessor, was blind to the advantage that
the Jews were to his Duchy, an advantage that
was quite clear to the unscrupulous but versatile
intelligence of his father Francesco. As the decline of Spain commences with the period of the
expulsion of her Jews, so the independence and
sovereignty of Milan were forfeited at the time
when she drove from her soil these, who were
among her best citizens. Only blind Chauvinism
sees in these events cause and effect, but fair judgment will not deny that the persecution and exile
of the Jews were symptomatic of political inepti-
tude and were the result of a policy based on far-
reaching evils. In 1500 Lodovico lost his throne
the Duchy its independence and thereafter for
three hundred and fifty years it was alternately
held by France Germany Spain and Austria until
it was finally incorporated with the present kingdom of Italy. In 1541 the Emperor Charles V
confirmed the ancient privileges of those Jews that
had returned after Lodovico's decree of exile and
in 1597 they were again driven into exile.*

Westernmost of the Venetian territories on the
boundary of Milan lay Brescia, the nearest great

* H. B. 1 : 18.

city to which the wandering Gerson Soncino could turn. Here he was temporarily safe under the protection of the Venetian Podestà, whose dignity like that of the ancient Roman procurator was derived from the great power of which he was the representative. Of all the territories tributary to Venice, none was more valuable to her than Brescia "the armed," for from her workshops famed for centuries and even to our own day came the most splendid specimens of the armorer's art, the weapons of war so valiantly used by the island republic in her many wars of conquest and defense. Like Ancient Rome, Venice stretched forth a grasping arm across sea and land for territorial sovereignty; her capital was a world city whose cosmopolitanism saved her from many of those excesses that disgraced more provincial and fanatical communities; her great trade saved her from insular narrowness; in her harbor lay the ships of all nations; on her piazzas met the representatives of all the world. Although the Church was likewise imperial in theory and practice and sought to lay the entire world under her dominion, she differed in one fundamental characteristic from Venice. For whereas the Church notwithstanding her universal empire touching all climes and times remained rigid intolerant and self-sufficient, Venice respected the opinion of others and looked with dignified tolerance upon those who differed from her in dress speech thought or religion.* Her

* Graetz, 8 : 234.

commercial prosperity instead of chaining her to the dull routine of mere money-making, expanded her ideas and enlightened her mind by contact with all the world, and during the fifteenth century even after the Ghetto gates were erected for them, the Jews of Venice enjoyed many privileges denied them by other States, excepting always those that patterned their policy after the brilliant example of the great Venetian republic.

Before following the fortunes of Gerson Soncino in his wanderings through Italy, let us pause a moment to look back at his early career in the city whose name he bore. We shall call him Gerson Soncino, although in the synagogue he was called to the law as Gershom ben Mosheh, and in his non-Jewish books he calls himself Hieronymus.* Ordinarily it may not be worth while to dwell on a mere name, but we are now speaking of the man who although not first in time was first in importance among Hebrew printers, and who for upwards of fifty years during several of which he was the only Hebrew printer in the world, printed about one hundred

* Soave, p. 12, citing S. D. Luzzatto, states that Joseph Almanzi first discovered the identity of Gerson and Hieronymus Soncinoi Manzoni points out that his Hebrew name is Gershom, (not Gershon, as in Jew. Enc. article "Soncino") and that the following forms of the name have been used by the bibliographers:—Gereshom, Gershom, Gersham, Gersam, Jersam, Gershon, Gerson and in Italian Gersone. Manzoni himself calls him Gershom. I have followed Sacchi and Steinschneider and call him Gerson. His Italian biographer Sacchi, his ear attuned to the music of Italian speech, preferred "Gersone" or "Gerson" to "Gershom" and it is not unlikely that he was so called even in his lifetime.

and fifty Hebrew Latin and Italian books, many of them of great size, many of them of great importance, all of them distinguished by brilliant execution and careful scholarly editing.

It is difficult to value a great man's career, since admiration for its brilliance is apt to lead into exaggeration of its importance; but the most temperate judgment will not deny the importance of Gerson's service to scholarship and the cultivation of good taste and to the development of the spirit of toleration and brotherhood between Jew and non-Jew, which is now the shining distinction of Italy. In modern Italy alone of all the great Christian nations of the continent anti-Semitism is unknown, and the citizen and patriot is judged by a truer standard than that which considers his attendance at synagogue or cathedral. In his lifetime Gerson consorted freely with his Christian fellows, and it is through this intercourse that we know of some of the most interesting episodes in his life. His life has likewise attracted the attention of Christian scholars, and indeed almost all that we know of him is due to the work of three of them the indefatigable and zealous churchman De Rossi,* the learned and cultured nobleman Manzoni,† and the scholarly litterateur Sac-

* 1742–1831. Appointed in 1769 Professor of Orientalia at Parma; for biographical sketch see Jew. Enc. 10 : 486.

† 1816–1889. Count Giacomo Manzoni commenced collection of Hebrew books at age of fourteen. Studied Hebrew and became an enthusiastic scholar and friend of the Jews and a defender of their rights. Berliner, "Aus meiner Bibliothek" p. IV. note.

ואומר משתבל חי עב אלדי הראשונים ומי ידמה לך ובלי ומתם מלך מיגלג כתשבחתיובולי
וקודם שיאמר קדיש אומר זה הקינות

יַה שמך ארוממך   רצדקתך לא אכסה
האזנתי והאמנתי   לא אשאל ולא אנסה
ואיך אומר כלי חומר   אליוצרו מה תעשה
דרשתדך פגשתידו   למגדל עוז וצור מחסה
הבהיר כאור מזהיר   באין מסך ולא מכסה

ישתבח ויתפאר ויתרומם ויתנשא

הדרת כבודך ועח ידך   מספרים השמים
בעת עלותם ובעת פנותם   ובעת שחותם, אפים
ומלאבים טהלכים   בתוך אבני אש ומים
יעידך ויודך   בוראניב שפתים
כי תסכול ולא אתבול   בלי זרוע ודים
תחתיות ועליות   ההחיות והכסא

ישתבח ויתפאר ויתרומם ויתנשא

ומי ימלל כבוד מחולל   השחקים באמרתו
חי עולם אשר נעלם   בגבהירום מעונתו
וברצותו בבן ביתו   באדלושת שבינתו
דשס מראות לנבואות   להביט אל תמונתו
ואין תבנית ואין תבנית   ואין קץ לתבונתו
רק מראיו בעין נביאי   כמלדרם ומתנשא

ישתבח ויתפאר ויתרומם ויתנשא

דבר גבורות בלי ספורות   ומיספר תהלותיו
אשרי איש אשר יחיש   להוכיר עוז גדולותיו
ויסמך באלתומך   עולם סעל גבולותיו
דעריצו טוב ורצוא   ויצדיק דיך עלילותיו
ויודה על אשר פעל   כי למענו פעולותיו
ובי יש יום לאל איום   ודין על כל המעשה

ישתבח ויתפאר ויתרומם ויתנשא

השתונן והתבונן   והבונן בסודך
והבטת מה אתה   ומאן יצוך
ומי הביגך ומי הביגך   וכחמי עירך
והבט אל גבורות אל   והעירה כבודך
חקור פעליו רק אליו   אל תשלח ידך
כי תורוש בסוף ובראש   במופלא ובמכוסה

ישתבח ויתפאר ויתרומם ויתנשא

ואומר חזן קדיש עד לעילא   כמנהג ואחר כך אמר יוצר של ראש השנה וזאת מלך אורנבורג

A page from the Mahzor

Soncino, 1486

chi,* and lest we be accused of ingratitude to a
great Jewish scholar, let us at this time acknowledge the debt we owe to the incomparable work of
Moritz Steinschneider, who in his "Jüdische
Literatur" "Jüdische Typographie und Jüdischer
Buchhandel" and his innumerable works in Hebrew Bibliography has built a monument that
shall endure as long as Hebrew books are read.
As a nonagenarian he was still working with the
same devotion as when fifty-five years ago he
wrote of Gerson Soncino, "the true founder of the
typographical fame of the family of the Soncinati,"
and he has but lately been called to eternal rest
after a life of extraordinary activity and usefulness.

The history of the Soncino press may be traced
for four generations in Italy and Turkey, but its
true fame rests as this greatest of Hebrew bibliographers has said on the work of Gerson.   As the
synagogues of Italy show the influence of church
architecture, so the Hebrew books of Italy bear
unmistakable evidence of its artistic atmosphere.
The presses of Gerson Soncino were set up in the
cities where Bellini, Perugino, Mantegna and Giulio
Romano painted; his types were cut by Francesco
Griffo one of the greatest engravers of his time; he
sought the patronage of Cesare Borgia, the Sforza
the Rovere and the Gonzaga and considered himself

* Federico Sacchi published "i tipografi ebrei di Soncino" at
Cremona 1877. He made investigations in British Museum and his
preface is dated at London. I am not quite sure that he was not a
Jew. See also Soave "Dei Soncino celebri tipografi italiani dei secoli
XV. e XVI" Venice 1878.

the rival of the great Aldo Manuzio. He went on journeys of exploration to distant cities seeking rare manuscripts and the society of learned scholars brilliant artists and celebrated priests. We find him in far-off Geneva and Cambrai, as well as in the brilliant environs of Padua and Venice, fortifying his talent with new ideas and bringing fresh inspiration to his work.

This intellectual strength and æsthetic taste did not chill his sympathy for the poor and oppressed, and it was not in vain that the victims of persecution appealed to his warm human interest. The virtues of his ancestry and the grace of mind and manner that was a blend of his Italian and Jewish culture, enabled him throughout his extraordinarily long career to suffer with equanimity "the slings and arrows of outrageous fortune" and to continue on his way with undiminished powers and hopefulness. Faithful to his ideal in his work, true to the call of his suffering kin, he remained steadfast in the faith of his fathers* bearing privation oppression and contumely, rather than speak the few words at the baptismal font that would have given him rest and riches and honor. True to his work his blood and his faith, he was loyal to the country that had exiled him, for when in the evening of his life he with many co-religionists left beautiful Italy and sought a

*Among his teachers were the French Rabbis Belvegna Trabot Mirabelle and Moses Bazla to whose influence he bears testimony later in his career. Sacchi p. 25.

new home under the Crescent of Mohammed, he ever after looked back with tearful longing to the land of his birth misruled by the Vicar of Christ.

The father and uncle of Gerson, Moses and Joshua Solomon sons of Israel Nathan Soncino were the founders of the press that bore their name. Israel Nathan was the inspirer of the enterprise Joshua Solomon the chief printer. Solomon son of Moses a brother of Gerson was also associated with the work and all these together with Gerson formed a notable printing house united by blood and affection and a common zeal for the "holy work." The first work bearing the name of Gerson is the "Great Book of the Commandments" of Moses of Coucy, issued in 1488 while the family was yet united, Israel Nathan and his son Moses yet alive and Joshua Solomon not yet gone to Naples. It seems that although Joshua Solomon's name appears in most of the books of the first five years of the press, the others were entitled to an equal share of the credit of their production and it may be that the younger men after serving their apprenticeship were rewarded by permission to attach their names to an occasional publication. Thus while Gerson appears as the printer of the Book of Moses of Coucy, his brother Solomon in 1490 appears as the printer of a new edition of that other great law book, the Turim of Jacob ben Asher. Gerson's grandfather Israel Nathan and his father Moses died within a year, his uncle Joshua Solomon went to Naples, and the ties of home thus broken Gerson yielded to slight pressure and departed for Brescia.   He had already printed two fine books, another great law book the "Strong Hand" of Maimonides in 1490 and a collection of allegories and fables in rhymed prose entitled "Ancient Fable" (Meshal Hakadmoni) by Isaac Ibn Sahula, in both of which the art of the illustrator was applied in decided violation of the traditional interpretation of the second commandment.   The book of fables lent itself readily to pictorial representation of beasts and birds and men; in the law book the illustration consisted of decorated initial letters, an arabesque title border and the use of figures such as an angel with a spear directed toward a devil's head and two angels on either side of a wreath* Without abatement of his interest in Judaism Gerson published with Olympian impartiality the most absurd monkish tales, Catholic books of devotion and books which set forth all the pretensions to infallibility that characterized medieval Christianity.†

For four years Gerson Soncino dwelt in Brescia and printed Bibles and prayer books, and there is great significance in the character of the productions of his press.   When men are in daily terror

---

* Z. H. B. 8 : 58.

† Gerson's brother Solomon seems, to have continued the press at Soncino. In 1495 three books appeared bearing his name, a Mahzor, a Prayer book and a book of penitential prayers. Perhaps the edition of Talm. Bezah of 1493 is also to be ascribed to him. According to Sacchi (p. 16). Solomon died in 1490, but this seems to be disproved by the books of 1495.

of their lives and in fear of the confiscating hand of the oppressor they have no inclination for the delights of literature, unless they belong to that very small class of higher natures who like the philosopher of old can live in the free world of spirit while their bodies lie bound in chains. In conditions of great trial and tribulation men pray but they do not study, they possess Bibles and prayer books but no libraries. As long as the Jew lived like his ancestors in Egypt with his loins girded his shoes on his feet and his staff in his hand, waiting the approach of a fanatical mob or the soldiers of some confiscating prince, a library of books and devotion to scholarship remained to him merely a millennial dream. Hence it was not until the end of the seventeenth century that large Hebrew libraries began to be formed, and even then only in some specially favored communities. The first book printed by Gerson Soncino at Brescia was a work of pure literature, the first and also the last of its class printed by him during those four years, the Mahberot of Immanuel of Rome a collection of poems novels epigrams and parodies. The books that followed were the necessities of the religious rather than the luxuries of the intellectual life. He printed Pentateuchs, from which the weekly portions were read in the synagogue, Psalms, always a favorite with those in affliction, prayer books for daily devotion, and penitential prayers for fast days now specially desired in these times of universal affliction and persecution.

The Brescia Bible of 1494 is a notable book. It was the text used by Luther in making his translation, and the great reformer's copy is now in the Royal Library at Berlin.*

On the broad board of Italian politics the Jews were insignificant pawns. Kings bishops and knights great and small keen-witted and unscrupulous, were playing the fascinating game of politics in which moves were guided by intrigue, plots met by war and counterplot. Sword in hand and lie on lip they faced each other, and chief among them all for unscrupulous faithlessness was the greatest of them Pope Alexander VI the famous or infamous Roderigo Borgia. The peace of Italy was destroyed; Charles VIII of France marched into Milan and destroyed the equilibrium of the entire peninsula; the Medici were expelled from Florence and Naples was taken. Finally the great league of Pope Emperor and Doge assisted by many of the minor powers, met and drove back the conquering Frenchman. Fighting was continuous, and in the trail of war came those barbarities worse than death itself. In the midst of these terrors by day

---

* There are but few copies of this book in existence. In 1896 but two copies were known. Berliner, "Einfluss" p. 4. In 1904 we hear of seven. Jew. Enc. Art. "Incunabula." The Prophets and Hagiographa of this edition are inexact in accents; this branch of Hebrew grammar was not developed until later. H. B. 1 : 41. It must have been one of the Soncino editions that is referred to in the following entry in the Diary of Marino Sanuto " 17 July 1509. On the way to my house I met a man having a beautiful Hebrew Bible on good paper value 20 ducats, who sold it to me as a favor for one marzello: I took it to place it in my library."

and terrors by night, Gerson Soncino continued
at the work of his press, making prayer books and
penitential litanies for the agonized worshipers
of the God of Israel. Even these books were in
paltry demand, for as he complained the Sacred
Scriptures were forgotten, readers were scarce and
purchasers few, desolation and misery reigned in
all the cities; through his art he hoped to supply
the text books for students, for the copyists had
ceased their work through persecution and suffering.* Suddenly we find that he has again taken
flight and has set up his press at Barco. Here too
the first work of his press was a volume of Selihot
(penitential prayers), but his second the last book
printed by him for five years was the Talmudic
treatise "Courts" (Sanhedrin), dealing with the
constitution and procedure of courts and the substance of criminal law. In this publication Gerson
showed how wisely he read the signs of the times.
Even in the cities in which they were most favored
the Jews were simply tolerated, and the wise man
sought refuge behind the sheltering wall of obscurity, for to attract attention was dangerous
often fatal,—to criticise the practice or theory of
the Church or the State was suicide. Therefore
Gerson following the practice of many scribes and
of his uncle Joshua Solomon Soncino, carefully
edited this Talmudic treatise "Courts," expurgating passages or words likely to offend some Christian adversary, even taking liberties with ancient

* Epigraph to Brescia Bible.

texts by substituting inoffensive phrases for dangerous ones. There was as yet no official censorship by the Church; that chapter in the history of human folly had yet to be written, but many Hebrew books had drawn the fire of ecclesiastical condemnation by reason of comparatively harmless and perfectly natural anti-Christian sentiments. Thus the commentary of Kimhi on the Psalms first published at Bologna in 1477 contained the learned author's bold protests against the arrogance of the faith that claimed all truth for itself and condemned all else as damnable error. When Rashi explained the meaning of the word "Goyim" as "disciples of Jesus of Nazareth"* he little suspected the burden of woe that he was thereby preparing for posterity, for the hatred of Jewish apostates as well as of unlearned ecclesiastics seeing in every use of the word "Goi" a direct reflection upon the Christian religion, triumphantly pointed to the authority of Rashi acknowledged as the greatest of Jewish commentators. So that in later years, when the ardent persecution of Hebrew books had become common, it became necessary in many cities to publish some such pathetic disclaimer of guilt as the following: "Be it known that if the reader finds in this book the word 'Goi' or 'strange worship,' or the like, it refers to the nations who lived in the days of the sages of the Talmud, who were the worshipers of stars and constellations, who denied Providence resurrec-

* Popper, p. 21.

tion of the dead and the law of Moses; but it does not refer to the nations of our own time among whom we dwell, who observe justice and righteousness and believe in Providence and the law of Moses and the prophets, a faith which should bring blessings upon them, and not a curse, God forbid." Wherefore, Gerson Soncino drew his pen through Rashi's explanation of "Goi," and to make it clear that Christians were not meant wrote "Those who do not believe in the law of Moses which he received from Heaven," a phrase to which none could take exception, for even the Popes were wont to say to the delegation of Roman Jews who came to congratulate them on entering upon their pontificate, "The Holy Law we praise and honor, ye Hebrews, for it was given unto your forefathers by Almighty God through the hand of Moses."*

Notwithstanding Gerson's care in expurgating his edition of "Sanhedrin," it met the common fate of Hebrew books, and to-day there is only one known copy, once the property of Rabbi Isaac Pardo of Verona, now in the collection of the British Museum.

After this service to his people, Gerson Soncino

---

* Part of the reply of Pope Leo X to the delegation of Jews. The rest of the reply is as follows:—"Your observance and interpretation of it we condemn and disapprove, since the Apostolic Creed teaches the advent of the Messiah, whom you still vainly expect, and preaches our Lord Jesus Christ, who lives with the father and the holy ghost and reigns as God for all eternity." Vogelstein and Rieger "Geschichte der Juden in Rom" II. 33.

apparently himself became a victim to the stress and strife of the time, and for five years from 1497 to 1502 his press was silent. During these last two years of his work in Brescia and Barco he was the only Hebrew printer in the world; all of the other presses of Italy had ceased, and those in Spain and Portugal were silenced forever, the Constantinople press did not begin until 1503, and in Northern Europe no press was established until 1513 when

A Typical Soncino initial **word**

Gerson Cohen ben Solomon began to print at Prague.*   The darkness of these five years in the history of Gerson the wanderer † is intensified by the insignificant fragments of information that have come down to us. We know that he did not remain at Barco nor even in Italy, but wandered northward into France and Switzerland visiting various Jewish communities and consorting with

* Zunz "Zur Geschichte und Literatur" p. 261.
† Depping p. 380.

their scholars and scribes. For notwithstanding the establishment of the printing press in Italy Spain and Portugal, books still continued to be multiplied by the slow process of the pen of the scribe. Hebrew manuscripts, always comparatively rare by reason of the time and care required in their production, had now become extremely rare in Italy, and after the persecution of Hebrew books was thoroughly organized in the sixteenth century they disappeared almost completely. Therefore when Gerson found a manuscript in some out of the way corner of France or Switzerland he purchased it to take back to Italy, in the hope that he might some day be permitted to resume his work. At some time during this period he lived at Venice and was attached to the ancient patrician House of Tiepolo whose palaces bearing two obelisks on the roofs, may still be seen on the Grand Canal. It was probably at this time that he met Aldo Manuzio, whose house on the Campo Sant' Agostino was near the palace of the "gran cavaliere", Bajamonte Tiepolo* and there arose between the two great printers an animosity, whose traces we shall see when we take up Gerson's activity at Fano. And here too he made another friend the Franciscan Padre Francesco Georgi to whom the first book published by him at Fano was dedicated by his corrector and friend Lorenzo Astemio.† The Padre Georgi was one of many

* Clement "Queen of the Adriatic" p. 326.
† Manzoni "Annales" part II p. 150.

Christian Hebraists entangled in the meshes of the Cabbala, that mystical science whose only real service has been the reconciliation of many Jews and non-Jews, who but for this union of interest might never have been brought together. In this way the Cabbala has served to help on the millennial day when the lion and the lamb shall lie down together.*

In studying the history of Gerson Soncino nothing is more to be regretted than the absence of any record of these five years of his wanderings. What an incalculably valuable book of travels he might have written, illuminating many dark pages, not only of Jewish history but of the general history of the times. For after all there is little known of the history of the people of the end of the fifteenth century, and our sources of information consist largely of the gossip of courts the records of military enterprises the debates of clergymen upon theological abstractions and the memoirs of the dilettanti in literature. Of the people we know nothing; they had no history, they existed merely for the purpose of furnishing soldiers and money for their rulers. Hence the chronicles of the times are meagre in those details, the customs the manners daily life and habits of the people that would be to us of supreme importance,† What happened to Gerson on his

---

* Manzoni p. 5.

† We have too few records to enable us to render an adequate verdict on the civil status of the Jews of this epoch in other parts of Italy. Depping "Die Juden im Mittelalter," p. 363.

wanderings, whom did he meet and converse with, what befell him at the inns on the roadside in the academies of learning at the houses of scholars and merchants and in the humbler habitations of his poorer brethren? There is left to us only a vast regret that a man so rich in intellectual gifts and so broad in his sympathies should have missed the opportunity to record these precious impressions of men and affairs and have left us practically nothing except a fleeting reference in the epigraph to one or two of his books.

CHAPTER V.

GERSON SONCINO (1501–1512).

IN the year 1501 our Jewish traveler passed under the old triumphal Arch of Augustus, and found himself at the city gate of Fano. He had wandered far and wide through the less hospitable plains of France and highlands of Switzerland, and at last had come back to "il bel paese," the land of his birth. From Venice where he had found noble patrons in the house of Tiepolo, he at last turned southward into the duchy of Urbino, whose capital city Duke Guidobaldo had made the meeting place of the choicest spirits of Italy. No longer did the noble house of Montefeltre bear sway, for a new master had arisen Cesare Borgia the famous son of the reigning Pope Alexander VI. Since 1497 the Duke of Romagna as he was entitled by his father, was mastering the Marches and developing ambitious schemes whose fruition was to make him the most powerful prince in Italy. Pesaro Rimini Faenza Forli and Fano had fallen before him, and the citizens of Fano had shown their loyalty to the usurper, whose rule they found lighter than that of their legitimate sovereign, by successfully defending the city against Duke Guidobaldo's attempt to retake it. For this they had been loaded with favors and pontifical privileges.* The policy of Borgia like that of all tyrants, was to conciliate the people while undermining the power of their rulers. The Jews of Fano of whom there were many enjoyed the favor of the terrible Borgia, who like the Malatesti of old treated them kindly and used their intelligence for the advantage of the State. Indeed thrice had the Malatesti suffered excommunication for their defiance of the Papal wishes regarding the treatment of their Jews.† Of course the son of the Pope with his father's statecraft before him had to fear no such danger, for the Pope acting as a temporal sovereign had received the Jews in his territories because of their value to his State at the very time when as head of the Church he had sanctioned their exile from Spain and Portugal because they were enemies of Christ. The policy of the princes of Italy simple enough though in its development it often appeared intricate and ob-

* Sacchi p. 52 n. 24.
† Jew. Enc. 5 : 340.

scure, is best known through the name of its ablest scientific exponent Machiavelli, and in the words of this crafty Florentine was designed "to secure the ruler against enemies, to gain himself friends, to overcome opposition by force or fraud, to make himself beloved or feared by the people and reverenced by the soldiers, to destroy and exterminate such as would injure him . . . to make kings or princes either obliged to requite him or afraid to offend him."* And as an example worthy of imitation, Machiavelli points to Cesare Borgia as the freshest and best model for princes.

What led our printer to Fano, into the jaws of the tyrant Borgia? Evidently contemporary opinion was not unanimous in condemning him and indeed there must have been something attractive in his personality or his rule to have warranted Gerson in placing himself and his art at his disposal. Why did Gerson not remain at Venice and seek to establish a Hebrew press there in the very heart of the world of letters, where he had friends and patrons. Perhaps it was lack of funds to buy the necessary privilege from the Signoria, perhaps it was the strength of Aldo's influence that prevented him from becoming the first of the Hebrew printers of Venice. After he had been established at Fano, he gives as a reason for settling in that city that he was pleased "with the air, the site and the fertility of your devoted city of Fano and the friendliness and wit of its inhabitants." Strange

* Machiavelli "The Prince" Chap. VII.

reasons indeed; fair enough in a letter to the reigning prince, but hardly convincing to us who know Gerson. He was not seeking fresh air and pleasant company, but was making a choice of a home under pressure of the stern law of necessity. It is true that Venice had many flourishing presses and Fano had none,* but even this alone was not a sufficient reason for the change. Who can doubt that he would have preferred brilliant Venice full of scholars and booklovers the book market of all the world, to Fano lately torn by fierce civil war and now under the rule of a prince whose presence was an invitation for plots and intrigues and possible war, the quintessence of instability, the very opposite of that peace and quiet needed for his work. Although Gerson printed all his Latin and Italian books in Fano under the name of Hieronymus Soncinus, he must have been known to be a Jew, for he printed Hebrew books and lived as a Jew, and as he had many friends and patrons among Christian scholars and literati who helped to make his exile bearable,† we may infer the friendliness of the Fanesians toward the Jews. He seems to have gained the good will of the Spanish Cardinal of Santa Balbina, the Apostolic Delegate in the Romagna, who notwithstanding that Spain had exiled and killed and baptized all

* Manzoni p. 14.

† His Hebrew name hyphenated showed that he considered himself an exile: Ger-shom "dwelling there as the stranger." Henceforth Gerson always used the hyphenated form of his name in his Hebrew books.

her Jews, graciously favored Gerson's plans to set up a printing press at Fano.* One of his earliest friends was Lorenzo Astemio of Macerata former librarian of Duke Guidobaldo of Urbino,† who had after the rise of Borgia left Urbino and settled at Fano as a teacher of grammar. He edited and corrected the Latin and Italian books printed by Soncino‡ and in many a phrase in dedicatory letters to various patrons showed his esteem for

Initial words from Soncino's Mahzor

the Jewish craftsman. Even in September 1503 "when all Italy was clashing with tumult" Astemio exhorted all who had unpublished manuscripts of good Latinity to send them to Hieronymus Soncinus, so that being printed by so well known a man the owner of the book should be honorably remembered by posterity.¶

* See dedication of Petrarca 1503 to Cesare Borgia.
† Manzoni p. 60.
‡ Manzoni p. 6.
¶ Introduction to Palaemon's "Ars grammaticae" Fano 1503. Manzoni p. 43.

Gerson's first book at Fano was a collection of Latin authors, principally fathers of the church, and the new era* began with the publication of Cyprian's "Cross of the Lord" Lactantius "Resurrection of Christ" Pope Pius II's "Hymn to the Virgin Mary" and the like. Lorenzo Astemio lauded the work in a letter to Soncino's friend Padre Francesco Giorgi, no doubt gaining the goodwill of churchmen for his patron the Jew who was prepared to devote his art to the service of the Catholic religion. For upward of a year after the appearance of his first book at Fano Gerson refrained from printing Hebrew, and devoted himself to Church Fathers scholastic philosophy Latin and Italian belles lettres and grammar, publishing them all under a name taken from the sacred name of St. Jerome (Hieronymus) "Qui proprium a sacro nomine nomen habet."† Perhaps his friend Lorenzo Astemio shared the secret of his dissimilation, when he wrote to the Bishop of Fossombrone that moved by his sense of the public good and by his admiration of the book he had persuaded Soncino to set aside his other work in order to print the Enchiridion of the Pythagorean philosopher Sixtus, highly recommended by St. Jerome and St. Augustine? The work contains only eight folios and could not have taken many hours to print, and it is difficult to understand why Gerson

---

* Freimann's statement, "Ueber heb. Ink." p. 4, that the Soncino family printed non-Hebrew books before 1500 is erroneous.

† From verses in edition of Epigrams etc. of Antonio and Giacomo Costanzi, Fano 1502.

should have been especially zealous to produce it except for its effect. Our printer was fighting for a foothold for a chance to strike root to establish himself in the good graces of the powers ecclesiastical and secular, and after securing the favor of the Cardinal and the Bishop, he turns to the Prince whom he boldly calls in the glaring flattery of the time "the Divine Borgia Caesar the Second."* To this "Divine Caesar" Lorenzo Astemio had dedicated the Life of Epaminondas issued by Soncino in 1502, and with fine Italian hand impaled the bloody Borgia on the keen point of this veiled reproof. "You (Caesar) have also this characteristic of Epaminondas, who though he might have led great armies and could have heaped up the greatest riches desired nothing more than an immortal name."† In July 1503 Gerson Soncino approached the foot of the Borgia throne with a fine volume containing the poems of Petrarca and dedicated to "the most illustrious and most excellent Prince Cesare Borgia, Duke of Aemilia and Valentino and Standard Bearer of the Holy Roman Church," prefacing this sonnet to the fierce patron of literature:

Each servitor of true and loyal thought,
    Whatever be the service he may bring,
    Who does not of his master's glory sing,
In failing this, has grievous error wrought.

* See colophon of "Invectiva in grammatistas" 1502.

† Hoc quoque Epaminundae habere videris, qui quom maximos ductasset exercitus potuissetque facile amplissimas coacervare divitias, praeter immortale nomen nil habere concupivit. Manzoni p. 7.

Whence we, in fear lest we may fail in aught,
    This new edition of our author bring,
    And to the steed of the Pierian spring
We dedicate the volume we have brought.

Mounting on Pegasus, soars thy valiant fame,
    O, Godlike Caesar Borgia, whose repute
        E'en now extends unto the farthest land.
So to thy excellence, thy noble name,
    We dedicate this work, the ripest fruit
        Of Fano's press, imprinted by our hand.*

Having published this adulatory poem, and presented to Borgia what he called "the first fruit of his exiguous lucubrations" but which was in fact his seventh publication at Fano, Gerson waited for the favor of the prince. But the wise and familiar words of that greater poet must have sprung to his lips, when within six weeks of the date of the publication of his eulogy, Pope Alexander lay dead of poison, his powerful son Cesare

---

*Translated by Beulah B. Amram. The original is given by Sacchi p. 56:—

    Deve ciascun deuoto e bon vassallo,
      De qualunque virtu sia possessore,
      Dar sempre laude & gloria al suo signore;
    E non facendo cio, faria gran fallo
    Onde noi, c'hauem sculpito nel metallo,
      La noua stampa del praesente auctore,
      Temendo non cader in tanto errore,
    La dedicamo Al pegaseo Cauallo.
    Sopra del qual si forte corre, e vola
      La fama tua, o Diuo Cesar Borgia,
      Che gia s'extende all' ultimo Oceano.
    Adoncha a tua Excellentia unica, e sola
      Sia dedicata questa noua forgia
      De stampa, Impressa in la Cita de Fano.

at death's door, his nascent power crumbling to ruins.

Put no trust in princes,
In the son of man, in whom there is no help,
His breath departeth, he returneth to his dust;
In that very day his purposes vanish.

In his dedication of the Petrarca to Borgia, Gerson discloses his rivalry with Aldo Manuzio the prince of Venetian printers, and the alleged wrong done by Aldo to Francesco Griffo the typecutter and inventor of the Aldine type. This dedication though somewhat lengthy may be reproduced here to tell its own story in the very words of our printer: "To the most illustrious and most excellent Prince Caesar Borgia, Duke of Aemilia and Valentino etc. and Standard Bearer of the Holy Roman Church! Two years, most excellent and invincible Prince, have passed since, being pleased with the air, the site and the fertility of your most devoted city of Fano and the friendliness and wit of its inhabitants, I decided to come to live in it and practice the art of printing. At that time I met here the Reverend Apostolic Legate the Cardinal of Santa Balbina, the distinguished preceptor of your Excellency, a man truly worthy of this dignity and a lover and patron of all learning. I recommended myself to his Eminence and made known to him my full intention to take up my perpetual domicile in this city and to bring here typecutters and printers, not ordinary and inferior but such as excelled all others. Since I was most graciously heard by his Eminence I desired to fulfill my promise, and through my persuasion there have come here not only the most notable and capable compositors whom it was possible to bring, but also a most noble cutter of Latin Greek and Hebrew type, called Messer Francesco da Bologna, whose skill I certainly believe to be unequalled in this work.   For he not only knows how to cut fonts most perfectly but he has invented a new form of letters called cursive or chancery, which neither Aldo Romano nor others who cunningly have tried to adorn themselves with the plumes of others, but this very Messer Francesco first invented and designed, and it was he who cut all the fonts of letters from which the said Aldo ever printed, as well as the present font with a grace and beauty that speak for themselves.   And now we are all most humble and devoted vassals of your Excellency, and it behooves our faithful service always to invoke your happy patronage, our most illustrious and merciful Prince, and to offer to you the first fruit of our exiguous lucubrations.   Wherefore we destine and dedicate this work to your Excellency, not as a new thing, nor as worthy of your Excellency who are devoted not to desirable gain but to military discipline which completes and adorns our age with its shining and admirable deeds; but only to give some proof to your Excellency of our devotion and humility and of this newly invented type, which we hope may not be displeasing to you; with the help of God and your favor we shall strive to dedicate works most famous and noble to your highness, to whom most humbly we recommend ourselves."

In order to understand the allusions to Aldo Romano and others who wore borrowed plumes we must go back a few years and enter the famous shop of Aldo on the Campo Sant' Agostino. At the time that Gerson was in Venice Aldo Manuzio Romano whose name is familiar to thousands who do not know of the man's existence through the adjective "Aldine" applied to so many books editions printing houses and things literary, had just begun his life's work of rescuing from oblivion the masterpieces of Greek literature. He acquired less renown through his Greek texts which are his real contribution to the humanities, than through his Latin and Italian texts printed in letters which are familiar even to school children; for the modern italics though artistically inferior are modified Aldine types, later called italic from the land of their origin. And through these types the great printer Aldo comes into relation with his fellow-craftsman Gerson Soncino. There was a famous engraver of Bologna Francesco Griffo*

* Pannizi "chi era Francesco da Bologna" and Gualandi "note intorno a Francesco Raibolini detto Il Francia" identify him as the famous painter. Manzoni "studi di bibliografia analitica I" differs with them. The question is settled by documents published by Adamo Rossi that he is Il Griffo and not Il Francia. Fumagalli p. 42.

who had cut many types for Aldo,* and to whom
Aldo showed one of his most precious possessions,
acquired from a Paduan scholar—a copy of the
poems of Messer Francesco Petrarca, written in
Petrarca's own beautiful hand. "Make me types
even like these letters of our divine poet!" and
forthwith Francesco cut the counterfeit of the
beautiful letters which enshrined the still more
beautiful thought of the poet. Thereupon young
Pietro Bembo, not yet the cardinal-poet sought in
all the courts of Italy, edited the text and there
appeared in July 1501 "Le cose volgari di Messer
Francesco Petrarca," first of all Italian "Aldine"
books. The novelty and beauty of its types excited the admiration of eager booklovers, and other
printers, quick to profit by the new fancy of their
patrons imitated these types and even sought to
have Francesco Griffo cut them similar fonts.
Then Aldo had recourse to the law, and we may
yet read his petition to the Signoria of Venice
wherein he supplicates "the most grave Senate
not to permit any other to make or imitate the
Greek and cursive Latin letters nor to print the
books made or to be made by your petitioner . . .
in your dominion for ten years." Nor was the
most grave Senate deaf to his appeal, but forthwith issued a decree granting his prayer. Now
consternation seized good Francesco who probably
said with show of reason, that by cutting types for
Messer Aldo he had not intended to deprive him-

* Manzoni, p. 30.

self of his livelihood; but as Messer Aldo had made his further sojourn within the domain of the Signoria irksome and dangerous, it behooved him to depart to other cities where he might cut his types and be at peace.

Then Francesco remembered his old friend Gerson the Jew, who now was established at Fano by the sea, in the domains of Cesare Borgia Duke

Medal of Aldo Manuzio

of Romagna. At Fano the old friends met and made a pact, and Gerson announced to all the world that he would publish books with types of much grace and beauty cut by the noblest of gravers of Latin Greek and Hebrew letters, Messer Francesco da Bologna "who has invented a new form of letters called 'cursive' or 'chancery' which neither Aldo Romano nor others who cunningly have tried to adorn themselves with the plumes of others, but this very Messer Francesco first invented and designed." It is difficult to determine the origin of the feeling between Gerson and Aldo,* and it was either as the cause or result of their quarrel that Aldo in his Hebrew Grammar published in 1501† announced that he hoped also to publish grammars, dictionaries and sacred books.‡ Had Aldo like his successor and fellow-townsman Daniel Bomberg, printed Hebrew books as he had threatened Gerson would have been seriously affected by the competition of this established friend of the rich and mighty and beloved son of the Church. Aldo's rights to the cursive types had been confirmed by letters of Popes Alexander VI and Julius II, and when Pope Leo X likewise confirmed them and recognized Aldo as the inventor of these types, threatening all who infringed upon his rights with the ban of excommunication, the wrath of Francesco Griffo rose again and we hear the last echo of this controversy in his indignant words. For after having worked long for Gerson and served other printers he returned in 1516 to his native city and printed an edition of Petrarca, in the preface to which he claims that he had first made for Aldo Manuzio Romano, the Greek and Latin types with which Aldo "had not only come into much wealth, but had assured himself of immortal fame with

---

* "Aldo Manutius und Hieron. Soncino" H. B. 1 : 125.

† "Introductio per brevis ad linguam Hebraicam." Hebrew type for this book was cut by Francesco. Jew. Enc. 1 : 335.

‡ Sacchi p. 54 note 31. Manzoni, p. 256–265, thinks that this Hebrew grammar was the cause of their disagreement.

posterity."* And had it needed confirmation he could have pointed to the testimony of Aldo himself, who when the types were fresh from the mold and the first Latin book a Virgil had been printed with them, wrote in the preface this tribute to the skill of his engraver:

IN GRAMMATOGLYPTAE LAUDEM.
QUI GRAIIS DEDIT ALDUS, EN LATINIS
DAT NUNC GRAMMATA SCALPTA DAE-
DALEIS FRANCISCI MANIBUS BONONI-
ENSIS.†

Although our sympathy goes out to Soncino in his unequal contest with the powerful Aldo we are obliged to admit the superiority of Aldo's Petrarca, not as regards the type, but the correctness of the text. The reason appears when we remember that Aldo's editor was one of the most exquisite scholars of the time the far famed Pietro Bembo, whereas Soncino had to be content with the modest skill of Astemio, who although a good Latinist was no match for Bembo in the living language.‡ After the edition of Petrarca, Gerson printed eighteen other books at Fano until his removal to Pesaro in 1506; the very next book being his first Hebrew publication, the "Hoshaa-

* Sacchi p. 20.

† Brown p. 47. Francesco cut various styles of italics. Manzoni Annali p. 30 considers the style used by Soncino finer than that used by Aldo. Francesco came to a bad end. He was hanged in 1518 for killing his son-in-law. Fumagalli p. 42.

‡ Manzoni p. 38.

not", hymns for the feast of Tabernacles.*   After
the fall of the Borgia family, referred to by Gerson in the epigraph of a grammatical work "printed
9 September 1503, 19 days after the death of Pope
Alexander VI," Gerson continued his work undisturbed by the tremendous political changes wrought
by the removal of Cesare Borgia. To him as to the
other craftsmen and scholars, the change of master simply meant a change of patron, and in his
dedicatory epistles instead of the Duke of Aemilia
and Valentino there appear Duke Guidobaldo of
Urbino, his duchess Elizabeth Gonzaga, Ramberto
Malatesta, scion of the ancient house that ruled
in Fano. What Manzoni considers the most
beautiful book of the press of Soncino appears
in 1506, the "Christian tenstringed harpsicord"
(Decachordum Christianum) by Cardinal Marco
Vigerio Bishop of Sinigaglia illustrated with ten
engravings of scenes from the life of Jesus by
Florio Vavassore, the beauty of which so impressed
the cardinal's kinsman the governor of Fano that
after Gerson had removed his press to Pesaro he
was especially invited by the municipal authorities
to print the Statutes of Fano.

The ancient port of Pesaro lies on the Adriatic,

---

* Of the twenty-five books printed 1502–1506 nine are in Hebrew.
The "Hoshaanot" were followed by "Musar Haskel" of Hai Gaon
in 1504, Sefer Harokeah (the Perfumer) by Eleazer of Worms, and the
Prayer Book in Italian and Hebrew letters "Sidur di tutto l'anno,"
in 1505, the Khosari of Jehuda Halevi, the book of Devotion, The
"Gates of Repentance" of Jona Gerondi, a Hagadah and the Roman
Mahzor in 1506.

out of the main path of the swarms of warlike rovers who under Spanish Swiss and German leaders overran Italy and for decades ravaged the land in the service of Pope and Prince.   Under the rule of the Sforza and of the Rovere it became an asylum for scholars and artists and its court was celebrated by Ariosto as the place where "with the author of the 'Courtier,' with Bembo and the others sacred to divine Apollo, exile was rendered less hard and strange."   After the fall of Cesare Borgia, Giovanni Sforza Lord of Pesaro reëntered the city from which the arms of Borgia had driven him, and shortly thereafter he married Ginevra daughter of Marco Tiepolo of Venice a lady whom Jacopo da Bergamo in his book on the celebrated women of Renaissance, lauds for her elegance of form her wonderful grace her calm and queenly bearing and her chaste beauty.*   This lady had been the patroness of Gerson Soncino when that wandering craftsman was in Venice just before his establishment at Fano; and it was in all probability her marriage to the Lord of Pesaro in December 1504 that turned Gerson's thoughts to that city. Giovanni Sforza was a cultivated gentleman, who though capable of deeds of violence was devoted to the study of philosophy,† and had gathered a notable library in his palace at Pesaro, vying with that of the Dukes of Urbino on their neighboring mountain top.   Compared with their

* Gregorovius "Lucretia Borgia" N. Y. 1903 p. 28.
† Gregorovius "Lucretia Borgia" p. 330.

cousins of Milan, the Sforza of Pesaro were humane rulers, their warlike and savage instincts tamed by the smallness and entrancing loveliness of their domain, then as now one of the most peaceful spots in all Italy. The desire to be at peace! We can well imagine how the heart of our printer swelled with the hope that good fortune might at last give him a shelter where he could pursue his work in happy seclusion. He would go and seek refuge under the Lord of Pesaro, relying on the good-will of the noble Ginevra his erstwhile patroness. He had not to travel far to make the change, for the towers of Pesaro may be seen from Fano rising out of the mists of the sea.* His first book he dedicated to his noble patroness, with words more literally true than is usual with such performances, "Thinking often of you, most Illustrious Lady Ginevra Sforza, and how I might show my loyalty toward your Excellency and your house in the famous city of Venice, all the more now that you are my lady and patroness and consort of my lord, the most excellent Giovanni Sforza of Aragon, by whose favor and with whose assistance and grace I am come to the city of Pesaro, . . . I have dedicated to your Serenity the Poems of Serafino newly printed in your city, with cursive letters."† With this splendid book, first printed by him in 1504 at Fano and dedicated to Elizabeth Gonzaga Duchess of Urbino, thereafter in 1509

* Gregorovius "Lucretia Borgia" p. 80.
† Manzoni p. 149.

dedicated to Galeazzo Sforza brother of Giovanni, who was then ruling, and in 1516 to Eleonora Rovere da Gonzaga wife of the Duke of Urbino, Gerson began his career in Pesaro. In this congenial atmosphere he printed without cessation from 1507 to 1515 and again in 1517, 1519 and 1520. The two famous libraries of Pesaro and Urbino attracted scholars and established a bookmart in these cities, and stirred by the rivalry of the great Aldo, Latin Italian and Hebrew texts flowed from Gerson's press. Had be been a Christian the world would have known him as a printer of fame equal to Aldo, for men of culture and discernment who were his contemporaries have left plain records of their opinion of his merit, an opinion fully sustained by the excellence of his productions. But he was a Jew, and until recently his name was barely known even to bibliophiles, who seem to have ignored the great books on Hebrew typography which the Abbot De Rossi wrote more than a hundred years ago. To the non-Jewish world the Hebrew printed book like the Talmud is little known, and bibliographers talk about Soncino books published at Prague or in Spain just as the monks used to talk about Rabbinus Talmud, as though it were a man. Perhaps the non-Jewish world may be excused for its lack of interest, but it is only just that his co-religionists should remember this Jewish printer, whose merits equal those which gained Aldo "immortal fame with posterity."

Gerson, first of all the Jewish printers to undertake the publication of non-Hebrew books, was probably forced to do so by an apathetic Jewish patronage; for the Jews were too poor to support the press. It is the brilliant success that crowned his non-Hebrew work that explains the anomalous fact that a Jewish printer could maintain himself for forty years in the midst of an always hostile jealous and sometimes dangerous Christian environment. No other Jewish printer in Italy at all approached this record. Although his press was transferred to Pesaro, his reputation among the Fanesians made it profitable to keep his press at Fano running, contemporaneously with that of Pesaro. His great book, the Decachordum of the Bishop of Sinigaglia was published at Fano on August 10, 1507, after he had removed to Pesaro, and it was this noble book which secured for him the contract to publish the Statutes of Fano under special agreement with the Priors of that city.* His skill at this work secured for him the contract to print the Statutes of the city of Jesi in 1516 and of Rimini in 1525, and competent experts the great lawyers Aurelio Superchio and Tommaso Diplovatazio recommended to the town council of Pesaro that Gerson be given the contract to print the

* The contract with the Priors of Fano is dated 21 February 1508. He agreed to print eighty copies of the Statutes using the same type as the Decachordum. The Priors agreed to furnish him with a house for his press, a corrector for the work and to pay him eighty gold florins, equal to about $192.00. Manzoni p. 140–141. He printed two other books at Fano in 1508.

Statutes they had revised. This however was never done.* In his edition of Cornazzano's "Military Affairs" dedicated to Giovanni Sforza he acknowledges "the great most ample and inestimable benefits patronage favor and kindness" shown to him and to his family. Making all due allowances for the exaggeration of this dedication we may reasonably conclude that it was well with him at Pesaro. A few Hebrew books published at this time (1507) indicate that he was not unmindful in the midst of his success with Christian books of the great purpose set before him: † "May God illumine my darkness and give me strength to commence . . . other holy books of the law of God and of his religion." ‡ One of these, the grammatical work "A walk through the paths of knowledge" contains an anonymous commentary, written by the famous Elijah Levita while he was at Padua. Many years thereafter Elijah told how while he was immured at Padua on account of the plague a servant stole the manuscript and had it printed at Pesaro, thus cheating him of the credit for the book besides robbing him of the financial benefit that he might have derived from it.¶

* Aurelio Superchio was in 1512 sent by the City of Pesaro to obtain from Pope Julius II the investiture of this dominion for Duke Francesco Maria of Urbino. Tommaso Diplovatazio was a distinguished lawyer and diplomat who revised the laws of Pesaro.

† In the epigraph of the Mussar Haskel of Fano 1504.

‡ These three Hebrew books are Bahya ben Asher's commentary on the Pentateuch, Kimhi's Grammar, the "Walk through the paths of Knowledge" and an anonymous grammatical work entitled "Entrance of my words," Petah Debarai.

¶ Manzoni p. 162.

The publication in July 1508 of a funeral oration delivered by a Paduan scholar on the death of Duke Guidobaldo of Urbino serves to recall the unsettled state of affairs in the principalities of Italy. Guidobaldo was the last scion of the House of Montefeltre, and the Borgias during the Papacy of Alexander VI had their eyes on his possessions. His sister was married to a brother of the Cardinal della Rovere, who subsequently ascended the Papal throne as Julius II.*

Guidobaldo married the noble Elizabeth Gonzaga of the ruling house of Mantua to whom Soncino had dedicated an edition of Serafino in 1504, not long after Guidobaldo had returned to his duchy, from which the ruthless Cesare Borgia had driven him. At the death of Guidobaldo, a nephew of the Pope Francesco Maria della Rovere who had been adopted by the Duke his uncle by the mother's side succeeded him to the duchy.† It was this Francesco Maria who became Lord of Pesaro. For Giovanni Sforza died July 27th, 1510, leaving as his heir an infant son Costanzo born November 4, 1505, during whose minority Galeazzo brother of the late Giovanni was regent. On August 15, 1512 Costanzo died. Julius II withdrew his support from Galeazzo and forced him to agree October 30, 1512, to surrender his castle and domain to the Duke of Urbino.‡ As long as the Sforza

* Gregorovius "Lucretia Borgia" p. 103.

† Guicciardini "History of the Wars of Italy" London, 1756. 4: 258.

‡ Gregorovius "Lucretia Borgia" p. 331.

ruled at Pesaro, Gerson was protected and honored by the court and the scholars. The Sforza, Duke Ercole of Ferrara and later their Highnesses of Urbino accepted his dedications. Alessandro Gaboardo of Torcelli edited and corrected many of his books, and testified to the skill of this "most accurate printer." He was the friend of the astronomer Camillo Leonardo the poet Giacomo Costanzi the printers Nicolo Brenta and Pietro da Cafa of Pesaro and Bernardino Oliva and Bernardo Guerralda of Ancona, no less than of the preaching Friar Innocente Bacchio. In the republic of letters in the world of thought the passport was excellence, and consideration of religion and race seems to have played but an unimportant part. It cannot be overlooked that at this time some of Gerson's books were introduced to the reading public by Innocente Bacchio, who belonged to the Preaching Friars a class of men chief among whom were men like Giovanni di Capistrano and Bernardino da Feltre whose business consisted largely in preaching personal virtue and morality, together with undying hatred and persecution of Turk, Jew and other infidels and heretics. Here surely is a millennial scene,—the preaching friar in the house of the Jew, recommending the worthy printer to the good will of the Lady of Pesaro.* This is all the more noteworthy, because this time saw the beginning of the Reuchlin controversy on the Talmud, soon des-

* See introduction to the " Medicine for the Soul " 1510.

tined to divide European opinion and for the time being make the Talmud of the Jews the banner, around which, for the most part unwillingly it must be said, the friends of enlightenment and freedom of thought gathered. Gerson was printing Talmudic treatises apparently without let or hindrance and without offense to his ecclesiastical friends in the Marches,* especially the treatise on Strange Worship (Aboda Zara) whose very title was found offensive to Catholic sensibilities. As the controversy proceeded the atmosphere at Rome cleared. Julius II was a warrior rather than a priest, his successor Leo X a scholar and man of the world, who despite all the vaporings of the godly men who saw religion and morality imperilled by the publication of the Talmud did not hesitate to grant a privilege to Daniel Bomberg of Venice in 1518 to print a complete edition.†

    * In 1508 Yebamot; 1509–10 Bezah; 1511–12 Baba Bathra and Megilla; 1513–14 Aboda Zara; 1515 Moed Katon, Sukkah, Erubin; 1519 Hullin.

    † The morality of the Jews may be best illustrated by reference to the Catholic work on the History of the Popes by Dr. Louis Pastor. (St. Louis, 1901.) He describes the morals of the Christian world, admitting unwillingly enough the corruption of Church and priesthood. He depicts the faults of the time unsparingly;—vainglory falsehood sexual vice superstition sensuality and the prevalence among all classes of society, even the priesthood and monks of a callousness to these vices that permitted the grossest indecencies to go almost unnoticed. Amid all this the author being an Austrian Catholic feels called upon to have his fling at the Jews. After finding them guilty of usury, he calls attention to the only immorality that he can charge them with:—a Jew first printed Boccaccio's novels! Pastor "History of the Popes" 5 : 119, a charge which if true is ridiculous if it is intended to show that the Jews had anything to do with the utter

One of Gerson's patrons was the Carmelite Monk Fra Battista, whose poem on the "Fortunes of Francesco Marquis of Mantua" was printed in 1509.*

Another and a greater contemporary is represented among the publications of Gerson Soncino. Some of the smaller works of Savonarola were

rottenness of society and clergy. As a matter of fact no authority is given for his statement and our studies of Jewish printers justify us in denying its truth: Jew. Enc. article "Boccaccio" 3: 279. Gerson Soncino who was the only Jewish printer of his time who published non-Jewish books was issuing Latin classics Catholic religious works books of grammar and rhetoric and there is not one book in his entire list that can be classed as immoral, unless the literature of miracle working saints and the abdication of reason to ecclesiastical authority be placed in that category.

* This Francesco was the brother of Elizabeth Gonzaga, Duchess of Urbino, to whom Gerson's Fano edition of Serafino's poem was dedicated in 1505, and it was his victory over the French at Fornuovo that was indirectly responsible for the famous "Madonna della Vittoria" painted by Mantegna and now hanging in the Louvre. As this is probably the only great Italian picture known to have been paid for by a Jew, it may not be uninteresting to sketch its history. The picture represents the Virgin and the infant Jesus, seated in a bower of flowers, on the one hand Saints Joseph and Michael, on the other the infant St. John and St. Elizabeth, The Madonna's right hand and the hand of Jesus are raised in blessing over the kneeling figure of Francesco Gonzaga, the captain of the League which was formed by the Pope Spain England Venice and Milan to oppose Charles VIII of France. At the battle of Fornuovo (July 6, 1495) the Marquis implored the aid of the Virgin, through whose intercession no doubt the French were obliged to retreat. Now it appears that one day while Francesco was campaigning, a religious procession through the streets of Mantua passed the house of Daniel Norsa, a Jewish banker in the Via San Simone. When Norsa had bought his house, he obtained episcopal consent, after paying a large sum of money, to remove an image of the Virgin which adorned the facade. When the procession passed the house it was noticed that the place formerly occupied by the image of the Virgin, had been defaced by some profane verses probably by some wag who delighted like so many of the time to sport with

printed at Pesaro by Nicolo Brenta* at the expense of Soncino, and at a later date (1519) Soncino commissioned Bernardino Oliva of Ancona to print another book of the great Friar, also at his expense.†

The Hebrew books printed by him were nearly all books by the old masters, and he very properly concluded it more meritorious to print a good old book than to write a poor new one. In one work however he essays authorship. "Introductio ad litteras hebraicas"‡ was the work of his youth,—

the things held sacred by the Church. The crowd seeing the verses, threw stones and broke the Jew's windows, and otherwise threatened him. He wrote to the Marquis, who, moved by the justice of the cause and no doubt also by financial consideration, gave the Jew his protection. After the victory of Fornuovo the Marquis wrote to his consort the famous Isabella d'Este who ruled in his absence, that as a thank offering for the aid given him by the Virgin on the field of battle, Daniel Norsa should restore the picture of the Virgin in a more splendid form; thus the mother of God would be fittingly honored at no expense to the Marquis. Whereupon Andrea Mantegna was ordered to paint the picture for one hundred and ten ducats and Daniel Norsa was ordered to pay within three days. Subsequently in order to make the thank offering to the Virgin more complete Girolamo Redini a preaching friar proposed that Norsa's house be torn down and a church built there, dedicated to the Madonna of the Victory. The justice of this at once appealed to all and it was done, and Mantegna's new picture was carried in procession and enshrined in its new temple, where it remained until Napoleon's day when the French whom she had helped to defeat three hundred years before took her picture amid much other plunder and carried it off to Paris where it still remains. For this account see more fully Cartwright's "Isabella d'Este."

* Manzoni p. 229.

† In addition to Brenta and Oliva, Pietro da Cafa printed for Soncino, producing a number of works at Pesaro in 1510. This Pietro, unlike the other printers, worked in the house of Soncino and seems for a time to have been in his employ. Manzoni p. 210.

‡ Mabo el otiot ibriot published 1510.

"hoc alphabetum jam pene puer composui,"—
and he introduces it to the Christian readers, for
whom it was intended, in simple unclassical Latin
phrase full of the idiom of the vernacular.*

Besides bookmaking he naturally was engaged in
bookselling, and at least two documents are extant
showing his business connection in Perugia. He
had patrons in all the great cities and his business
prospered except when it was checked here and
there by the perpetual warfare, which was the
outcome of the policies of the League of Cambrai.†

* Lectori.

Lector si placet hebraicam linguam condiscere. Hoc alphabetum,
et litterarum combinationes et quaedam alia ad hanc rem facientia,
tibi et studiosis condonani (sic). His. n. (nam) nisi Ameles angulus
dici mauis hebraice Legere poteris. Hoc alphabetum jam pene puer
composui. Sed his cui dederam hebraicae Linguae ignarus non recte
apposuit nunc uero correptum (sic) habes: Deinceps psalmorum
Codicem hebraice graece et latine Pisauri excussum expectato A diuo
Hieronymo de uerbo ad uerbum secundum ueritatem hebraicam traduc-
tum, additis nonnullis nostris glossis Loca plurima a scriptoribus in-
ductis corrupta aperientibus. Adde et Lector Candidissime. His
psalmorum codex poterit tibi ad linguam hebraicam graecam et latinam
pro dictionario succurrere. Vale, et haec plusquam Tantali Talenta
ficito: Pisauri. Manzoni p. 257.

† Guicciardini, 4 : 211.

CHAPTER VI.

GERSON SONCINO (1513–1534).

Ancona—Political Upheaval—Battista Guarini's Verses on the Jew-badge—At Ortona-a-Mare—Pietro Galatino's "Mystery of Catholic Truth"—Gerson's Tolerance—At Rimini—The Invitation of the Ecclesiastical Council—Gerson's Book-mark—His Controversy with an Apostate in Bomberg's Shop—His Last Book in Italy, 1527—The Sack of Rome—Gerson in Turkey—List of Soncino Publications.

IN the year 1513 the infant Costanzo Sforza died, and his uncle the Regent Galeazzo retired in favor of the Pope's nephew Francesco Maria della Rovere, Duke of Urbino, who is mentioned in the epigraph of Soncino's books as "Duke of Urbino and Sora and Prefect of Rome." The Pope died in February and was succeeded by Leo X, in whose honor Soncino published the poems of Lorenzo di Medici his father. Whether Leo X's well known friendliness to the Jews stimulated Hebrew printing cannot now be determined. It appears however that not only did Soncino's business increase but that two other presses were established, that of Samuel Latif of Mantua of mere passing importance,* and that of Daniel Bomberg of Venice destined to rival and finally to supplant that of Soncino. The business of Soncino war-

---

* He printed a few books in 1513, 1514, to wit:—Seder Olam Rabba Vezutta, Megillot Taanit, Sefer Hakabbalah, Tanya, Shulhan Arba. See Schwab "les incunables" p. 61; Zunz "Zur Gesch. u. Lit." 250.

ranted his establishing a new connection at Ancona, a well known and important seaport lying to the south of Pesaro, where presses were in operation under charge of his friends Bernardino Oliva and Bernardo Guerralda, with whom Soncino placed orders for a number of books during the years 1513–1517. At the same time Soncino's sons were taken into the firm and the books now appear by "the sons of Soncino". * What may be taken as an indication of lightheartedness produced partly by the general happy aspect of his affairs, is the publication of two jolly books belonging to that peculiar class published solely for the joyous Festival of Purim, "The Treatise on Purim" † and the Book of Habbakbuk "the bottle", a broad parody of the Book of Habbakuk.‡

Since 1510 when the output of Hebrew books of Soncino's press had been rather meagre, he printed the Bible and the Earlier Prophets. Besides the Talmudic treatises and the Purim books mentioned, the following five years yielded only commentaries on the Pentateuch by Nachmanides 1513–14, by Bahya and Levi ben Gerson 1514, and a Mahzor, German rite in 1515. Among his non-Hebrew books was a departure into the books on chivalry, the publication of one of those foolish and extravagant romances which were held up to

---

* Ramban "Commentary on Pentateuch"; Talmud Babli, Abodah Zara ; etc.

† Z. H. B. 9 : 153.

‡ Sacchi p. 39; Catalogue of Schwager and Frankel of Husiatyn.

the ridicule of posterity in the immortal work of Cervantes, the "Book of the Giant Morante, of King Charles and all the Paladins, and of Orlando's Conquest of the City of Sannia."

Now he seems to have given up his press at Pesaro—why, we do not know—and returned to Fano, where he remained for two years. The reason for his removal could hardly have been political for the towns were so close together as to be affected similarly by the political changes or military campaigns of that turbulent time.* There was an improvement in the general condition of the Marches for several decades rent by wars and political changes. Francis I of France almost immediately after his accession in 1515 invaded Italy and after a short campaign became master of Lombardy. In Pesaro and Urbino the general discontent with the rule of the Rovere finally resulted in their expulsion in 1516 and as is usual in such crises, a period of great unrest and disturbance ensued. Amid all this Gerson no doubt suffered in his business along with his fellow countrymen, and in addition had to bear the ignominy of the Jew hatred which had been growing as the result of the Reuchlin controversy. In an edition of Pindar's Trojan War he was obliged to print a versified stupidity of the poet Battista

---

*In addition to many non-Hebrew books, he printed the following:—in 1516, the Turim; in 1517 only Hebrew books; a Bible, the Arukh of Nathan ben Yehiel, the commentary of Bahya on the Pentateuch (reprinted by him for the third time) and the grammar of Moses Kimhi.

Title page of Kolbo
Soncino, Rimini, 1525

Guarini, who unworthily descended from his Olympus to fling a stone at the much suffering Jews:—

To Caecilianus.

Why the Jews wear the letter O.*

Why does the Hebrew wear the fourth vowel on his breast ?
  Caecilianus was wont to be asked by many.
He thought, that, condemned to eternal torment,
  The Hebrew bears it as a sign of his grief;
Or perhaps this vowel is used as a Zero
  Indicating his nonentity among men.
Or since Jews get rich through usury
  It indicates how they get much out of nothing.†

How our printer must have suffered under this indignity! Perhaps he too was obliged to wear the distinguishing badge, and though laden with years and honors, submit to the attack of every street ruffian. The personal sting in these verses must have grieved Gerson because of the injustice of the attack. The Soncino family began their career in Italy as money lenders, the fruit of whose

* The Jew-badge, a mark required to be worn by the Jews, consisted of a piece of yellow or red cloth cut in the shape of the letter O.

† Battista Guarini ad Caecilianum Cur Judaei ferant litteram O.
    Cur ferat hebraeus vocalem in pectori quartam
        A multis quaeri Caeciliane solet.
    Addictum aeternis ut se cruciatibus esset
        Cogitet, haec secum signa doloris habet
    Aut quia pro nihilo numeris apponimur illam,
        Inter mortales se sciat esse nihil.
    Aut, quod judaeis augentur faenore nummi
        Major ab hac numerus nam solet esse nota.

intelligence was enjoyed by the all-powerful Duke of Milan, who permitted them to accumulate money in order to take it from them when reasons of State required. Under Francesco Sforza they lent money to farmers, merchants and nobles, they furnished the sinews of war for the Duke and were permitted by him to retain a fair amount as the profit of their enterprise and the reward of their toil. After Israel Nathan Soncino abandoned money matters and turned to the press, neither his sons nor his grandsons nor his great-grandsons ever thought of exchanging the happy labor of the printer's shop for the opulence of the banker. As keen of intellect and adroit of wit, they might have, had they so chosen, rivalled the success of their forebears in the enterprises of finance, but instead of yielding to the allurements of this more envied vocation, they printed their books and oft repeated the words of Gerson and the other pioneers of the press, "May God vouchsafe unto us to print other books, many of them, without end. Amen. So may it be His will."

The situation in the Marches grew steadily worse and Gerson again girded his loins and sought a new home, this time within the domains of the King of the Two Sicilies Charles V of Spain afterwards the Emperor Charles I, who though no friend to the Jews * evidently seemed to Gerson a safer master than the shifting sovereignty of the

* Graetz 9 : 281.

Marches. To Ortona by the Sea Gerson turned his face, and in 1518 we find him vainly attempting to establish himself in the Abruzzi, that rough mountainous land that formed a great natural barrier, protecting the kingdom of Naples on the north, and stretching through Abruzzi Citeriore in a poor sandy plain to the sea. Here lay Ortona, noted for its wines but poor in those products of the mind that made the Marches and Venice so attractive to the scholars and the printers. No doubt our printer had reasonable peace and quiet at Ortona, for he even contemplated moving to Chieti the capital of this province, but peace and quiet though essential are not the exclusive desiderata for a printer, especially when purchased at the price of utter abasement to an insignificant princeling like the Count of Montorio who as vassal of Charles V ruled over Ortona. In the language used not only by the printers but by all the craftsmen and scholars Christian and Jewish, Gerson after reciting that he has brought his family and household to this part of the Abruzzi, to this noble city "like the royal eagle among the birds," servilely dedicates an edition of Cornazzano's "Military Affairs" to the Count "whose innumerable virtues and nobility he would be able to describe only in part if he had the fertility of Cicero the majesty of Virgil and the ease and sweetness of Ovid."* Thus to obtain a mere living the best men of that day had to abase themselves before

* Manzoni p. 472.

the worthless men of might, whose dominions founded by military skill were handed down to unscrupulous descendants, whose illegitimate birth was an indication of their divorce from all real virtue or nobility of character. Their vices and weaknesses are hidden beneath a sumptuous exterior, and the selfishness and immorality of their lives forgotten in the noble poems and glorious pictures dedicated by the men of genius whom they patronized.

During his sojourn at Ortona Gerson printed four books, one of them in Hebrew.* Most interesting of all of these is the work of Petrus Galatinus the Franciscan "On the Mystery of Catholic Truth" with its subtitle, "Most useful work in all Christendom concerning the mysteries of the Catholic truth against the obstinate perfidy of the Jews of our time; recently excerpted from Talmud and other Hebrew works and elegantly presented in four languages." One may forgive the scholars, who confused by the name Hieronymus assumed by Gerson Soncino in his non-Hebrew books thought that there were several members of the same family printing in the Marches, and afterwards when it was determined that there was but one, believed that he had been converted to Catholicism.

How shocking to orthodox Jewish minds must have been the catholicity of taste and interest of this master printer. Ancient Talmudic texts had

* Grammar of Moses Kimhi.

gradually under the pressure of a hostile environment been interpreted by the rabbis so as to prohibit the reading of works of belles lettres and history, lest the reader be led to scoffing apostasy and evil desire. It was a natural and almost instinctive method of defense developed by the minority to preserve their religion their view of life and their racial identity against the powerful encroachment of a hostile and enormous majority. But a few years after Gerson's time Joseph Caro the last great codifier of the laws of the Jews, after citing these restrictions against reading, and including specifically the works of Immanuel of Rome, added "and those who compose them and edit them not to say those who print them lead the multitude into sin." The views of this Palestinian scholar no longer were a true measure of the situation in Italy, where Gerson Soncino one of the advance guards of the new era, was indicating unerringly the direction of the path of civilization. He deemed nothing that was human foreign to him, and we find among his publications the ancient classics as well as Catholic publications of most unimpeachable orthodoxy, and most remarkable of all this book of Galatinus, which was not only Catholic but distinctly anti-Jewish in purpose, introduced to the public in Hebrew verses by the author or some apostate editor as a book filled with loveliness, expounding the secrets of the Talmud in which may be found the very foundation of Christian Messianism the unity of

Father Son and Holy Ghost.* Manzoni, with true nobility, says "We should pity this sincere Jew who in order to live amidst intolerant hypocrites and fanatical and greedy persecutors (although the Evangel is the law of toleration and love) was obliged to publish books which instead of humiliating him rather cover those who ordered them, with contempt."†

After his brief and unsatisfactory attempt to find a permanent home in the Abruzzi, Gerson returned to Pesaro where he dwelt during 1519 and 1520 printing no Latin or Italian books and only four Hebrew books.‡ His failure to print other than these few Hebrew books cannot be explained for the records are silent. He had been well established at Pesaro and had been well liked, but the hideous head of anti-Jewish feeling was raised again and this together with the baneful effect of militarism and the pernicious activity of the Dominicans now roused throughout the world as the result of the Reuchlin controversy, may have made the Jew persona non grata and the practice of his art impossible. As the sun set for him in

* The desire to find support in the Hebrew books for the doctrine of the Trinity arose out of the spread of Cabbalism, a so-called science, through which Jewish mystics attempted to explain the mysteries of heaven and earth, and which had many Christian devotees among them the famous Cardinal Egidio of Viterbo, who in this very year 1518 had assisted in the establishment of a Hebrew press in the city of Rome.

† Manzoni p. 465–6.

‡ In 1519 Talmud Babli Hullin and Midrash to the Megillot; in 1520 Pirke Eliayahu and the Later Prophets.

one place it rose in another, and thus we find our courageous and much tried printer leaving Pesaro in 1520 to go to Rimini, whither he had desired to go in 1518 at the time when he was obliged as a second choice to settle at Ortona.

On the 24th day of October 1518, "the Consuls and Ecclesiastical Council of Rimini assembled according to custom and in the usual place" the Palazzo del Comune, considered the petition of one Hieronymus Sonzinus an excellent printer of books (librorum impressore egregio) who sought a residence in the city and privilege to exercise his craft. After due deliberation they solemnly decided that as all public or private business among which the printing of books is to be worthily included, should be encouraged for the honor and benefit of the State, and as the cities of Rome Venice and Naples have favored printers of books "we owe it to the greater honor and benefit of our city Ariminium to follow in their footsteps; and as we should not only admit the said Magister Hieronymus to our city but should also assist him with favors, exemptions and subventions as much as possible; Now therefore," etc. etc.* Without going into further detail, suffice it to say that the worthy Ecclesiastical Council of Rimini in the States of the Church, showed marks of unusual favor to Gerson Soncino the Jew. It is possible that these ecclesiastical councillors were taking their cue from the Vatican where at that moment

* Sacchi p. 22; where the whole document is quoted.

there was enthroned a Pontiff who was distinguished above all others for liberality culture and freedom from the general mania for persecution—the same Pope whose sympathy went out to Johannes Reuchlin in his contest with the Obscurantists; who in the same year 1518 notwithstanding the influence of the Men of Darkness permitted Daniel Bomberg to print a complete edition of the Talmud at Venice, and in his own city of Rome authorized the establishment of a Hebrew press for Elijah Levita. The men of Rimini must have known that Gerson Soncino was a Jew, for he had been printing for upwards of fifteen years in the neighboring cities of Fano and Pesaro. We must therefore conclude that this Ecclesiastical Council presided over by some mitred dignitary did, with full knowledge, admit the Jewish printer into its city and accord him exceptional privileges; to their great and everlasting credit be it recorded. If this liberal act be an indication of the character of the rule of the Church in Rimini, it helps us to understand why Pandolfo Malatesta last of the ancient house that for so many generations ruled over Rimini tried in vain for several decades to recover the city of his fathers, from which he had been ousted by the redoubtable Cesare Borgia. Like the citizens of Fano, who after the defeat of their lawful sovereign the Duke of Urbino, remained loyal to the victor Cesare Borgia because of the latter's milder rule, the people of Rimini probably preferred the rule of the Popes to that of the ancient and legitimate but petty and vicious tyrant Pandolfo. Had the Church continued through the following centuries to rule its provinces in the same spirit of liberality and toleration, the temporal power would probably never have been forfeited and the Pope would to-day be something more than "the prisoner in the Vatican."

In the best location in Rimini on the old Roman Bridge of St. Peter one time the Bridge of Augustus, where artists and craftsmen nobles and merchants were wont to pass and repass all day long, the Council assigned a bookshop to Gerson Soncino rent free for one year. They exempted him from all taxes and imposts (datio et gabella) so that he might import his paper and export his books without let or hindrance or financial strain, and to cap it all they did solemnly promise to pay twelve ducats out of the city treasury for one year's rent of an appropriate dwelling house in the city for him and his family.* In full faith and testimony of which they caused letters patent to be issued, with the great seal of the Comune of Ariminium written and sealed under their direction by Johannes Postumus Secretary of the Municipality.

Perhaps it may be interesting to remember this old war-worn city, not only for the fierce tales of medieval life under the half savage Malatesti, not only for the tale of that sad pair whom Dante saw driven by the stormy blast of hell, but also

* This contract resembles the one made with the Priors of Fano when they engaged Gerson to print their Statutes.

for this gracious act of courtesy and good will offered by a Catholic community and accepted by a Jew.

Not until two years thereafter did Gerson accept the hospitality of Rimini, though tendered so handsomely. We do not know why he lingered at Ortona, returned to Pesaro and then waited there in comparative inactivity when this opportunity was offered him at Rimini. As if to mark this period of his life he adopted as his book-mark the tower of Rimini, flanking it with a Hebrew motto from Proverbs "A tower of strength is the Lord; into it shall run the righteous and be saved" —the first Hebrew printer's mark in Italy. Although we are not concerned with that branch of bibliographical science which deals with book-marks nor with the pleasant hobby of collecting them, we may pause for a moment to contemplate the mark of the greatest of Jewish printers, wherein with characteristic ingenuity he combined loyalty to his faith and gratitude to the Catholic city that harbored him.* The freedom from the limitations of his time which led him to publish Catholic books is paralleled by his liberal inter-

---

* True printers' marks are as a rule seals and often in the form of a seal and without words. These marks consist for the most part of figures of animals, taken from the coat-of-arms of the place of publication or in connection with the name of the printer; and appear on the title page and also of other pages of the book, such as the epigraph or introduction, or the beginning and end of various parts. Such are the peacock of Sabbioneta, also used at Mantua and Venice; the small white lion in the black square, used at Constantinople; the lion with

pretation of another old law regarding the representation of "anything in the heavens above, on the earth beneath or in the waters under the earth." It was quite unusual for the Jews to have anything to do with graphic arts, and an occasional departure from the ancient custom always required explanation and apology. Not all were able to explain as wittily as Abtalion ben Solomon who when charged with the offense of having a picture of his teacher Rabbi Samuel Katzenellenbogen of Padua on the wall of his study turned to Isaiah 30 : 20 reading, "and thine eyes shall see thy teachers."* The Soncino books, even those published in the lifetime of Israel Nathan Soncino the founder of this press, were often ornamented, not only with the interlacing geometrical designs with which Mussulman artistic fancy contented itself but with flowers Cupids and animals notably two hares whose cunning forms are seen so often in these books. How was it possible for a cultured man living in the Italy of Leonardo Rafael and Michelangelo, to name only the greatest of the multitude of great artists of the time to fail to respond to the influence of their

the double tail and two globes, in the prints of Prague, taken from the coat-of-arms of Prague; the half lion and half eagle crowned, of Salonica; the lion battling with the horse, of Ixar; the griffin, of Grifio, of Venice; the elephant of Cavalli; the candelabrum of Meir Parenzo; the temple of Giustiniani, also used in Prague editions, also in Safet and Lublin, etc. Some of the prints of Salonica have a tower. Ersch & Gruber 28 : 25.

* Jew. Enc. 1 : 137.

genius, notwithstanding the prohibitions of centuries of legislation which had trained the eye of the Jew to see in the pictorial representations of an alien faith not art but false theology?

Another device used by Gerson at Rimini was a title page whereon was pictured a portal with two columns and an arch designed and ornamented in true Renaissance style. Above the portal a small tablet contained the printer's name. This design was after Gerson's death freely used by other printers, who substituted for Gerson's name the motto "This is the gate of the Lord, the righteous may enter into it." Nor can they be accused of plagiarism, for the design was probably not original with Gerson. In early days when books circulated in manuscript the author retained no property in them and the owner took all sorts of liberties with the texts. Thus copyists incorporated emendations additions and notes with the original text and innocently made "new" books out of old ones. When books began to be printed the printers "borrowed" each other's title pages and devices almost without objection, and Aldo Manuzio's acquisition of literary copyright and exclusive right to use the cursive types is one of the first instances of what has become the universal rule in modern times. Gerson's Hebrew books at Rimini are not numerous but important. A Mahzor according to the Roman rite (1521) was followed (1522) by the Book of Roots. Daniel Bomberg, who was now actively printing at Venice and gradually encroaching on Gerson's book trade had brought out an edition of this work in 1521, and Gerson in his edition prompted rather by business competition than unselfish zeal for letters bitterly criticises its many flagrant errors. Following these books he published the Kolbo, Bahya's and Rashi's commentaries on the Pentateuch, the Melizat Efer ve Dinah, Landau's Agur and the Abkat Rohel, a poor output for six years and an

תמו דברי והמחבר ספר וכל כו תהלה לאל יתעלח •
ותה השלמתו ע״ צעיר והמתוקקים מבני שונצינו והוא גרשם
אריסנו והקריה   ח׳ יה׳ יתן לנו לשון למורים ודרי׳כנובאשתנ
אמן :

From Colophon of Kolbo
Soncino, Rimini, 1525

indication of the inroads made by the competition of Bomberg.

It was in the shop of Bomberg in January 1525 that Soncino met his fate, and excited the final cause which added to those that had been gradually developing resulted in his expatriation. Let Soncino tell the story in his own words.* "In January 1525 a Marrano apostate came from Rome to Venice speaking all day against God his law and his people. He wickedly discoursed against our young and old leaping like a goring ox. His dreams and words caused fear. It happened that while I was in the house of Messer Daniel talking

* On last page of Melizat Efer ve Dinah 1525.

business to him in the presence of Cornelio Israel
(Adelkind), Camillo the Greek and a Flemish
servant, that the shameless one was there abusing
me and daring me to write verses with him . . .
I went into a shop and hastily wrote these few
words:—

This man proposes to write verses
I am amazed at this idolater
This nobody who is blind to his limitations.
As impossible, this, as for me to go to Rome and apos-
    tatize!
Why bawl with a loud voice
There being no reason ? You ignoramus,
Who dare to vaunt yourself above me,
You, whose pen is fetid with its vileness.
I, not being a Christian, believed you wise;
I find you an imbecile.
I, not being a Christian, consider your pride and folly
Before the multitude of strangers."

We fear that Gerson's language was little better
than his opponent's, but he was pouring out his
long-pent sense of outrage suffered at Christian
hands upon this apostate who weakly sought
refuge in the bosom of the Church, and **then** not
content with enjoying freedom from persecution
himself tormented his former brethren in faith.
It is said that this apostate revenged himself on
Gerson by denouncing him at Rome for printing
Talmudic treatises without a license and making
sport of the Christian religion.* It is most likely

* Rabbinovicz's Maamar, p. 27. Manzoni denies Rabbinovicz's
theory; see also Freimann in Z. H. B. 9 : 22; and Sacchi p. 25.

that Gerson lost his fortune and his peace of mind in defending himself against these charges, and in 1526 as if to combat them and seek support at the Roman Court published the "Mirror of the Holy Mother Church" by Cardinal Ugo di San Vittore. But we find him now fairly at the end of his career in Italy. It was probably at this time that he became of service to his unfortunate brethren in faith, who, to escape persecution fled to the Orient with his aid and assistance. In the preface of his Miklol* he says, "God be praised and may he be my support and the prop of my old age; may He record it to my credit that I helped the Marranos of Spain and Portugal. With all my strength will I endeavor to the end of my life to free them from the hand of their destroyers and lead them to a safe refuge under the shadow of the Mighty One, there to dwell under His protection." In 1526 he contemplated his removal to Cesena and in 1527 we find him there printing the last of his publications in Italy, which curiously enough is a love-letter writer (Formolario di lettere d'amore) by Andrea da Gubbio.†

Discouraged by the success of Aldo Manuzio and later by that of Daniel Bomberg, persecuted for his religion's sake and harried by financial distress, his final determination to leave Italy was hastened by the sack of Rome and the events which immediately followed it. In 1527 under

---

* Constantinople 1532–4.

† Sacchi p. 25.

an absurd pretext of right against the protest of
Pope Clement VII. the Constable de Bourbon
entered Rome which was sacked and destroyed by
the adventurers that composed his army. The
Jews as usual bore more than their share of the
horrors of this capture, and the scenes enacted in
the densely populated district beyond the palace of
the Cenci must be covered with the decent veil
of oblivion. All Italy was shocked, all Jewry
rent its garments and mourned. Gerson Soncino,
in far away Cesena saw in this event the end of
safety for the Jews of Italy, and with thousands
of his co-religionists he took ship for the Orient.*

In the realm of the Sultan Solyman the Magnificent the noblest monarch in Europe, Moham-
medans Jews Greek and Roman Catholics lived
and enjoyed religious rights under the protection
of a strong arm and a wise head. At Salonica,
one of the principal cities of the Mussulman power
the sons of Gerson who had parted from their
father had already established a flourishing press.
Hardly had Gerson landed greeted his children
and inspected their press, when the smell of

* "Through the uninterrupted persecutions and exiles of the
Jews   .   .   ." says the historian Jost, Geschichte d. Judenthums u.
seiner Sekten 111, 125 "through destruction of their writings, in the
repeated terrors on the Iberian peninsula and burnings in France
and Italy, Judaism was in decay, the number of the faithful diminished
by death and apostasy, the spirit clouded, the most spiritual and learned
obliged to seek for mere bread. A complete dissolution seemed
imminent. Two events almost contemporary saved it from destruction,
the invention of printing and the capture of Constantinople by the
Turks."

printer's ink aroused the old instinct and forthwith the veteran craftsman began a new edition of the Mahzor.*

For some reason however he continued his journey to Constantinople, where for upwards of five years he produced many excellent books. The presses of Constantinople had been active since 1503, and Gerson found many fellow-craftsmen in the Turkish capital.†

In 1534 bowed with old age he left Constantinople to return to Salonica‡ to die in the arms of his children, and at the very brink of the grave he began the publication of another book the grammar (Miklol) of David Kimhi which was finished by his son Eliezer¶ after his death. But although he had found rest and comparative happiness in the land of the Crescent, he ever looked back with hopeless longing to the land of the Cross. His love for his native land was too deep ever to be

* In the Melizat Efer ve Dina published at Salonica, he uses the Christian month "Gennaro" with the Hebrew year a reminder of his earlier practice (see Mussar Haskel of 1504 where he uses "Ottobre"); although printing for Jews in a Mussulman land he still uses the Christian chronology.

† The Constantinople Soncino books were imported into Italy, and Turkey became an important printing centre in the sixteenth century. Elijah Levita reports to Widmanstadt that books wanted by him were not to be found in Venice and were only printed in Turkey and that a number of Soncino editions had just arrived in Venice from Turkey. Perles, Beitrage p. 159.

‡ His son Moses had published at Salonica as early as 1521. Two of his prints are known, the Yalkut Shimeoni 1521 and a Mahzor 1526.

¶ Eliezer returned to Constantinople and printed about 20 books there until 1547 when his press came into the hands of Eliezer Parnas.

forgotten. He had given up his life his thought and his means to the prosecution of the arts of peace, and to the attempt to contribute his portion toward the establishment of peace on earth and good-will among his Christian and Jewish fellow-men; he had sought to live in amity with his neighbors while the lives of his people were destroyed in fanatical persecution; and in spite of many years of trial in Italy looking back from his quiet resting place in Turkey, his heart turned with longing and love to the land of his birth. Nor could the loving kindness of his children and the comparative ease of his life make him forget the bitterness of his exile and separation from his beloved Italy. "At the sunset of my life," he says, "I am come into a strange land and I am like the herd that perishes."* Of this admirable man, Sacchi says "He was second only to Aldo in the sumptuous novelty and perfection of his works printed in Latin and Greek, and he ransacked the most hidden resources of typography and type cutting for his Hebrew texts. Although the publications of Bomberg in Venice seriously competed with his, nevertheless the beauty and variety of his types both in the square character and in the rabbinical the beauty of his ornaments and the variety of his works fully establish the great reputation which he acquired. To a man so celebrated whose name has so splendidly enriched the land in which he was born there is due

* Sacchi p. 26.

the greatest respect, and in concluding our notice of him we trust that the discovery of other unknown works and the more careful research of bibliographers will bring to light other interesting particulars of the life of our printer."*

A LIST OF HEBREW BOOKS PUBLISHED BY THE PRESSES OF THE SONCINATI.

SONCINO.

1483	Talmud Babli Berakhot
	" " Bezah
1484	Ibn Gebirol, Mibhar Hapeninim
	Bedersi, Behinat Olam
1484–5	Abot with Maimonides
1485 (?)	Talmud Babli Megillah
1485	Mahzor (Roman rite) vol. I.
	Earlier Prophets with Kimhi
	Albo, Ikkarim
1486	Later Prophets with Kimhi
	Tefillat Yahid
	Haggadah

CASAL MAGGIORE.

1486	Mahzor (Roman Rite) vol. II.

SONCINO.

1486–7	Talmud

* Apostolo Zeno called him "impressoria arte primarius et doctissimus rerum reconditarum". Sacchi p. 27.

1487	Seder Tahanunim
	Talmud Babli Gittin
	Rashi to Pentateuch
	Talmud Babli Baba Mezia
1488	Bedersi, Bakashat Hamemmin, etc.
	Bible
	Kimhi, Mahalak Shebile Hadaat
	Moses of Coucy, Semag
1489	Talmud Babli, Shabbat
	" " Baba Kamma
	" " Hullin
	" " Niddah
1490 (?)	Tefillot
	Asheri, Turim
	Maimonides, Mishneh Torah
1490–1	Ibn Sahula, Meshal ha-Kadmoni

NAPLES.

1490 (?)	Landau, Agur
1490	Psalms, Proverbs, Job
1491	Bible
	Pentateuch with accents

BRESCIA.

1491	Immanuel, Mahberot
1492	Pentateuch with Megillot

NAPLES.

1492	Mishnah with Maimonides

SONCINO.

1493   Talmud Babli, Bezah

BRESCIA.

1493   Pentateuch
        Psalms
1494   Bible, with accents

BRESCIA OR SONCINO.

1495   Mahzor (Roman rite)
        Tefillot (German rite)
        Selihot ("   ")

BARCO.

1497   Selihot
        Talmud Babli, Sanhedrin

FANO.

1503   Hoshaanot
1504   Hai Gaon, Mussar Haskel
        Ezobi, Kaarat Kesef
1505   Eleazar of Worms, Rokeah
        Sidur de tutto l'anno (Italian in Hebrew
            letters)
1506   Jehudah Halevi, Kuzari
        Seder Tahanunim
1504–6 Jonah Gerondi, Shaare Hateshubah
        Hai Gaon, Mussar Haskel
        Jonah Gerondi, Sefer Hayira
1503–6 Haggadah
1504–6 Mahzor (Roman rite)

PESARO.

1507	Bahya Biur al Hatorah
1507–8	Kimhi, Mahalah Shebile Hadaat
	Petah Debarai
1508	Tefillah Mikol Hashana
	Talmud Babli, Yebamot
1509–10	" " Bezah
1510	Soncino, Mabo al otiot ibriot; introductio ad letteras hebraicas
1510 (?)	Talmud Babli, Berakhot
	" " Baba Kamma
1511	Bible, 1st part
	Earlier Prophets with Kimhi
1511–12	Talmud Babli, Baba Bathra
	" " Megillah
1512	Earlier Prophets, with Abrabanel
1513–14	Nahmanides, Perush al hatorah
	Talmud Babli, Abodah Zarah
1514	Bahya, Biur al hatorah
	Gersonides, Perush al hatorah
1515	Later prophets with Kimhi
	Talmud Babli, Moed Katon
	Mahzor (German rite)
	Talmud Babli, Sukkah
	" "" Erubin

FANO.

1516	Asheri, Turim

PESARO.

1517   Bible (2nd part)
             Nathan ben Yehiel, Arukh
             Bahya, Perush al Hatorah

PESARO.

1517 (?)   Kimhi, Mahalah shebile Hadaat

ORTONA.

1518   Kimhi, Mahalah shebile Hadaat

PESARO.

1519   Talmud Babli, Hullin
             Midrash Hamesh Megillot
1520   Pirke Eliayahu
             Later Prophets

SALONICA.

1520   Albo, Ikkarim
1521   Yalkut Shimeoni

RIMINI.

1521   Mahzor (Roman rite)
1522   Albo, Ikkarim
1525   Kol-bo
1526   Bahya, Biur al Hatorah
1525   Rashi to Pentateuch
             Benveniste, Melizat Efer ve Dina
1526   Landau, Agur
             Machir, Abkat Rokel

SALONICA.

1526	Mahzor
1526–7	Yalkut Shimeoni
1529	Mahzor

CONSTANTINOPLE.

1530	Siddur Tefillot
1530–1	Bulat, Kelal Kazer
	Bashyazi, Aderet Eliyahu
1531	Hai Gaon, Musar Haskel, etc.
1530–2	Kimhi, Miklol
1532–4	Kimhi, Miklol
1532	Almoli, Shaar Hashem Hehadash

SALONICA.

1532–3	Kimhi, Shorashim

CONSTANTINOPLE.

1532–3	Yabez, Hasde Adonai
1533–4	Mizrahi, Sefer ha-Mispar
1533	Nissim, Derashot
1535	Immanuel, Mahberot
1536	Vital, Keter Torah
1537	David Cohen, Responsa
1536–7	Kalaz, Sefer hamussar
1538	Aboab, Nehar Pishon
	Shalom, Neve Shalom
1539	Illescas, Imre Noam
1539–40	Asheri, Turim
1540	Algaba, Amadis de Gaul (?)

CONSTANTINOPLE.

1542	Ibn Yahya "Leshon Limmudim"
1543	Shabbetai "Minhat Yehuda"
	Shabbetai "Milhemet hahokma vehao- sher"
	Benjamin of Tudela "Mas'ot"
1543–4	Ibn Yahya "Shiba Enayim"
1543–45	Job
1545	Ibn Gebirol "Diwan," (Shirim uzemirot)
1546	Pentateuch (Aramaic Hebrew, Persian & Arabic)
1547	Pentateuch (Aramaic, Hebrew Greek & Spanish)
1546–7	Barfat "Responsa"

CHAPTER VII.

DANIEL BOMBERG (1515–1522).

The Primacy of Venice in Typography—Germans at Venice—Bomberg and Adelkind—The Latin Psalms of Felice da Prato—When Did Bomberg Begin Printing Hebrew Books?—The Early Printing Laws—The Jew-badge and the Ghetto—The Great Rabbinical Bible—Bomberg's Difficulties in Securing Renewal of His Copyright—Press Regulations —Papal Decrees Against the Talmud—The Reuchlin Controversy and Pope Leo X—The First Printed Talmud— Bomberg's Letters to Reuchlin.

GERSON Soncino had one rival who, unlike Aldo not merely promised to publish good Hebrew books, but attained an excellence in the field long dominated by Gerson that ultimately led to the ruin of that devoted printer and sent him into Turkish exile. True, a wealthy Christian living in Venice, could succeed where the best Jewish printer in the world could not even gain a foothold; but besides these mere fortuitous advantages Bomberg's love for Hebrew letters would have led him to success had he been less wealthy or less favorably situated than in the very heart of the world in beautiful and powerful Venice.

At the beginning of the Sixteenth century under Doge Leonardo Loredano the Queen of the Adriatic was at the height of her glory and power. With marvelous energy she had recovered from the disasters inflicted on her by the League of Cambrai, and re-established her hold on the mainland, while her unrivalled power at sea made her mistress of the Mediterranean and the centre of the commercial activity of the world. Her institutions were led by the most brilliant scholars, her great university at Padua harbored the most learned professors of the sciences, in her studios were the greatest colorists of the day. Every line of trade, every move in the great world game of politics received final direction and shape under her influence. She was one of the first cities of Italy to establish a printing press, and her first printers, John of Speyer and Nicolas Jensen, contested the pre-eminence of the German printers of Subiaco.*

The printers of Venice, among the first in time, were undoubtedly the first in excellence. Besides the influence of a highly developed art and a great world commerce, Venice gave to her citizens the assurance of a safe refuge where they could follow their peaceful occupations under the guarantee of a strong and stable government, and furthermore, the opportunity of a ready market for their work. The artistic craftsmen of Venice could count not only on the large and cultured community of merchant princes and ecclesiastics whose palaces covered her islands, but on the continuous influx of foreigners, whom trade or

---

* The date of the first Venetian book 1461 is now supposed to be an error for 1471. John of Speyer printed "Epistolae Familiares" in 1469 and Nicolas Jensen printed "Decor Puellarum" in 1471. Brown, "The Venetian Printing Press" p. 8.

diplomacy brought to the city of Saint Mark. Venice encouraged her children to do all things well, to neglect nothing, to execute their purposes with an artistic idea expressed in every detail. No other city in the world has taken such pains to decorate herself; a glance at the façades of the palaces on the Grand Canal shows to what extreme this love of ornamentation was developed; even the gondola posts in the water are colored and blazoned with armorial bearings, and the buildings themselves on all sides present a bewildering mass of beautiful interlacing design.   In such an atmosphere her publications,* exact and perfect in scholarly and artistic details, established a standard in typography that prevailed in Europe for several generations.   Here it was that Aldo Manuzio reached such admirable perfection in his work, here it was that Daniel Bomberg earned the title bestowed upon him by a representative scholar of his time "the Aldo in Hebrew books."†

In the stream of craftsmen migrating to Italy we note the great number of Germans.   "A variety of reasons contributed to draw these Germans to the capital of the Republic.   Her geographical position—her proximity to one of the great passes, the Brenner, which led right into the heart of Germany—and as a consequence of this geo-

* "One of the reasons which induced so many foreign printers to settle in Venice was the excellence of the paper and the ease and cheapness with which it could be obtained."   Brown "Venetian Printing Press" p. 24.

† In a letter of Andrea Masio cited by Perles "Beiträge" 226.

graphical position, the large and powerful colony of German merchants who frequented the city; the presence of the great German exchange, the Fondaco dei Tedeschi, where every German had an opportunity of meeting his fellow-countrymen, of receiving and transmitting news, of despatching and receiving goods—all these advantages tended to draw German printers to Venice upon their first arrival in Italy."* With these German Christians came German Jews in large numbers, followed by Jews from the Iberian peninsula after the edicts of expulsion of 1492 and 1496, who settled not merely at the capital but in many of the large towns on the mainland under Venetian sovereignty. The tide of immigration brought into Venetian territory the Christian Daniel Bomberg and the Jewish family of Adelkind, the former coming direct to Venice, the latter first to Padua and thereafter to the capital, where Cornelio Adelkind entered the shop of Bomberg and contributed mightily to the great and well deserved fame of his master.

Daniel Bomberg was born probably in the eighth decade of the fifteenth century,† the son of a rich burgher of Antwerp, one Cornelius Van Bomberghen. It is said that he learned something of typography in his native city, where the press was first established in 1482, but whether this be true or not, it seems certain that he removed to

* Brown, Venetian Printing Press, p. 28.
† His son printed Treatise "Shekalim" in 1527.

Venice about the beginning of the sixteenth century.* He was soon diverted from his intention of engaging in mercantile enterprises by his association with an apostate Jew, Felice da Prato, who directed his attention to the press, and in 1515 he began his career as a printer by publishing at the press of Herman Liechtenstein Felice's Latin translation of the Psalms "Psalterium ex Hebraeo ad verbum fere tralatum", a translation made by Felice in fifteen days.†

When did Bomberg begin to print Hebrew books? Here as in so many instances tradition and written records disagree. According to the evidence of the published dates in the Bomberg books the earliest is the Pentateuch, Five Scrolls and Prophetic Portions issued in quarto on November 30, 1516 (15 Tebet 5277). Yet the Jewish chroniclers assign to him an earlier date. Gedaliah Ibn Yahya in the "Chain of Tradition"‡ David Gans in the "Branch of David"¶ Yehiel Heilprin in the "Order of the Generations"** and H. D. Asulai in the "Name of the Great"†† all give 1511 as the date of the beginning of the Bomberg press. These are all based on the "Chain of Tradition" of Gedaliah, sometimes called the "Chain of Lies"

* Wolf B. H. 2 : 945.

† Vogelstein & Rieger "Geschichte der Juden in Rom" 2: 37 note 4; de Gubernatis "Materiaux pour servir a l'histoire des etudes orientales en Italie" p. 37–38.

‡ Ed. Venice 112 b.

¶ Ed. Frankf. 42 b.

** p. 239.

†† 2: 48.

by harsh critics who reject his record of oral traditions gathered at Salonica and Alexandria with rather undiscriminating impartiality. It has been shown however that as usual the critics are wrong.*

Disregarding the tradition recorded by Gedaliah probably after Bomberg's death, we have the testimony of Bomberg's contemporary the careful and scholarly Joseph Hacohen who in his "Chroni-

Initial word from Rabbinical Bible
Bomberg, Venice, 1517-1518

cles of the Kings of France and the Kings of the House of Ottoman the Turk" records that "in this year (1513) Daniel Bomberg of Antwerp began to print," and the testimony of Bomberg himself who in 1515 applied for a patent in his Hebrew type and copyright in his Hebrew books, for it had cost him much money to have the Hebrew letters cut and to obtain men learned in Hebrew to set up and correct the books.† It is probable therefore that the chroniclers are pretty near to

* Jew. Enc. 12 : 582.
† Brown, Ven. Print. Press, p. 105.

the truth when they assign a date earlier than 1516 to the first Bomberg books. Of these books however, nothing remains. It is possible that they were entirely consumed by the pyres of the Inquisition, notwithstanding that their printer was a Christian by birth and their editor one by conversion. We shall see that not even the laws of the Republic of Venice were strong enough to save from the relentless hands of the Inquisition, the property right of the children of Daniel Bomberg in the stock of books left by their father, although law, justice and the influence of mighty men all spoke in their favor. Bomberg, entering a new field until then dominated by Gerson Soncino, probably followed the usual practice, dictated by caution, of issuing his first books in small editions which, distributed only in Italy, might easily have been reached by the Inquisition.

There appears to be no record of any license granted to Bomberg to print Hebrew books, but the fact that it was found necessary to obtain such minor privileges as copyright and patent in type, makes the supposition of an official license to print almost a certainty. Felice da Prato had been baptized in 1513* and having thus made himself persona grata with the churchmen who were beginning to assume authority in matters temporal and quasi-spiritual outside of the ter-

* Z. H. B. 10 : 32, not in 1518 as stated by Vogelstein and Rieger 2 : 37. Although the latter give some circumstantial details, the actions of Felice in Venice as far back as 1515 indicate his apostasy at that time.

ritorial limits of the States of the Church, he presented a petition to the Venetian authorities setting forth that in order to publish his books properly it was necessary to have four Jews to superintend the printing; but that unless they were permitted to discard the yellow cap it would be impossible to secure them because of the insult to which they would be subjected in the streets.* Existing regulations in Venice, originally inspired by the Fourth Lateran Council, required all Jews and Jewesses to carry in a prominent place on their outer garments a mark to distinguish them from their Christian fellows. During the wars of the League of Cambrai, the common danger uniting all Venetians regardless of creed in defense of the State had somewhat relaxed the anti-Jewish regulations, but with peace ecclesiastical influence again asserted itself, re-enforced the old measures to separate the sheep from the goats, and not only compelled the Jews to wear a yellow hat, but assigned them to that special quarter in the northwestern part of the island city which to this day bears the name of Ghetto and which remained the exclusive dwelling place of the Jews from March 29, 1516† until Napoleon Bonaparte tore down its gates and proclaimed equal rights unto its inhabitants.

We are not concerned with scholarly speculalation as to the origin of the Ghetto and of its

* Brown, Ven. Print. Press, p. 105.
† H. B. 1 : 17.

name.   Although the origin of the name appears
to be unknown, the institution itself was represented in nearly all the cities of Italy, and the
regulations concerning it were all based on the
fundamental principle that a Jew as an enemy
of Christ, hence of the government of Christ on
earth, must be kept from too close association with
those good Christians who had, through the course
of centuries learned to accept the government of
the church as the fixed and unalterable will of
God.   Jews, being heretics, might sow seeds of
dissension in faithful hearts, and lead innocent
Christian souls into danger of hell fire.   Commercial communities like Venice cared less for
the spiritual aspect of the question or its effect on
ecclesiastical sovereignty than for the monetary
profit to be derived from the Jews.   Whereas in
Rome the House of the Neophites was established
just outside the Ghetto precinct, and all sorts of
lures and threats were used to win converts, in
Venice there is little record of conversionists'
activity, and restrictive measures were designed
for revenue only.   Although Christian money-
lenders of Venice were permitted to charge forty
per cent. interest, the Jews, always conceived to
be rich beyond the dreams of avarice, were compelled to conduct three public loan offices at their
own expense and make loans at only five per cent.
interest; the economic effect of which was to
end the career of the Christian money-lenders, and
to circulate only Jewish capital.   When Venice

became the centre for the Jewish book business, the privilege of printing books was never conferred upon a Jew. Only members of patrician houses could obtain the right to establish presses, and although many distinguished Jewish printers printed at Venice, it was always under the name of some Christian publishing house, Di Gara, Zanetti, Bragadin, Vendramin and others. Thus when Bomberg employed Jewish workmen he had to obtain for them the privilege of making themselves inconspicuous by discarding the yellow cap. And so difficult was the acquisition of this privilege that Felice in his first application asks for it for four months only and revocable at the pleasure of the College of the Senate.* In 1515, at the same time that the service of Jewish workmen was obtained, Bomberg applied for and obtained the copyright in the books and patents in the Hebrew types, "lettere cuneate si in rame come in stagno o in altra materia improntate."† Felice da Prato had obtained from the Pope a copyright which authorized his books for Rome and the States of the Church and also assumed to grant him rights in all states outside of Papal temporal domination.‡ Bomberg very prudently concluded that the Papal privilege did not run into Venice and disregarding Felice's privilege he applied to the College of the Savii.¶ This grant of copyright

* Brown, Ven. Print. Press, p. 105.
† Brown, Ibid. pp. 98, 105.
‡ Brown, Ibid, p. 63.
¶ Brown, Ibid.

to Bomberg involves the beginning of a conflict of jurisdiction between the Church and the State which ultimately resulted in the dethronement of Papal supremacy in all save matters of faith.

The first great work published in large folio by Bomberg (1517–1518), great in design as well as in execution, was the rabbinical Bible (Mikraot Gedolot), the complete text of the Bible, with many old and new commentaries and additional legal and liturgical matter in the appendices,* edited by Felice da Prato, who wrote the dedication to Pope Leo X. and prepared the massoretic notes.† The work however required such great erudition and accuracy that even this finely executed edition was severely criticized by the great grammarian, Elijah Levita, after he had come to Venice and connected himself with the press of Bomberg.‡ About the same time that he issued the rabbinical Bible, Bomberg published the Biblical text in two parts, and the Pentateuch and Five Scrolls, all during the sixteenth year of the reign of Doge Leonardo Loredano. In the meantime the Senate passed a general law relating to the repeal of privileges granted to printers which recited in its preamble that formerly there had

---

* "Without Bomberg, the great Massora would perhaps not have been published for a hundred years." Zunz "Zur Gesch." etc. p. 10.

† The collection of traditional information by which the text of the Biblical books was fixed beyond the possibility of change, either through the ignorance of scribes or the failure of human memory. Vogelstein and Rieger 2 : 37 note 4.

‡ Jew. Enc. 3 : 158.

שִׁיר הַשִּׁירִים אֲשֶׁר לִשְׁלֹמֹה׃ שְׁבַּחִי מְנַשִׁיקוֹת פִּידוּ בְּי טוּבִים דֹדֶיךָ מִיַּיִן׃ וְתוּשְׁבְחָן דִּי אֲמַר שְׁלֹמֹה נְבִיָּא

קֳדָם רִבּוֹן כָּל עָלְמָא יְיָ עֲשַׂרְתֵּי שִׁירָתָא אִתְאֲמַרַ בְּעָלְמָא הָדֵין שִׁירָתָא דָא מְשַׁבַּחָא רַיח מִכֻּלְהוֹן שִׁירָתָא קַדְמֵיתָא אֲמַר אָדָם בְּזִמַן דְאִשְׁתְּבִיק לֵיהּ חוֹבְתֵיהּ וְאָתָא יוֹמָא דְשַׁבְּתָא וָאֲנַן עֲלוֹהִי פָּתַח פּוּמֵיהּ וְאֲמַר מִזְמוֹר שִׁיר לְיוֹמָא דְשַׁבְּתָא׃ שִׁירָתָא תִּנְיֵיתָא אֲמַר מֹשֶׁה עִם בְּנֵי יִשְׂרָאֵל בְּזִמַן דִּי בְּזַע לְהוֹן מָרֵי עָלְמָא יַת יַמָא דְסוּף פָּתְחוּ כֻלְהוֹן וְאֲמַרוּ בְּחַד פּוּמָא שִׁירָתָא וְדַכְבַר חַנְכִיב נָבַן שַׁבַּח מֹשֶׁה וּבְנֵי יִשְׂרָאֵל אֲמַרוּ בְּנֵי דְיִשְׂרָאֵל בְּזִמַן דְאִתְיְהִבַת לְהוֹן בֵּאָרָא רְמָא דְהֵכְרֵין כְּתִיב נָבַן שַׁבַּח יִשְׂרָאֵל׃ שִׁירָתָא רְבִיעָאָה אֲמַר מֹשֶׁה נְבִיָא כַּד אַתָא זִמְנֵיהּ לְמִפְטַר מְאַלְמָא וְאוֹכַח בָּהּ יַת עַמָא בֵית יִשְׂרָאֵל וּדְהֵרֵין כְּתִיב אֲצִיתוּ שְׁמַיָא וְאֶמַלֵּל׃ שִׁירָתָא חֲמִישָׁאָה אֲמַר יְהוֹשֻׁעַ בַּר נוּן כַּד אֲגַח קְרָבָא בְּגַבַעוֹן וְקָמוּ לֵיהּ שִׁמְשָׁא וְסִיהֲרָא תְּלָתִין וְשִׁית שָׁעִין וּפָסַק מִלְמֵימַר שִׁירָתָא פָּתַח פּוּמֵיהּ סַטְיָא וְאֲמַר שִׁירָתָא וּדְהֵרֵין כְּתִיב אֱדַין יְשַׁבַּח יְהוֹשֻׁעַ קֳדָם יְיָ׃ שִׁירָתָא שְׁתִיתָאָה אֲמַרוּ בָּרָק וּדְבוֹרָה בְּיוֹמָא דְמַסַר יְיָ יַת סִיסְרָא וְיַת מַשִׁרְיָתֵיהּ בְּיַד בְּנֵי יִשְׂרָאֵל וָאֲמָרִין כְּתִיב וְדַבְרַת דְבוֹרָה וּבָרָק בַּר אֲבִינוֹעַם׃ שִׁירָתָא שְׁבִיעָאָה אֲמַרַת חַנָּה בְּזִמַן דְאִתְיְהִיב לַהּ בַּר מִן קֳדָם יְיָ וּדְהֵרֵין כְּתִיב וְצַלִּיאַת חַנָּה בִּנְבוּאָה וָאֲמַרַת׃ שִׁירָתָא תְּמִינֵיתָא אֲמַר דָּוִד מַלְכָּא עַל כָּל נִיסַיָא דְעֲבַד לֵיהּ יְיָ פָּתַח פּוּמֵיהּ וְאֲמַר שִׁירָתָא וּדְהֵרֵין כְּתִיב וְשַׁבַּח דָוִד קֳדָם יְיָ׃ שִׁירָתָא תְּשִׁיעֵיתָא אֲמַר שְׁלֹמֹה מַלְכָּא דְיִשְׂרָאֵל בְּרוּחַ קֻדְשָׁא קֳדָם רִבּוֹן כָּל עָלְמָא יְיָ׃ וְשִׁירָתָא עֲשִׂירֵיתָא עֲתִידִין לְמֵימַר בְּנֵי גָלוּתָא בְּעִדָּן דְיִפְקוּן מִגָלוּתָא וּדְהֵרֵין כְּתִיב מְפָרַשׁ עַל יְדוֹי דִי יְשַׁעְיָה נְבִיָא כְתִיב וּדְהֵרֵין כְּתִיב שִׁירָא יְהֵא לְכוֹן כְּלֵילַת אִתְקַדַּשׁ חַגָא וְחֶדְוַת לִבָּא כְּעַמָא דְאָזֵיל לְאִתְחֲזָאָה קֳדָם יְיָ תְּלַת זִמְנִין בְּשַׁתָּא בְּנֵי וְקַל זַמַר וְכַבֵּל לְמֵיזַל מַלְכָא דְיִשְׂרָאֵל וּלְמִצְלַח קֳדָם יְיָ תַּקִּיפָא דְיִשְׂרָאֵל׃ שִׁקְנִי׃ אֲמַר שְׁלֹמֹה נְבִיָא בְּרִיךְ שְׁמֵיהּ דַּיְיָ הַכָּל אוֹרָיְתָא עַל יְדוֹהִי דְמֹשֶׁה סָפְרָא רַבָּא כְּתִיבָא עֲלֵי תְּרֵין לוּחֵי אַבְנַיָא וְשִׁיתָּא סִידְרֵי מִשְׁנָה וְתַלְמוּדָא בְּגִירְסָא וַהֲוָה מַלֵּיל עִמָן אַפִּין כָּל אַפִּין כִּגְבַר דְּנָשֵׁיק לְחַבְרֵיהּ מִן סַגִּיאוּת חִבְּתָא דְחַבֵּיב יָתַנָא מִן שַׁבְעִין עַמְמַיָא׃ לְרֵוַח

דִּבֶּר אֱלֹהִים סְתָיוֹם זֶה סַמְכוּנֵי׃ מִקְרָא אֶחָד יוֹצֵא לְכַמָּה טְעָמִים וְסוֹף דָּבָר אֵין לְךָ מִקְרָא יוֹצֵא מִידֵי פְשׁוּטוֹ וַחֲסָמֵנוּ׃ וְאַף עַל פִּי סַדְּרָן הַנְּבִיאִים דִּבְרֵיהֶם בְּרוֹגְזָא צָרִיךְ לְיַשֵּׁב הַדְּבָרִים עַל אוֹפָנֵיהֶם וְעַל סֵדֶר כָּתוּב מַחַר הַקְּרָאֵם פָּרוֹדִים זֶה אֶחָד זֶה׃ רָאִיתִי לְסַפֵּר הַזֶּה כַּמָּה מְדָרְשֵׁי אֲגָדָה יֵשׁ סְדָרִים יֵשׁ בְּמִדְרָשׁ אֶחָד וְיֵשׁ מְפֻזָּרִים בְּכַמָּה מִדְרְשֵׁי אֲגָדָה מִקְרָאוֹת לְבַדָּם וְאֵינָם מִתְיַשְּׁבִים עַל לְשׁוֹן הַמִּקְרָא וְסֵדֶר הַמִּקְרָאוֹת׃ וָאֹמַר אֲנִי לֶאֱחֹז מַרְאֶה שְׁלֹמֹה בְּרוּחַ הַקֹּדֶשׁ שֶׁעֲתִידִין יִשְׂרָאֵל לִגְלוֹת גָּלוּת אַחַר גָּלוּת חֻרְבָּן אַחַר חֻרְבָּן וְלְהִתְאַבֵּל בַּגָּלוּת זֶה עַל כְּבוֹדָם הָרִאשׁוֹן וְלִזְכּוֹר חִבָּה רָאשׁוֹנָה אֲשֶׁר הָיוּ סְגֻלָּה לוֹ מִכָּל הָעַמִּים לֵאמֹר אֵלְכָה וְאָשׁוּבָה אֶל אִישִׁי הָרִאשׁוֹן כִּי טוֹב לִי אָז מֵעַתָּה וְיִזְכְּרוּ אֶת חֲסָדָיו וְאֶת מַעֲלָם אֲשֶׁר מָעֲלוּ וְאֶת הַטּוֹבוֹת אֲשֶׁר אָמַר לָתֵת לָהֶם בְּאַחֲרִית הַיָּמִים׃ וְסוֹף סֵפֶר הַזֶּה בָּרוּחַ הַקֹּדֶשׁ בְּלָשׁוֹן אִשָּׁה בְּחוּרָה אַלְמְנַת חַיּוּת מִשְׁתּוֹקֶקֶת עַל בַּעֲלָהּ מִתְרַפֶּקֶת עַל דּוֹדָהּ כְּלִדְרִיהָ מַזְכֶּרֶת אַהֲבַת נְעוּרֶיהָ אֵלָיו וּמוֹדָה עַל פְּשָׁעֶיהָ אַף דּוֹדָהּ צַר לוֹ בְּצָרָתָהּ וּמַזְכִּיר חַסְדֵי נְעוּרֶיהָ וְנוֹי יוֹפְיָהּ וְכַשְׁרוֹן פְּעָלֶיהָ אֲשֶׁר בָּהֶם נִקְשַׁר פְּמָהּ בְּאַהֲבָה עַזָּה לְהוֹדִיעָהּ כִּי לֹא מִלִּבּוֹ עִנָּהּ׃ וְלֹא שִׁלּוּחֶיהָ שִׁלּוּחִין׃ כִּי עוֹד הִיא אִשְׁתּוֹ וְהוּא אִישָׁהּ׃

הַשִּׁירִים אֲשֶׁר לִשְׁלֹמֹה׃ פֶּן רַבּוֹתֵינוּ כָּל שְׁלֹמֹה הָאֲמוּרִים בְּשִׁיר הַשִּׁירִים קֹדֶשׁ מֶלֶךְ שֶׁהַשָּׁלוֹם שֶׁלּוֹ׃ שִׁיר מֵהוֹא עַל כָּל הַשִּׁירִים אָמַר נִבְחָר לְהַקָּבָּ"ה מֵחַד עֲרָקִיָּה לֹא הָיָה הָעוֹלָם כְּדַי בְּיוֹם שֶׁנִּיתַן בּוֹ שִׁיר הַשִּׁירִים לְיִשְׂרָאֵל מִכָּל הַכְּתוּבִי' קֹדֶשׁ׃ וְסֵדֶר הַשִּׁירִים קֹדֶשׁ הַקֳדָשִׁים׃ אָמַר רַבִּי אֱלְעָזָר בֶּן עֲזַרְיָה לְמָה הַדָּבָר דּוֹמֶה לְמֶלֶךְ שֶׁנָּטַל סְאָה חִטִּין וּנְתָנָהּ לְנַחְתּוֹם אָמַר לוֹ הוֹצֵא לִי כָּךְ סֹלֶת כָּךְ כֵּן מֻרְסָן כָּךְ כֵּן סֻבִּין וְסַלֵּק לִי מִתּוֹכָהּ גְּלֻסְקָה אַחַת מְנֻפָּה וּמְעֻלָּה׃ כָּךְ כָּל הַכְּתוּבִים קֹדֶשׁ וְסֵדֶר הַשִּׁירִים קֹדֶשׁ הַקֳדָשִׁים׃ מָשָׁל לַדְּלִי יְדַע לָם סַמְכוֹ יִקְבֹּל עַל הַבּוֹעֵל וְחֵם סְפוֹג׃ יִשְׂמְצֵי וֹמְנֻפָּרֵק עִינָא׃

Page of Song of Songs from First Rabbinical Bible
Bomberg, Venice, 1517-1518

been many printers in Venice who directly and indirectly greatly benefitted the Republic. But the custom of obtaining privileges (copyright) had grown to such an extent that many printers finding no road open to their industry emigrated, to the great damage of public and private interests. The Senate therefore revoked every privilege granted and permitted any one to print any of the books mentioned in these privileges. And the law furthermore provided that in the future only new books, or books never before printed, "solum pro libris et operibus novis, nunquam antea impressis et non pro aliis", could be protected by copyright and these only by a vote of two thirds of the Senate. Thus Bomberg lost the copyright in his Hebrew work which he had obtained in 1515.*

Bomberg having now decided upon a still more brilliant enterprise, namely the publication of a complete edition of the Talmud, was obliged to protect himself from possible competition by a renewal of his copyright. He made his application in 1518 and the Senate by a vote of 113 ayes against 17 noes and 7 doubtful granted it.† It may be that the adverse minority were merely watch-dogs of the treasury, who took advantage of every opportunity to replenish a treasury that was being constantly drained by the expenses of the Turkish wars, for there were no other Hebrew printers in Venice who might have exercised an adverse in-

---

* Brown " Venet. Print. Press ", p. 74.
† Brown, Ibid, p. 105.

fluence. Perhaps his opponents were friends of the "clerical" party, at that time roused to great activity through the great controversy between Reuchlin and the Dominicans. Perhaps they know of his attempts, about to be successful, to obtain a license from the Pope himself to print the bitterly hated Talmud. We, who are accustomed to the unbridled license of the press, can hardly realize the meaning of censorship, except through what we know of conditions still existing in Russia. To print a book was a privilege accorded to few, and exercised under supervision of those whose first care was the suppression of anything in the slightest degree questioning the authority of God and the King. The status quo was maintained by the zealous and eternal vigilance of the servants of church and state, who pounced upon the slightest attempt to minimize their authority. In the states in which the zeal of churchmen was greater than the interest of the secular power, this supervision of actions and speech approached a condition of absolute inhibition on public utterance of any sentiment except that of unreserved submission to the constituted authorities and their interpretation of that which was permitted and forbidden. In the days of Pope Leo X., during the preliminary skirmishes of the Reformation the dominant power in Rome was the Dominican order, who, furiously incensed at their unsuccessful attempts to suppress Reuchlin and the humanists and to stem the rising tide of Lutheranism and revolt, were fanatically embittered against the Talmud, which had by reason of its defense by Reuchlin become the symbol of free thought and opposition to monastic intolerance.

The natural liberality of Pope Leo X. and the many influences friendly to Jews that surrounded him prompted his interest in Jewish literature and not only moved him to grant permission for a Jewish Press at Rome but resulted in his open advocacy of the Talmud.

When Pope Benedict XIII., deposed in 1409 by the Council of Pisa, sought refuge in Spain, where he was still acknowledged the legitimate successor of St. Peter, he showed his zeal for religion by the well-worn practice of an attack on the Jews. With truly paternal zeal for their spiritual welfare he published a bull in May 1415, forbidding them to read or teach that damnable book the Talmud and ordering all copies of it to be destroyed; but in 1417 before his benevolent purpose could be accomplished the Council of Constance representing a reunited Church ended the Papal career of Benedict by electing Pope Martin V. This new Pope soon renewed the decree of his predecessor against the Talmud but, as had happened so often, events of greater practical importance put this question temporarily in the background. At this time the entire attention of the Church was occupied by the growing power of the Sultan who was not only, like the Jews, the enemy of Christ, but also a constant danger to the power of his earthly representative. So the Turk saved the Talmud by simply being a Turk, and although all the good Christians of Italy who had never read the book continued to take it for granted as a very wicked and damnable thing, they made no serious attempt to suppress it. When in 1483 the Soncino press produced two Talmudic treatises no one seems to have paid any attention to them, or to the many other treatises that followed.

Toward the beginning of the sixteenth century Joseph Pfefferkorn, a Moravian Jew, finding himself in straitened circumstances, his trade as a butcher apparently proving unprofitable, attempted to improve his condition by burglary. After he had served a term of imprisonment, he embraced Christianity and, as a violent and bloodthirsty Jew hater, seems to have flourished for many years thereafter. We are not so much concerned with his successful method of earning a living as with the fact that his attacks on the Talmud, encouraged by the Dominicans of Germany, the most illiterate and stupid of all the monastic brethren, led to the conflict between the Humanists and Obscurantists, which brought out the noble Reuchlin's temperate and well-considered defense of the Jews and their literature. The charge of heresy brought against Reuchlin by the Dominicans raised the issue of the relation of the Talmud and rabbinical writings towards Christianity. The trial of the case dragged from

Mainz to Speyer, and thence to Rome, but long before the final decision was rendered, Pope Leo X gave unmistakable indication of his position in the controversy between culture and ignorance. This noble son of Lorenzo di Medici, whose plastic intellect had been moulded by the master hand of Poliziano of Florence, who had been initiated into the mysteries of the Hebrew tongue and its literature, was deaf to the importunities of ignorant monks and overzealous apostates. To the great consternation of the faithful, he followed the suggestion of his friend, Cardinal Egidio of Viterbo, to permit the establishment of a Hebrew press at Rome and he officially endorsed Daniel Bomberg's project to print a complete edition of the Talmud, "Mihi" says Bomberg, "a Summo Pontifice demandatum".* Whereupon Messer Daniel, within five years, completed this magnificent work, sparing no expense in the execution of what he called "opus certe magni et laboris et impensae"—to the delight of Jews and Christian scholars and to the chagrin and despair of the pious multitude. But good Popes die and periods of enlightenment are followed by drastic reaction. Thirty years after

---

* "Hac occasione sententiam contra libellum Capnionis extorserunt (Cardinalis Prierias et tota Praedicatorum factio) quamvis paullo ante Pontifex quosdam exhortatus fuisset, ut Talmut imprimerent ac adeo privilegiis exornasset". From a Rescript from Rome 1521 cited in Riederer's "Zur Kirchen, Gelehrten und Buchergeschichte." 1 : 180; see Graetz 9 : 197; Vogelstein and Rieger 2 : 37 note 3; see also letter of Bomberg to Reuchlin printed in Wolf B. H. 4 : 142 and given in translation on p. 165.

ורבי

מאי

שהיא גבוהה למעלה מעשרים אמה פסולה
ורבי יהודה מכשיר ושאינה גבוהה עשרה
טפחים ושאין לה שלשה דפנות ושחמתה
מרובה מצילתה פסולה: גמ'   תנן
התם מבוי שהוא גבוהה מעשרים אמה ימעט
רבי יהודה אומ' אינו צריך מאי שנא גבי סוכה
דתני פסולה ומאי שנ' גבי מבוי דתני תקנתא
סוכה דאוריתא תני פסולה מבוי דרבנן תני
תקנתא ואיבעית אימא בדאוריתא נמי תני
תקנתא מיהו סוכה דנפישי מילה' פסק ותני
פסולה מבוי דלא נפיש מילה תני תקנתא
מנא הני מילי אמר רבה דאמ' קרא למען ידעו
דורותיכם כי בסוכו' הושבתי את בני ישראל
עד עשרים אמה אדם יודע שהוא דר בסוכה
למעלה מכ' אמה אין אדם יודע שדר בסוכה
משו' דלא שלטא בה עינא רבי זירא אמ' מהכא
וסוכה תהיה לצל יומם מחורב עד עשרי' אמה
אדם יושב בצל סוכה למעלה מעשרים אמה
אין אדם יושב בצל סוכה אלא בצל דפנות
אמר ליה אביי אלא מעתה העושה סוכתו
בעשתרו' קרנים הכי נמי דלא הוי סוכה אמר
ליה התם דל עשתרות קרנים איכא צל סוכה
הכא דל דפנות ליכא צל סוכה ורבא אמר
מהכא בסוכות תשבו שבעת ימים אמר' תורה
כל שבעת הימים צא מדירת קבע ושב בדירת
עראי עד עשרים אמה אדם עושה דירתו דירת
עראי למעלה מעשרים אמה אין אדם עושה
דירתו דירת עראי אלא דירת קבע אמר ליה
אביי אלא מעתה עשה מחיצו' של ברזל וסיכך
על גבן הכי נמי דלא הוי סוכה אמר ליה הכי
קאמי' לך עד עשרים אמה דאד' עושה דירתו
דירת עראי כי עביד ליה דירת קבע נמי נפיק
למעלה מעשרי' אמה דאדם עוש דירתו דירת
קבע כי עביד ליה דירת עראי נמי לא נפיק
כולהו

Page of Sukkah, First Edition of Talmud
Bomberg, Venice, 1521

Pope Leo X came Pope Paul IV., the gloomy Caraffa of Naples, founder of the Roman Ghetto, scourge of the Jews, censor of the press, enemy of liberty, the best hated man in all Christendom, who in the intoxication of his fanaticism ruthlessly tore down all that the scholarship and humane liberality of Leo had built up. For by his renewal of the numerous decrees against the Talmud and rabbinical writings, and his whole-souled energy in directing their practical execution, thousands of manuscripts and printed copies of the Talmud and other books were confiscated and publicly burned to the glory of God, and so effective was the work of destruction that some of the Soncino editions of Talmudic treatises have utterly disappeared and only one complete manuscript copy of the Babylonian Talmud, now at the Royal Library of Munich, survives.*

Beginning 1519 with the treatise Pessahim (Passover)† the work proceeded steadily until on June 3, 1523 the last treatise the Mishnah Taharot (Purification) issued from his press. Nothing was allowed to interfere with the work not even the desire of Bomberg to comply with Reuchlin's request for an edition of Psalms, Proverbs and Ecclesiastes. A letter of Bomberg to Reuchlin

---

* This single brand plucked from the burning, together with the Bomberg printed edition, has become the basis for the much criticized but, nevertheless, important attempt at a scientifically revised modern edition of the Talmud, now in process of publication under the direction of Lazarus Goldschmidt at Berlin.

† Rabb. "Maamar" p. 31 note 36.

reprinted by Wolf* may here be allowed to speak for the great printer.

"You have asked me to send you a copy of the Psalms, Proverbs and Ecclesiastes in one handy volume, printed with accents. God knows I would gladly do this, did not the Talmud, a work involving the greatest labor and expense entrusted to me by the Pope, hinder me from complying with your wish, for as long as I have the Talmud in hand, I can not meet your request without the greatest personal inconvenience. You are not the only one to whom I must write this. However God willing, at some future time I shall be able to print all the more beautifully what I cannot do now. But I should consider myself ungrateful and rude did I not, as much as lies in my power, have a care for your immortal fame, and the work which I shall commence at your order, shall end in your praises (inadequate though they be). Your virtues however are so illustrious that I might even pass over your name in silence, for as is well known you are famous in Hebrew and Greek literature and nature can be said to have made you more just to others than to yourself, always seeking to profit others rather than yourself. Your diligence and vigilance have brought to light many most useful things that were hidden in a prison house of shadows; now they can be seen and read everywhere. But my courage fails me, for in attempting to sound your praises I am merely spoiling what

* B. H. 4 : 142; and see ed. of Psalms 1521.

the most eloquent Fabius is about to expound.
Farewell.

Venice, October 9, 1521."*

Though delayed by the pressure of other work,
Bomberg did not forget Reuchlin's request and
in 1522 he published an edition of Proverbs Canticles
and Ecclesiastes, prefacing it with a letter to
Reuchlin† in which he expressed his unfeigned

* Daniel Bombergus Joanni Reuchlin Phorc. legum doctori S. D.

Petiisti a me ut uno volumine Psalmistam cum Salomonis Pro-
verbiis & Ecclesiaste in enchiridii forma cum accentibus impressum ad
te mitterem, quod medius fedius libenter effecissem, nisi me Talmud,
opus certe magni & laboris & impensae, mihique a Summo Pontifice
demandatum, tuis vetuisset desideriis satisfacere, quoniam non sine
meo magno incommodo (dum Talmud est in manibus) quod rogasti
posset expedire; hoc tamen non solum ad te mittitur; reliqua vero
alias, Deo dante, commodius excudentur. Nunc autem ingratus &
inhumanus mihi videar, nisi tuum nomen, quantum in me est, aeterni-
tati mandandum curem, ut, quod tuis jussis coeptum est, tuis etiam
(quamvis multo plures ac majores merearis) laudibus absolvatur,
Quem enim patiuntur tuae virtutes praeclarissimae tuum silentio
nomen praetermittere, quum de Hebraeis Graecisque literis (ut late
patet) sis ad eo bene meritus, quod justius dici potes aliis natus, quam
tibi ipsi, nam alienam tuae semper utilitatem praetulisti; tua enim
industria tuisque vigiliis multa perutilia, quae a tetro tenebrarum
carcere claudebantur in lucem prodierunt, eaque nunc ubique videntur
et lectitantur. Sed, quo progredior nimis audax, tuas dum conor
laudes enarrare, deterens quas nedum Fabius ille facundissimus se
speraret explicaturum. Vale.

Venetiis nono Kal. Oct. 1521.   Wolf B. H. 4 : 142.

† Dan. Bombergus Jo. Reuchlino Phorcensi L. L. doctori S. D.

Etsi Talmud e Rab Alphes impressione praepeditus, nedum hinc
ad septem menses, me sperabam tuis posse desideriis respondere quibus
tunc ultimam (ut spes est) sumus manum imposituri. Vicit tamen
quod videbatur difficillimum ac minime tentandum, magna, qua
tecum connexus sum, benevolentia, hacque coactus non potui, quin
tuis jussis obtemperans (gravis licet obstaret Talmud & Rab Alphes
et opera & impensa) Salamonis Proverbia, Canticum Canticorum &
Ecclesiasten in enchiridion simul (ut jussisti) noviter cum accentibus
excudenduum curarem. Nam quid tuum arduum, quidve tam operosum

admiration for that splendid protagonist of intellectual liberty, whose defense of the Talmud had excited the admiration of all lovers of learning. "Now (the Torah) is saved for the second time by Reuchlin," writes the scholarly Cardinal Egidio of Viterbo "for in this cause of yours for which we are laboring during the dangerous heat of the summer, we know that we are defending not you but the law, not the Talmud but the Church, that we are not serving Reuchlin but that Reuchlin is serving and defending us."*

mihi potest objici, quod, te jubente herculea audacia non aggredior, nec clam me est, quam mihi sit & tutum & utile, tuis justissimis petitionibus satisfacere. Quod igitur a me per literas petiisti (quamvis adhunc usque diem distulerim) nunc ad te missum tanto libentius accipies, quanto me fateor id ardentius exegisse. Quis nunc mihi (ut hic locus erat) maximas et plurimas laudes satis commemoret, quae tibi procul dubio debentur, sed ingenii mei imbecillitate non exsolvuntur; exactum autem putetur, quod, si possem, libenter darem. Tu enim (taceo caetera) pro sacrae linguae instauratione quid non fecisti ut non immerito alter ejus pater sis appelandus. Vale.

  Ven. 11 Kal. Febr. 1522.   Wolf B. H. 4: 143.

  * Data hominibus "Torah baesch" doctrina igne Sinaitico, erepta primo nobis est a deo ex igne, cum Abraham exigue servatum esse volunt. Nunc secundo a Reuchlin servata est ex igne, cum libri illi servati sunt, quibus stantibus lex panditur et lucem capit, intereuntibus autem tenebris aeternae noctis offunditur. Denique in hoc judicio tuo, ubi hac aestate periculoso aestu laboravimus, non te, sed legem, non Thalmud, sed ecclesiam, non Reuchlin per nos, sed nos per Reuchlin servatos et defensos intelligimus.

  From letter of Reuchlin in 1516, cited by Graetz 9 : 155 note 1.

  It was Reuchlin who by his Rudimenta Linguae Hebraicae (1506) the first book by a Christian writer to interest Christians in Hebrew drew Hebrew into the larger circle of the Humanities and gave it a place beside the classics; Bacher "Hebr. Sprachwissenschaft" 103. See also Gubernatis "Materiaux etc." 32.

  Reuchlin used the Bomberg Bible of 1517 for his lectures at Tubingen. Z. H. B. 10 : 80, note.

CHAPTER VIII.

DANIEL BOMBERG (1523–1536).

Bomberg's Editors—The Eulogy of Abraham de Balmes —Bomberg's Struggle for Renewal of License—Opposition of Marino Sanuto—Bomberg's Enormous Losses— Bomberg and Soncino—The Home of the Venetian Printers —Scenes from the Press Rooms—Cornelio Adelkind—The Qualifications of the Early Printers—Eulogies of Bomberg— Elijah Levita and Cardinal Egidio of Viterbo—Did Cornelio Adelkind Apostatize—The Year of the Plague, Its Effect.

THE editor of the Talmud was the learned Rabbi Hiyya Meir ben David for many years Judge of the Jewish Court at Venice. With almost incredible industry he corrected the proofs of the Talmud and all of the commentaries after comparison with manuscripts and the printed texts of Soncino.* And not only the Talmud but also the other great books published by Bomberg at this time, the Responsa of R. Israel Isserleim; of Joseph Kolon; of R. Solomon b. Adret; (an immense mass of Jewish "Case Law",) the great code of Alfasi, itself an enormous task, besides smaller works,† were edited and corrected by this indefatigable scholar. ‡ Meanwhile Felice da

---

* Gerson Soncino complained that the Venetian printers reprinted his texts. This charge is only partly true. See Soncino's introduction to Sefer Miklol, Constantinople, 1533.

† Rabb. "Maamar", p. 36.

‡ After his work was done he left Venice in 1522 and became Rabbi at Lepanto. Rabb. "Maamar" p. 33 note 41; see also Jew. Enc. 6 : 432 and Nepi and Ghirondi "Toledot Gedole Israel" p. 57.

Prato left for Rome,* to take up missionary work to his former brethren in faith, and for reasons unknown he declined the invitation of Pope Leo X to take charge of the Hebrew Press about to be established there under Papal patronage.† It is possible that he was so offensive to Elijah Levita for whose benefit the Roman press was established that Elijah's patron Cardinal Egidio may have induced the Pope to intimate to Felice that he was expected to decline the invitation. The Hebrew press at Rome was established and ended in 1518, a year in which Bomberg printed only one small book, the Psalms,—apparently devoting himself to preparation for the great activity of the following years.

With the completion of the Talmud Bomberg lost his second editor Rabbi Hiyyah Meir b. David who left Venice for the East. He still had as printers the Adelkind family, of whom Cornelio had virtually become his righthand man. But new assistants correctors and editors now joined his press, Jacob b. Hayyim ibn Adonijah the Tunisian, Abraham de Balmes, distinguished physician and scholar, Hayyim b. Moses Alton and David Pizzighettone. Abraham de Balmes whose grammar the "Mikne Abraham" was printed by Bomberg shortly after the author's death in 1523, was distinguished in many fields, as physician

* Z. H. B. 10 : 33.

† Vogelstein and Rieger 2 : 37.

to Cardinal Grimani of Venice,* as translator of scientific and philosophical works from Hebrew into Latin,† and as lecturer at the University of Padua‡ where he attained renown as an Aristotelian.¶

In Venice he met Bomberg whose warm interest especially by contrast with the coolness with which some of his own coreligionists had received him, so deeply touched the old scholar that there sprang up between them a friendship that lasted till De Balmes' death. It is most probable that the fine scholars of the type of De Balmes and Levita who mingled freely in high Christian circles were looked upon with no great favor by some of their brethren. "When I came to Venice," says de Balmes,** "the congregation of princes and magnates, I saw our people engaged in pious conversations, and diligently attending the House of Study, but I found no heifer that would be yoked with mine for no one sought any knowledge that had not already been long expounded. . . . Each one thought only of increasing his wealth. . . . and I concluded that it was time for me to embrace the bosom of a stranger, to worship at a foreign shrine. . . . And behold there came to me Daniel Bomberg, a man greatly beloved of

* He was privileged by Pope Innocent VIII. to practice medicine at Naples. Vogelstein and Rieger 2 : 22.

† Perles "Beitraege", 193.

‡ Jew. Enc. 1 : 199 and Graetz 9 : 46 & 215. Graetz's statements are somewhat inaccurate.

¶ Jost III. 119.

** Introduction to Mikne Abraham.

ספר דקדוק שחבר החכם

המלס הפילוסוף האלהי המפורסס ברבניס זה כמה שניס יושב על כסא
ההוראות למופת ולאות כמהֹר אברהם דבלמס יצֹו אשר בו כלל כל
מכסכי ועכפי וכופי מלאכת הדיקדוק במעט הכמוֹ ורב האיכות
בסדר ובשלמות' איס על ידו לרגליהס · מכל אשר היו לפכיו
במלאכה הזאת כי הר אמוכיס אספו בחפניהס הרבה ·
ועלה ארבה'מי הוסף ומי ג רפ'תמידין שלא כסדרן
ומוסכין שלא כהלכתן'והחכס יצֹו הסקיף בעיוכו
ובשכלו הכמרץ וחבר זה הספֹ הכותן חמרי
ספר ופתח בו חֹ שערי'אשר כמעט מבכי
עמכו היו סגוריס   כי המפתחות היו
אבודיס ולהכנס בו אינס יכוליס
וכשארית סוגרת ומסוגרת א
אבת מעריס· לבן בסדה
בעקה הכערה ואין
מוסיע לה עד מקס
מארי דחקלא
הוא הסדה
אמר
קנה אברס בשכלו הדיק
והרס' ולכן קרא שמו מקֹנה אברֹס ׃

Title page of Abraham de Balmes' Hebrew Grammar
Bomberg, Venice, 1523

whom glorious things were spoken. . . . He was a Christian and he feared his God. . . . The feet of his father did not stand at the foot of Sinai but to him did I turn all my fountains, for he was one of those who spend their money freely in the service of God, . . . to print Bible, Mishnah and Decisions beyond all other printers. He also studied Hebrew and crowned himself therewith and all his deeds shine like the splendor of the sky. And when he saw me . . . he asked me to write a book, a Hebrew grammar. . . . And as the nation among whom we were exiled think ill of us because there is none of us to serve in this sanctuary I determined . . . to obtain the favor of Daniel in the service of my Creator." And inspired by the good will and assistance of Bomberg, de Balmes wrote his grammar and although he died before it was completed, Bomberg printed it and subsequently published a Latin translation.* Bomberg's strongest editor and corrector after the departure of Hiyyah Meir was Jacob b. Hayyim ibn Adonijah of Tunis, a victim of persecution in northern Africa, who found his way into Italy and eventually like Felice da Prato found rest in the bosom of the Church.†

In addition to minor works he corrected the Jerusalem Talmud (1523) the second edition of the Rabbinical Bible (1525) and together with David Pizzighettone the Yad Hahazakah (1524).

* Bacher "Hebräische Sprachwissenschaft" 106; Wunderbar "Lit. Bl. des Orient" 7 : 2103; De Gubernatis "Materiaux" 45.

† Graetz 9 : 219; Jew. Enc. 7 : 32; Rabb. "Maamar" p. 37.

And now Bomberg is obliged again to lock horns with the power of the authorities. It seems that in 1525 his privilege to print expired, whereupon he petitioned for a renewal. Notwithstanding the powerful endorsement of the Chiefs of the Council of Ten and an offer of one hundred ducats by Bomberg "the motion was put and lost", says Marino Sanuto in his Diaries, "and this for the second time; and it was well done, and I had a good hand in it; for he printed books in Hebrew that were against the faith." The next day the vote was put again with Bomberg's offer of one hundred and fifty ducats and again was lost.* Had Sanuto merely recorded his opposition to Bomberg without assigning a reason we might more easily understand it for he was always in opposition. In recording his speeches in the Senate he usually begins "Io Marin Sanudo contradixi", and his vote against Bomberg might have been set down as the natural expression of his constitutional inability to allow any proposition to be adopted. The reason of Sanuto's opposition is not to be found in his piety, for his library, the most wonderful in Venice, contained all things Christian and Heathen and he has recorded the purchase of Hebrew books. It was probably inspired by the calumnies still circulated by the Men of Darkness against the Talmud despite the Pope's permission to have it printed. On March 8, 1526 Bomberg's offer of three hundred ducats was refused, but on

* Brown "Venet. Print. Press" 105.

March 27 the religious scruples of the Senate were overcome by the princely sum of 500 ducats * and Bomberg was voted a renewal of his privilege for ten years and a copyright for all his books.

When it is remembered that twelve ducats were paid by the Council of Rimini for one year's rent of the dwelling selected for Gerson Soncino, the magnitude of the sum of five hundred ducats, merely for the right to print, will be better appreciated. It not only reveals the extent of Bomberg's wealth and zeal, but it explains how his great patrimony could be devoured by the ravenous maw of the press. According to Scaliger, Bomberg lost three or four millions in gold in his printing enterprises; probably an exaggeration, yet an indication of the great resources with which he was credited and the sums which must have gone toward the perfection of the many magnificent editions which he produced. His Talmud editions alone are said to have cost one hundred thousand dollars.†

It was during the year 1525, that the two great Hebrew printers were brought face to face in Bomberg's shop, though it is more than probable

* Brown, "Venet. Print. Press," 105.

† Fumagalli, p. 478, says 300,000 ecus for the Talmud and 3,000,000 ecus for all the books, Wolf, quoting Scaliger, B. H. 2 : 895 says: "Bombergue qui etait d'Anvers et duquel le fils est venu a venise, et la a tout consume son bien, a si bien imprime les livres Hebreux; les juifs corrigeoint et praesidebant a l'imprimerie, Il a imprime des livres pour plus des 4,000,000 d'or". And again, "Bombergus edidit ter Talmud: nunquam semel edidit, quin constiterit 100 millibus coronatorum. Edidit libros pro 3 millionibus et sunt correctissimi."

that they had met on other occasions of which we have no record. Soncino's bitter criticism of Bomberg's books after he had been obliged to leave Italy and his charges that Bomberg had used his Talmud texts from which to reprint many of the Treatises of the first Venice edition,* show traces of that jealousy that seems inevitably to affect persons who are dependent on the same patron. The law of the printer was the law of the jungle, "eat and be eaten." The presses of Conat and Abraham b. Hayyim disappear before the presses of Soncino, who in turn goes down before Bomberg. After Bomberg's death the press of his heirs succumbs to that of Giustiniani who is in turn driven out of business by Bragadini. When Gerson Soncino came up from the small town of Rimini to Bomberg's shop at Venice, he must have been impressed by the air of cosmopolitan culture that prevailed there.†

In those days the printers' shops were a sort

---

* Sacchi p. 35.

† The printers of Venice lived, for the most part, in the parish of San Paternian. Aldo removed to San Paternian from the house he first occupied at Sant' Agostino, and the Estimo or assessment rolls of the various parishes give us, under San Paternian, a variety of printers' names. In the Estimo of 1514 we find Andrea da Axolla in this parish, living in a house belonging to the Doge Nicolo Tron, for which he paid sixty ducats a year. From the same source we learn that Lazzaro de Soardi stampador et compagni also rented a house in San Paternian, the property of Alvise Ruzier, for which they paid thirty-one ducats a year. But though San Paternian was the great centre of the printers, we find them scattered all over the town, at Sant' Angelo, at San Stin, at SS. Apostoli, at San Lio, at San Giacomo dall' Orio, and very many in the parish of Santa Maria Formosa. Brown "Venet Print. Press" 100, 101.

of clearing house for the intelligent public opinion of the time, the meeting places for the scholars and the lounging places for the elegants. Here congregated painters craftsmen merchants travelers, all who were interested in the things of the intellect, and what man of wealth or station in the Venice of the days of the Doges Loredano, Grimani and Gritti was not interested in those things that give zest and new meaning to life? We may easily picture the scene in Bomberg's press room, busy with workmen of half a dozen nationalities, typical of the cosmopolitan character of Venice and the universality of the press. As the press is unscrewed, a skillful hand pulls the sheet and passes it still moist under the eye of the critical foreman of the shop, Cornelio the son of Baru'h Adelkind late of Padua. Scholars and noblemen crowd around, looking over his shoulder to inspect some new typographical effect and express their criticism or admiration in the lively and spirited manner of the Venetian. In one corner a group of grave scholars is handling some books and discussing fine points of scholarship, in another, Moses del Castellazo, illustrator of the Bible* is discussing wood engraving with some dilettanti. Cornelio turns from group to group, devoting himself principally to the practical work of the shop, for he is a little beyond his depth in the very learned talk of the scholars. Among them all moves the master of the shop, the stately Bomberg, in broidered robe

* R. E. J. 22: 290; Brown p. 103.

and high cap, with the dignity of the successful man and the urbanity of the cosmopolite. In this company are found some who have forced their way into the company of their betters in order to shine by reflected light. One of these was the apostate who challenged Soncino to write Hebrew verses and who was so fiercely abused by that indignant craftsman.*

In some respects, the contrast between Daniel Bomberg and Gerson Soncino is striking; Bomberg the Christian permanently established in rich Venice, printing splendid books for Jewish readers,

* This fellow was probably one of that class who so annoyed and embittered Aldo Manuzio, and compelled him to take somewhat drastic means to protect himself. In 1514, a year before his death, Aldo wrote a letter to a friend in which he says: "I am hampered in my work by a thousand interruptions. . . . Nearly every hour comes a letter from some scholar, and if I undertook to reply to them all I should be obliged to devote day and night to scribbling. Then through the day come calls from all kinds of visitors. Some desire merely to give a word of greeting, others want to know what there is new, while the greater number come to my office because they happen to have nothing else to do. 'Let us look in upon Aldo,' they say to each other. Then they loaf in and sit and chatter to no purpose. Even these people who have no business are not so bad as those who have a poem to offer or something in prose (usually very prosy, indeed) which they wish to see printed with the name of Aldo. These interruptions are now becoming too serious for me and I must take steps to lessen them. Many letters I simply leave unanswered, while to others I send very brief replies; and as I do this not from pride, nor from discourtesy, but simply in order to be able to go on with my task of printing good books, it must not be taken hardly. As a warning to the heedless visitors I have now put up a big notice on the door of my office to the following effect: 'Whoever thou art, thou art earnestly requested by Aldo to state thy business briefly and to take thy departure promptly. In this way thou mayest be of service even as was Hercules to the weary Atlas. For this is a place of work for all who may enter.'" Putnam 1 : 437.

Gerson the wandering Jew laboring now with success now with failure with so paltry a clientele that, to get a living, he was obliged to turn to the publication of Latin and Italian books. The remark of Abraham de Balmes, that the Christian Bomberg is to be preferred to pious Jews, who allow their industrious co-religionists to die of starvation, was perhaps justified by conditions existing in Venice, although when we contemplate the Jews locked up in their Ghetto we may pardon their remissness in patronizing the finer arts. The oppressed persecuted and plundered Jews in the territories through which Gerson had wandered, may certainly be pardoned for their neglect of their distinguished co-religionist.

About the time that Bomberg was printing his first Rabbinical Bible Gerson Soncino at Ortona-by-the-Sea published the book of Galatinus on the "Mystery of Catholic truth." We may not question the Judaism of Gerson nor the Catholicism of Bomberg, for their publication of books of an alien faith merely illustrates the amenities of literary taste and the catholicity of intellectual interest, which, in the higher circles of a reawakened society, broke down the barriers of century old ecclesiastical restrictions. Perhaps, however, there is some significance in the fact that although the "Mystery of Catholic truth" printed by the Jew has sunk into absolute oblivion, the rabbinical Bible printed by the Christian is still used, not only among Jews, but, more and more, among scholarly non-Jews for whom the literature of the past two thousand years of Judaism is gradually being unsealed. These two men share the highest place in the history of Hebrew typography. Although in the number and importance of his publications Bomberg stands first, Soncino's career extended over a longer period and when Bomberg's circumstances are contrasted with Soncino's it is seen that the difference in the output of their presses does not really represent any substantial difference in their importance.*

* The following synopsis of their presses does not pretend to be entirely accurate but it represents approximately the relative output of the two presses.

CLASSES OF HEBREW BOOKS.	NO. OF EDITIONS.	
	SONCINO.	BOMBERG.
Palestinian Talmud	none	1
Rabbinical Bible	"	3
Code of Alfasi	"	1
Mishnah	"	1 & part of 2nd ed.
Responsa & Novellae	"	10
Khozari	1	none
Ikkarim	2	"
Kolbo	1	"
Aderet Eliyahu (the Talmud of the Karaites)	1	"
Code of Maimonides (Yad)	1	1
Code of Moses of Coucy (Semag)	1	2
Code of Jacob ben Asher (Turim)	2	1
Babylonian Talmud	part of 1st ed.	2 & part of 3rd ed.
Midrashim	1	6
Bible (complete)	3	4
Bible (parts)	7	25
Biblical commentaries	7	8
Prayer Books & Books of Devotion	13	12
Grammars	7	11
Dictionaries & Concordances	2	4
Rabbinical, philosophical, ethical, etc.	13	15

The Bomberg press since its establishment had employed the family of Adelkind, father, sons and grandsons, another family of craftsmen who under different circumstances might have established a famous press like that of the Soncinati. Most prominent among the clan of Adelkind was Cornelio the friend and associate rather than the subordinate of the master, in whose press room he served for upwards of three decades. So great was his merit as a printer that Bomberg permitted their names to be associated on the title page of many a book, and in some of them even allowed Cornelio's to appear alone; witness the following colophon to an edition of the "Choice of Pearls" of Ibn Gabirol issued from the press of Bomberg in 1547:

And the work was finished on the eve of Sabbath, in
the month Shebat, in the year 307, in the great
city of Venice which is under the rule of
the Signoria, may God increase their
glory, and in the first year of
the principate of Francesco
Donato, by the hands
of Cornelio Adelkind.

Cornelio's father Baru'h the Levite of Padua* his son Daniel† and his brother, whose name is unknown but who is one of "the brothers of the seed of Israel the sons of Baruh" ‡ were his some-

* See Psalms published 1524.
† He printed Job and Daniel in 1527.
‡ Mentioned in the colophon of the Responsa of Joseph Kolon published 1519.

time associates at the press, but beyond a few
facts concerning their career as printers little is
known of them. The very name Adelkind (noble
kin), descriptive like all ancient names, indicates
the standing of a family that was well known and
honored in Germany for several centuries. An
Adelkind had given up his life for the 'Sanctification

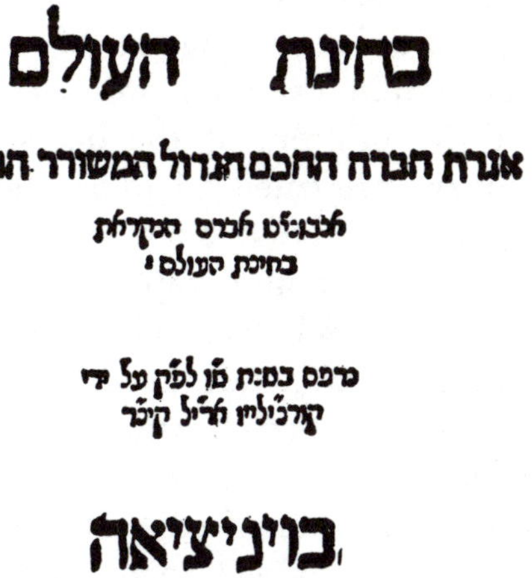

בחינת העולם

אגרת תברה החכם תגדול המשורר הנלדש׳

אבנביט אברם יזקרית
בחיכת העולם ׃

נדפס במכת מו לפֿק על די
קארנֿיוליו אֿדיל קינֿד

בוניציאה,

Title page of "Investigation of the World"
Adelkind, Venice, 1546

of the Name' at Nurenberg;* another had recited
the Shema on the rack at Weissensee,† and Baru'h
Adelkind the father of Cornelio, was among those
who fled from Germany to seek an asylum in the
cities of the plain of Northern Italy. From Padua
the printers came into Venice in the days of Aldo
Manuzio's greatest fame, and may have been

* Z. H. B. 10 : 35 note.
† Jew. Enc. 1 : 189.

among the many craftsmen whom the numerous presses of Aldo employed. After the death of his father, Cornelio continued at the press of Bomberg, and under his critical eye his son Daniel served his apprenticeship. In after years, Daniel in appreciation of his debt to his father dedicated to him one of his publications, praying him to accept it as the gift of a devoted son.

Perhaps the familiar figure of our American printer, Benjamin Franklin, may serve as an exemplar of the printers of the old school. They were not mere pressmen adept in the mechanical details of their business; they were readers of the books they printed and kept up a lively intercourse with the scholars who produced them. Knowledge then was not as diversified as it is today and modern specialization had not yet made it impossible for the scholar to know everything. Hence, the printers acquired that information and experience which enabled them to render a good account of themselves in argument and discussion with trained scholars.

Cornelio, indeed, was enough of a scholar to arrange the vocalization of Elijah Levita's "Harkabah", and to edit and arrange the text of the "Midrash Tanhuma." This was the man to whom the work of Bomberg's press owes much of that excellence, which gained for it the admiration of contemporaries and established it as a model for later craftsmen. About the year 1527*

* See treatise Shekalim printed by David son of Daniel Bomberg.

Bomberg's son David began his work at the press of his father, afterwards to become his partner and to be among those who inherited his press. It seems to have escaped bibliographers that there was more than one Bomberg although Guillaume le Bé* speaks of "des Bombergues" and Cornelio Adelkind† of "Li nostri siniori bombergi". The fact that Daniel Bomberg as well as his son David had Biblical Hebrew names and that they printed only Hebrew books may well have been the cause of the belief in their Jewish origin and it gave point to the emphatic statement of Joseph Hacohen that in them "there was no drop of Jewish blood."‡

The eulogy of Abraham de Balmes¶ the many expressions of devotion and admiration of Elijah Levita may be taken to be the tributes of those who enjoyed his favor, and therefore perhaps open to the suspicion of friendly exaggeration. But the words of Joseph Hacohen who was in no way connected with Bomberg or beholden to him leave no room for doubt of the justness of the tribute of his friends. Says Joseph:**

"In this year (1513) Daniel Bomberg, of Antwerp, began to print, and he brought forth from darkness unto light many books in the holy tongue. Constantly there went in and out of his house many

* Omont p. 6.
† In his letter to Masio, Perles "Beiträge" p. 209; see p. 209.
‡ See p. 184.
¶ See p. 170–172.
** In his Chronicles of the Kings of France & Turkey.

learned men and he never withdrew his hand from giving unto all in accordance with their demands and to the extent of the means with which God had endowed him. The said Daniel was born a Christian; neither in his parents nor in his forebears was there a drop of Jewish blood."

Between the years 1526 and 1531 the principal work of the shop was the production of the second edition of the Babylonian Talmud some portions of which were printed at Adelkind's expense.* The force at Bomberg's command was strengthened by the accession of Elijah Levita who had been driven from Rome by the terror of the year 1527 when n the sack of the city by the soldiers of the Constable de Bourbon he lost all his property, his books and his manuscripts and with his family snatched from death escaped to Venice to earn his bread as a corrector at Bomberg's press and a teacher of Hebrew to many Christian dignitaries. His great reputation had made him the friend and teacher of many of the eminent Christian Hebraists of his time and had led him to the palace of Cardinal Egidio at Rome where he dwelt for ten years. For this he had to defend himself against co-religionists who charged him with apostasy, and in the Preface of his Massoret Hamassoret he says:

"Now, I swear by my Creator that a certain Christian, (Cardinal Egidio of Viterbo) encouraged me and brought me thus far. He was my pupil

* Rabb. "Maamar" 41.

for ten years uninterruptedly. I resided at his house and instructed him, for which there was a great outcry against me, and it was not considered right of me, and several of the Rabbis would not countenance me and pronounced woe to my soul because I taught the law to a Christian, owing to the interpretation assigned to the words "And as for my judgments, they (the Gentiles) are not to know them" (Psalm 147, Verse 20). When the Prince, (The Cardinal) heard my statement, he came to me and kissed me with the kisses of his mouth saying 'Blessed be the God of the Universe who has brought thee hither. Now, abide with me and be my teacher, and I shall be to thee as a father, and shall support thee and thy house, and give thee thy corn and thy wine and thy olives and fill thy purse, and bear all thy wants.' Thus we took sweet counsel together, iron sharpening iron. I imparted my spirit to him and learned from him excellent and valuable things, which are in accordance with truth." * The apostasy of Cornelio Adelkind is almost assumed by no less a

* From the introduction to Ginsburg's edition, page 96 cited by Abraham's Jewish life in Middle Ages, 423.

In his practice to teach the law to Christians, he had the authority of Rabbi Moses Botarel who answered the charge of having taught Cabbalah to a Christian scholar named Maestro Juan, on the ground that his friend Maestro Juan was so distinguished a scholar that he was worthy of being inducted into the most mysterious realms of the so-called sacred Cabbalistic lore, and in his introduction to the Book of the Creation, Botarel cites the rabbinical doctrine that a Gentile who engages in the study of Torah is like unto a high priest.

See also Elia Menahem Halfan on Jews teaching Hebrew to non-Jews. J. Q. R. 9 : 500.

scholar than Steinschneider who considering the phrase "brothers of the seed of Israel" used of the sons of Baruh Adelkind together with the word of Cornelio himself "Israel was my name and as Cornelio I will be remembered",* says that is "almost an inducement to believe that Cornelio was an apostate who considered himself specially qualified for his work by his Jewish descent."† The fact that at least three distinguished apostates, Felice da Prato, Jacob b. Hayyim and Isaiah Parnas served at Bomberg's press strengthens the suggestion. It is denied however by Rabbinovicz‡ and to his argument may be added the internal evidence of an introduction to a Judaeo

* See Cornelio's epigraph of Petah Debarai 1546.

† Ersch & Gruber 44 note 56.

‡ "Maamar," p. 34, note 43, where his argument is that we have no right to presume that he was an apostate for he was the manager of Bomberg's press until 1549, and then worked at the press of Giustiniani where he printed the Talmud. How could an apostate have been taken for this work. But if it be said that Bomberg and Giustiniani being Christians would not be particular about this, we must note that Joshua Boaz printed the Talmud at Sabbioneta in the house of the pious R. Tobia Foa and sent for Cornelio to manage it. It is to be presumed that these men would not use an apostate for this purpose, although the apostate Vittorio Eliano corrected at the press of Cremona. The printer there was a Christian. (It is not unlikely that Conti was a Jew). After 1554 the printers were afraid of the apostates and took them into their service, to prevent them making trouble. In most of the books up to 1554 Cornelio signs "Cornelio of the house of Levi." If he had been an apostate why should he continue to say "of the house of Levi." In colophon of Bahya 1546, he says "Blessed be God who has not forgotten his mercy unto his servant and has permitted us to finish this holy commentary and we raise our eyes and hands to Heaven and pray unto the Rock to complete, etc." These pious words do not indicate apostasy.

German edition of the Psalms translated by Elijah Levita and published by Cornelio and Meir Parenzo in 1545:—

Cornelio Adelkind writes this to the pious young women and to men who have not had time to study:—

During my youth I devoted all my energies to helping to print many great and precious books, as may be seen in all books printed at Daniel Bomberg's press, in which my name is inscribed in front and in back. When I grew old I considered that I had done nothing for pious young women and for men that had not time to study in their youth, but who would like to spend their time on Sabbath or Festivals reading appropriate matters and not "Titrich of Bern" or the "Schoene Glueck." And for the sake of those that want to read God's word, for there are few (Jewish) books written in German, that are well and correctly translated, I went to Rabbi Elijah Levita and entered into agreement with him to translate several books for me and first of all the Psalms according to rules of grammar. And soon God willing I shall print Proverbs and Job and Daniel well translated. And if God lets me live yet awhile I shall make it easily possible for young and old to know what is written in the Bible, which is now, alas for our sins!, better known to others than to ourselves. Therefore I beg you dear pious young women and men buy the Psalms cheerfully and kindly and give us money that we may soon begin to print Proverbs.   Amen.

This we beg of you, your servants

Cornelio and Meir Parenzo.*

There is nothing in this introduction to indicate that Cornelio was anything else than a very pious Jew like his associates Elijah Levita and Meir Parenzo.   But after all the arguments against his apostasy we are confronted by a piece of evidence which while not necessarily conclusive is strongly persuasive.   Guillaume le Bé a young French en-

---

* Epigraph of Elijah Levita's Jüdisch Deutsch translation of Psalms (1545).   Cornelio Adelkind schreibt das den vrumen Bachuros und den Baalebatim die da nit haben zeit gehat zu lernen:

In meiner jugent hab ich vil Koestliche un' grose Seforim helfen drueken, un' hon al meinen vlais druf gelegt, as man wol mag sehn in ale Seforim, die man hot gedruekt in Daniel Bombergs drukrei, da ich bin inen gechasmet vornen und hinten.   Izunder as ich bin in die elter kumen, da hon ich mir gedocht, wie ich nichs hab gemacht vor die vrumen Bachuros un' vor itliche Baalebatim die da nit haben zeit gehat zu lernen in irer jugent, noch denochter wolten sie gern ire zeit vertreiben an am Shabbos oder am Jomtov mit leien goetliche Shemuos un' nit von Titrich von Bern oder von der Schoenen Glueck. Un' den selbigen zu lib, die da gern wolten leien von gots wort, un' doch vint man wenig Seforim in teutscher sproch geschriben die da wol un' recht geteutscht sein, bin ich gangen zu Reb' Elia Bochur, un hon mich mit im vertragen er soll mir itliche Seforim teutschen un' zum ersten das Tehillim noch dem Dikduk.   Un' bald wils got so wil ich drueken das Mishle un' Iyov un' Doniel wol geteutscht. Un' lost mich got noch eine zeit leben, so wil ich machen, das kleine und grosse wern moegen gerinklich wissen was im Esrim vearba stet geschriben, daz izunder baavonos iderman weiss men dervon wen mir. Dorum bit ich euch libe vrume Bachuros un' Baalebatim Kaft vroelich un' mit gutem herzen von den Tehillim un' gebt uns gelt das mir moegen bald anheben Mishle zu drueken.   Omen.

Das verheisen euch eure diner Cornelio un' Meir Prenz. Grünbaum Jüd. Deutsch Chrest. p. 553.

graver sojourning in Venice 1546–48 and again in 1556 cut Hebrew types for Marc Antonio Giustiniani and Meir Parenzo (whom he calls Maz de Perense). He made a collection of specimens of Hebrew types cut by other engravers among them types used in a Hebrew Commentary of "Messer Cornelio, Chrestien baptisé, correcteur en l'imprimerie des Bombergues". There can be no doubt of the identity of this Messer Cornelio and it justifies the theory that some time after 1545 he apostatized.*

After 1527 the press of Bomberg was chiefly occupied with the second edition of the Talmud. Nothing was printed in 1528 except Talmud and Mishnah. In 1529 the Karaite prayer book in four volumes for the Crimea Turkey Poland and Lithuania, a prayer book according to the German rite, Kimhi's Book of Roots and seven Talmudic

* Steinschneider scents apostasy in these words of Cornelio printed in the epigraph of Petah Debarai 1546:
And thus was finished the book Petah Debarai
In the name of the living god my redeemer and rock
 In the year of the creation 306
On the 29th day of Tishri
Edited by the Hebrew grammarian
Elijah the Levite, the lonely man,
Printed in the house of the master, the Christian
In Venice the Capital whose standard is a lion,
Who is now printing Sifra and Sifre
And may my hand not cease from putting forth fruit
Israel was my name and as Cornelio I will be remembered.
One might suppose, Steinschneider argues, that after nearly thirty years service in Bomberg's shop he would take the fact of Bomberg's Christianity for granted. Again why "Israel was my name," unless he had then definitely abandoned it?

treatises constituted a substantial output. In 1530 the plague broke out in Venice,* and although the press of Bomberg continued fairly active a marked decrease is observable in the publications. In 1531 the output had dwindled to four Talmudic treatises. The years 1532 and 1533 saw but two books issuing from Bomberg's press and there follows a hiatus of three years in which they printed nothing. We do not know the reason for this cessation of activity, nor how the printers occupied themselves in the interim. It was not until 1537 that renewed life appears and one book a volume of Psalms is issued contemporaneously with the new press law of Venice and the beginning of the press of the Silkweavers of Bologna.

* Serapeum 1851 p. 63. "All infectious diseases were at that time, and indeed till much later, classed together under the one name of the Plague, while the common people called them simply the death. The misery consequent on incessant wars, the close packing of the population during prolonged sieges, and the absence of police regulations or any attention to cleanliness in the towns, produced very unfavorable conditions from a sanitary point of view. Added to this was the danger from the constant unguarded intercourse with the East, with the result that Italy was never wholly free from infectious diseases smouldering in one place or another, and ever ready to burst into flame." Pastor 5 : 6.

CHAPTER IX.

DANIEL BOMBERG (1537–1549).

The Venetian Press Laws of 1537—Ecclesiastical Censorship—Elijah Levita's Grammatical Works—His Distinction and Influence—Bomberg's Rival, Giustiniani, and the Presses of Dei Farri and Brucioli—Growth of Ecclesiastical Influence at Venice—The Laws of 1544–1545—The Executors Against Blasphemy—Cornelio Adelkind's Ascendancy —Two of His Letters to Andrea Masio—The Last Year of the Bomberg Press—His Types and Influence—List of Bomberg Publications.

IN 1537 the laws of Venice advertise the decline of the Venetian press.* The city in which the art had reached its highest perfection now officially proclaims the humiliating fact that after seventy years of printing the art has sunk to such a low level as to disgrace the Republic. The printers had cheapened their books until the government had to step in with a law that acknowledged in its preamble that the printers of Venice, once the best in the world, had now become the worst. Foreign books came into Venice printed on good paper, but Venetian books were printed on such vile paper that when one made marginal notes it merely resulted in blots, and the Senate was obliged to decree that all who obtained copyrights must use paper that would not blot, under penalty of one hundred ducats, forfeiture of the copyright and

* For the following on this subject see Brown "Venetian Printing Press " pages 76–77.

confiscation of the books which were to be publicly burned in the Piazza San Marco. Lest there be any doubt, the Senate defines itself with minuteness: If five copies out of any edition blot the law has been violated; if five leaves of any book blot the copy may be counted among the five. Pamphlets and books worth ten soldi or less are not to be considered. Another section of the law re-enacted the law of 1517 regarding copyright, and defined a new book as one that had never been published before; this to defeat the trickery of the publishers who secured copyrights on old books by making a few corrections alterations or additions. But all this legislation passed over the house of Bomberg. Here was no vile paper* nor any cheapening of values nor any fictitious claim of copyright. In no respect did the general condition which attacked the Christian press of Venice affect the Hebrew press until well on in the seventeenth century. Then, too, the cheapening process resulted in poorly printed Hebrew books, and the inroads of the presses of Holland Germany and Bohemia made the cheapening an economic necessity. For the rich and cultured patrons of the earlier day had disappeared, their riches swallowed up by the greedy Church, their culture lost under the stress of harrying persecution and daily fear of exile; and for the poorer and simple folk

*The fine paper used in the Bomberg books was used later at Mantua as appears by comparison of the quality and water mark an anchor in a circle with a star above it.

who needed Hebrew books, the badly printed
volume was the more welcome because the cheaper
and more easily obtained. The paper of the sixteenth century Hebrew books is yellowed with age
but still strong and tough. One may make marginal notes on the time stained pages, even after
the lapse of nigh four hundred years, without fear
of blots. The censors of the Church have inked
the pages in thousands of volumes and the paper
has proved more durable than the ink, for the ink
has faded and the once deleted printed words are
now again legible, to prove that Dominico Iero-
solomitano, Fra Luigi da Bologna and Giovanni
Dominico Carretto (three of the most active ex-
purgators) lived and inked in vain.

Notwithstanding or perhaps because of the
competition of the Bolognese press, the house of
Bomberg showed renewed activity and in 1538
published nine books. If it be true as reported
by Scaliger that Bomberg died poor, the two long
vacations that his press took between 1531 and
1538 * and again between 1539 and 1544, may be
explained on the theory that during the interval
since 1531, during which he had published only
three books, Bomberg had been selling out his
accumulated stock and thus acquiring new capital
to continue his press.

Among the books of 1538 appeared two new
books, both by Elijah Levita, the more important
of which is the "Fettering of Tradition" (Massoret

* Bomberg was in Antwerp in 1538. Z. H. B. 10 : 34.

Hamassoret) wherein Elijah, true to the independent spirit that led him to dwell in the palace of a priest and teach Cabbalah to Christians, overthrows the generally accepted orthodox Jewish and Christian belief that the vowel points are as old as the Hebrew letters. He proves his theory that they are not older than the fifth century of the Christian era, and the passage containing his statement is marked by a hand on the margin pointing to the text, "for," says he, in his introduction, "in every place in this book in which I have stated something new or any matter in which no one has preceded me," a nice distinction such as one might expect from a careful scholar, "you will find the image of a hand on the margin of the page with the finger pointing as though to say: Look at this! Here is a new thing!" The other book of Elijah is called "Good Judgment" (Tub Taam) and deals with the accents. It was written by him after he came to rest in Venice and in fulfillment of a vow made during the horrors of the sack of Rome in 1527, a vow to which his Chaldaic Lexicon (Meturgeman) published by him at Isny likewise owes its origin. "Then" 1527, "came the evil days" he says,* "and the city", Rome, "was taken," its inhabitants "despoiled and driven away, no man seeing what happened to him, and behold, I vowed that if God granted me life I would write a grammar of the Targum 'Chaldaic' as I had written one of the

* Introduction to Meturgeman.

ולא אמרו ורד חולם ורד שורק וכן כ"ז מלין דכתיבין אי וכל. ורד לית
וכוותיה כגׄ לליׄן לית יפֿיל לית ולא אמרו דכתיבי׳ חירק ורגוסראׄ
שנמצא בהן חולם או חירק או שורק אינו מלשון בעלי המסורת.
רק התחכמות הסופר שכתב כן כרי להראׄ שהוא הבין המסורת.
ועתה אודיעך הטעם למה לא קראו להן סטות כמו שקראו לקמץ
ולפתח. חת לפי שהתנועות האחרות יש להן סימן אותיות המשך.
ר"ל הוֹיׄ והיוׄדראׄ או אי וֹה וספיקו בשמוׄ האלו ולא קראו להן סמות
אחרים. אבל הקמץ והפתח שאין להן אות המשך הוצרכו לקרא
להן סמות מיוחדין וכן הקמץ קטן ופתח קטן. שאין להן אותיות
המשך על הרוב כמו שבארתי בפׄ שירה לפיכך קראו להן שמות
מיוחדי שהן קמץ קטן ופתח קטן ואח"כ קטו מדקדקים אחרים ושנו
את שמותן וקראו לקמץ קטן צרי ולפתח קטן סגול נלדעת אלה
הסכים רעות כלן בשוה אבל שמות של שאר הנקודות לא הסכים
עליה: רעות כלן בשוה ויש שקורא לנקודות או חולם ויש שקורא
לו מלא פום וכן קרא לו רבינו שלמה יצחק כמו בסלת יכסימו
ופעלו לניצוץ עׄש ואנחנו האשכנזים קוראין לנקודת או מלא פום   שמות טו   ישעׄ ל
ודא ידעתי מאין הוציאנוהו כי אין בכל ספרי המדקדקים והנקדנים
שקראו לו כן אֿך קראו לנ שורק ואנתנו קורין שורק לנכׄורת אֿ
והמדקדקים קורין לוֹ שלשה נקודות או קבוץ והעיקר שקראו לו
קבוץ שפתים ויש קורין לו קבוץ פום. ונקרות אי קראן לו חירק
ויש שקורין לו שֿבר וכן קרא לו ראֿע בדרבה מקומות וכתב שהוא
נקרא כן בלשׄן ערבי והחכם הכוזרי קרא לחירק שבר גרול ולצרי
שבר קטן וברור לי כי החירק של תנועה קטנה ר"ל שהוא בליוֹד
הוא שקראו לו שבר ואותו שהוא עם היוד קראו חירק סתם:

והנה הארכתי עד הנה ביותר עד שבארתי ובררתי
שהנקודות והטעמים לא נתנו מסיני וגם אנשי
כנסת הגדולה לא המציאום כלל ואינם אלא מעשי ידי בעלי המסורׄ
שקטו אֿתכ כמו שבארתי והכלל כי הם העסידו התורה והמקרא
על עמדם ובלי ספק לולי באו כבר כלהֿת הותרה ונעשית התורה
כשתי תורות ולא היו שני ספרים בכל ספרי המקרא שהיו מסכים׳
יחד כאשר קרה לשאר ספרי המחברים ולא תראה כמה שנויים

From Elijah Levita's Massoret hamassoret

Bomberg, Venice, 1538

Hebrew." He gave his "Good Judgment" to Daniel Bomberg "a man greatly beloved * who prints the books of revelation, by the hands of approved and good workman," † in whose employ he had found bread for his family and that friendly reception which Bomberg gave to all impecunious scholars who sought his aid. Like Abraham de Balmes, whose glowing tribute to Bomberg may yet be read in the introduction to his Grammar,‡ Elijah lost no occasion to testify to his gratitude to this prince of printers, at whose press he was to spend the last two decades of his long and picturesque career. For to him Daniel Bomberg was "the master printer, a craftsman whose like is not known in Israel," "learned in the law of God." ¶ No need for laws to keep his press up to its highest mark, for when Bomberg printed the "Book of Roots" of Kimhi, it was worthy of comparison with the early Neapolitan and Soncino editions, and indeed surpassed them; Elijah Levita's praise that it differs from all other editions as the eagle from the fly, that it is perfect without fault, is perhaps a little high strung, but he is quite within the truth when he recommends it for "the beauty of the paper and the ink" and the editorial work of the "master corrector Isaiah b. Eleazar Parnas." ** Nor did Elijah's friendship with the

* Daniel 10 : 11.

† Epigraph of Tub Taam.

‡ Mikne Abraham 1523.

¶ Epigraph of Sefer Hashorashim 1529.

** A brother of the Moses Parnas who at one time assisted at the press of Soncino.

Patriarch of Venice Marco Grimani and the French Ambassador affect his simplicity or his loyalty to Bomberg, and although he was the guest of the Patriarch* and through the Ambassador was offered by the King of France the Professorship of Hebrew at the University of Paris,† he preferred to remain at Venice, leaving only when the Bomberg presses had stopped, (in 1540) and returning after they had resumed (in 1544).

After printing five books in 1539 including the "Paths of the Wilderness" Shebile Tohu of Gerardus Veltuyck, the only anti-Jewish book that Bomberg printed, his press suddenly again came to a standstill and did not resume until 1543, nor did it regain its wonted activity until 1544. The cessation of Bomberg's press prevented Elijah from printing his Tishbi‡ in Venice and he contemplated sending it to Bologna to the press of the Silkweavers.¶ But an invitation from Paulus Fagius at Isny in Algau to superintend his press induced the heroic old man at the age of seventy to leave Venice before his manuscript was quite ready, and he finished it while on the road. "If there is any error in this book** I hope I may be weighed in just scales, for this book is the fruit of

* R. E. J. 27 : 42.

† Jew. Enc. 8 : 48.

‡ "Tishbi contains 712 Hebrew, Chaldaic, Arabic, Greek and Latin words not easily found in dictionaries and used in Hebrew and Jewish literature; their origin and correct use explained. Printed and translated into sacred Latin by Paulus Fagius in Isny in Algau in 1541."

¶ Vogelstein & Rieger 2 : 91.

** Epigraph of Tishbi, Isny 1541.

haste. I hurried to come hither and when I left my home the work was not finished. Indeed when I was on the road, on mountains and hills, in rain and snow, I thought of the words and wrote them on the tablets of my heart and when I came to the inn I opened my traveling bag and took out my book and noted the words which God had placed in my heart. Here I did nothing because of the lack of necessary books. Therefore although I know that they are few and valueless, I went over them again and gathered them from all places in which they were scattered and wrote them down under their roots, where they may be found, so that he may run that readeth."

Here at Isny in obedience to the vow of 1527 he published his Meturgeman* followed by other books at Isny and Constance. But the Bavarian Alps and Lake Constance had no attraction for the old man who in his loneliness longed for his home on the Lagoons and for his wife, to whom he devotes these touching lines at the end of Meturgeman:

Oh my God, to me and my wife show this loving kind-
  ness
That she be not a widow and I not a widower
Let us die together . . . and let us be destined to
  awake
To eternal life together.

* Meturgeman: Lexicon Chaldaicum authore Eliia Levita quo nullum hactenus a quoquam absolutius aeditum est, omnibus Hebraeae linguae studiosis, imprimis & utile & necessarium. Excusum Isnae An. MDXXXXI Mense Augusto cum gratia et privilegio Caesaro ad Decennium.

And so in 1544 he returned, never to leave again. Conrad Gesner, who was in Venice in 1543, reported that no one up to that time had printed Hebrew there except Bomberg, but that a new press was being talked about from which a new edition of the Talmud was expected.* This was the press of Giustiniani which produced its first book in 1545.† At the same time two other Hebrew presses were in preparation, that of the

From Asheri's Commentary on the
Pentateuch
Dei Farri, Venice, 1544

brothers Dei Farri and of Francesco Brucioli. Let Bomberg look to it therefore that his press remain idle no longer, lest these new men supplant him without a struggle. As if in response to this stimulus Bomberg begins again in 1543 with an

* "Venitiis hactenus Hebraica nemo quod sciam praeter Danielem Bombergum excudit, nunc autem novam illic officinam extructam audio, ex qua Talmud proxime proditurum expectatur." Z. H. B. 10 : 28.

† This gives an idea of the preparation required for the establishment of a new press.

edition of the Pentateuch Megillot and Haftarot, serving notice on the new men that he is still in the field; and in 1544 he resumes his wonted activity by producing a Bible two Pentateuchs other Biblical books and a Mahzor (Spanish rite). Some explanation is necessary of the relation of the Bombergs to the new presses. There certainly was no competition between the Bombergs and the Dei Farri and Brucioli. Cornelio Adelkind printed all of the books of the Dei Farri during 1544, the one year that they published Hebrew books, at the same time presiding over the press of the Bombergs, and the types used were either Bomberg types or clever imitations of them. Perhaps the Bombergs had intended to give up their press and after selling out in part to the others had then changed their plans and resumed work themselves. Perhaps they had joined with the new men in some partnership relation, seeing that they could not prevent their obtaining a license to print Hebrew, and had thus mitigated the severity of their competition. Whether this be so or not, it seems that the competition of Giustiniani finally overthrew Bomberg, if the testimony of Alvise Bragadini is to be believed, when he says of Giustiniani "This was his method with the Bombergs. He planned to force them to stop printing, to the damage of the Jews; for their work was excellent and when they stopped, the good books stopped and books became dearer."* Giovanni

* Perles "Beiträge" 230.

Dei Farri and Brother were a well known firm of printers at Venice.* With the help of the master printer Cornelio Adelkind, who was also corrector and compositor,† they printed ten books in one year,‡ and then suddenly stopped further publication. Among the printers employed at the Dei Farri press may be named Judah ben Isaac Halevi of Frankfurt and Yehiel ben Yekutiel Ha Cohen, scholars, type founders and press builders¶ who probably helped to establish this press as well as that of Giustiniani.** Francesco

* One of them was probably the father of Pietro Farri, who printed at Venice, Fano, Sinigaglia and Jesi between 1590 and 1612. Fumagalli, p. 120.

† See Ikkarim & Bahya, Dei Farri 1544. Midrash on Psalms, Bomberg 1546.

‡ Steinschneider gives the following list:—

      Ikkarim
      Asheri's Commentary on Pentateuch
      Bahya
      Iggerot Rambam
      Ben Sira
      Pirke d' Rabbi Eliezer
      Halihot Olam
      Menorat Hamaor
      Sefer Hayashar (Ersch & Gruber 44)

to which may be added:

      Yosippon.

¶ Rabb. "Maamar" p. 47.

** It is sometimes difficult to distinguish the several functions of the employees of the Hebrew presses. As a rule the printer is known as "madfis" or "mehokek"; in later times at the smaller presses he was the same as the master of the press, "baal madfis" or the owner of the press, "baal hadefus". His name is usually introduced by the word "bidfus" corresponding to the Latin "excudebat" or by the words "al yede" equivalent to the Latin "opera". Some masters of the press spoke of themselves as "called to the press", "hukam al hadefus". The printing office is usually introduced by the words "bebet," "in aedibus", although the latter designation often indicates

Brucioli* merely dipped into Hebrew printing; only one Hebrew book appeared at his press.† The Brucioli family were long suspected of heresy by the Church authorities, a suspicion that the publication of the "Spirit of Grace" by Francesco Brucioli might well confirm, for it was a glossary of philosophical terms used by Maimonides and other philosophers, and, as is well known, it is under the guise of philosophy that heresy makes itself known.‡ As

merely the house in which the press was established. At the larger presses in addition to the owner there was a foreman or inspector or factor, such as Adelkind, of Venice, "nizab al hadefus", also "ben meshek", administrator; "neeman beto", procurator. The proof reader or corrector is the "magiha", (cura, studio.) Sometimes the factor and the proof reader were the same person. The compositor is known as the "mezaref" and also "mesader". The actual printer has no Hebrew technical name and is included in the general word "poel" or "omen", ("confectus ab" or "compositus per") workman. This also includes the compositors. Christian workmen are frequently used as compositors; and it may be noted that the proof readers frequently complained of the latter on account of the numerous mistakes caused by their ignorance of the Hebrew. Jewish converts to Christianity and Christian converts to Judaism are not uncommon among the workmen at the press. Thus Di Gara at Venice had only Christian compositors; on the other hand, Moses of Modena in order to improve his press at Salonica sent for Christian compositors from Venice; two of whom became converts to Judaism. The publisher is the "mebi lebet hadefus", he may furnish the cost of publication, in which case the work is issued at his "hozaot", "impensis", "sumptibus", or in his name "beshem", "nomine".

See Ersch & Gruber 29; Steinschneider Cat. Bodl. LXII–LXIII; Brown "Venet. Print. Press" p. 24.

*Not Brucello, as Steinschneider has it. Ersch & Gruber 44. There is no Brucello printing in Venice according to Cicogna's list of printers given by Brown "Venet. Print. Press" Appendix VI.

† Ruah Hen, 1544.

‡ Antonio Brucioli, the brother of Francesco, was one of the frequenters of the philosophical symposia in the gardens of Rucellai at Florence.

if in defiance of his persecutors he published at the press of his brother at Venice a Bible translation in Tuscan in 1532, two years before Luther's German translation appeared. The mere translation into the vernacular was damnable, and the books swarmed with heresies, that is to say, corrections of the official Vulgate. The author had the temerity to dedicate his book to Francis I of France, but the King did not have the courage of his convictions and declined to acknowledge the dedication, leading the irrepressible Aretino to remark that perhaps the King did not consider the book sufficiently well translated,—or bound.* In due time the outraged Church had its revenge. In 1546 Antonio Brucioli was in the prisons of the Inquisition and when the fierce bigot Caraffa ascended the Papal throne as Paul IV, he honored Brucioli alone among all Venetian printers by placing his name and his publications among those condemned in his Index Librorum Prohibitorum of 1559.† It was at the time of Brucioli's venture into Hebrew typography that the Holy Roman Church began to make itself strongly felt in the history of the book trade,‡ through the Inquisition haereticae pravitatis. The Venetian Republic always maintained a position of independence towards Rome, but desiring to assist the Church in

* Michaud "Biog. Univ." sub. tit. "Brucioli." Cambridge Modern History 2 : 383.

† Brown "Venet. Print. Press" 128.

‡ For the following account of the Venetian laws of 1544–45 I am indebted to Brown "Venetian Printing Press" pp. 79–80.

the suppression of heresy she created the necessary machinery of government for that purpose, thus maintaining her claim to be the sole ruler in her own dominions. The Lutheran heresy and its numerous offspring were flourishing and spreading, and the successor of St. Peter, face to face with the bewildering fact that a doubting generation was no longer convinced by the mere statement of his God-given power, was very fully occupied in devising ways and means to retain his ecclesiastical supremacy.

The series of laws of the years 1544–45 by which Venice established a censorship of books, resulted in the establishment of a new element in the history of the Venetian press, the presence of the three Savii sopra l'heresia among the administrators in charge of books and printing. The first of the press laws of this period was the establishment by the Council of Ten of the three Rifformatori dello Studio di Padova, or University Commissioners, who examined all books submitted to the Ten for leave to print. This was followed by a law forbidding anyone to print or sell any work without first having presented to the Rifformatori dello Studio documentary proof of the consent of the author or of his nearest heirs. All books printed without this consent were to be confiscated and immediately burned, and the printer fined one ducat for each book and each author injured, and imprisoned for one month. Books of this nature imported into Venice were to be forfeited and the

importer fined fifty ducats.   The Executors against
Blasphemy, Esecutori contro la Bestemmia, were
charged, as usual, with the execution of the decree,
and with them were associated the three Savii
sopra l'heresia, for the surveillance of the press
upon the matter of religion.

Neither the laws of Venice nor the competition of
Giustiniani affected the activity of the Bomberg
press, and the number and character of the books
produced would indicate that the press was quite
prosperous.   Ten books are to be credited to the
press during 1545 and thirteen during 1546.   The
Dei Farri press ended its career in the same year
in which it was commenced, but Giustiniani
printed ten books in 1545 and eight in 1546.   The
Bomberg press was strengthened by the accession
of Johanan Treves and of Meir Parenzo, the latter
destined to occupy a place in the House of Bragadini similar to that of Cornelio Adelkind in the
House of Bomberg.   In 1546 the Bomberg press
issued a novelty in Hebrew bookmaking, a series
of little grammatical works uniform in size and
style.   Gabriele Giolito had been the pioneer in
this field with his series called "Collane", neck-
laces, each necklace composed of anelli, links, and
gioielli, gems of excursuses in explanation of the
author's text.*   The Bomberg grammatical series
included works by Elijah Levita, Zedekiah Anau
and Abraham ibn Ezra and the anonymous Petah
Debarai, corrected by Elijah Levita.   The Harka-

* Brown "Studies" 2 : 96.

bah, first printed at Rome, was now reprinted with vowel points added by Cornelio Adelkind "in order to obtain favor of students."* This grammatical series may be said to have closed the career of Elijah Levita, poet and grammarian, for though he lived for several years it was as a sick old man, bereft of his mental powers and suffering from exhausting ailments. Cornelio had widened his horizon. He was no longer the mere printer but a corrector of the press, who expresses opinions on the relative correctness of manuscripts and printed texts,† who improves his editions and whose improvements are pirated by others who in his opinion "do not know the difference between right and left."‡ Withal he never loses his native modesty and the sense of his inferiority in scholarship to the great men whose books he prints and with whom his house is in correspondence. We are fortunate in having preserved for us several letters written by this good craftsman. The paucity of contemporaneous records, especially of biographical interest, may justify the reproduction of these letters in full, as some indication of the kind of man Cornelio was. Not that we may do more than guess at his individuality, through these means, for at best in our judgment of most men,

---

* See title page.

† See colophon of Midrash Shoher Tob, 1546, where he is mentioned as "haomed al hamelakhah vehamesader umagiha otha", and expresses the opinion that the old Constantinople edition is least defective.

‡ See end of Mahzor, Spanish rite, 1544.

even contemporaries, we are forced to be content with a few general impressions created at some particular time under special conditions, although we know that a safe judgment can be based only upon an omniscience that is vouchsafed to no man, and that can be only approximated with the most extraordinary advance of all conceivable scientific inquiry, method and analysis. Our rough and ready method of judgment may serve for certain practical purposes, but in the last analysis man must ever remain an insoluble mystery, and the truest word spoken of him is the word of that ancient Proverbialist, "From the Lord are the goings of man; but man—how can he understand his own ways?" From the record of the simplest daily acts some idea of a man may be gained, for in all that he does he makes history; in everything he says he recites it. And, therefore, it is to be regretted that most philosophical historians, content with sweeping views of masses of men and events, have "only glanced dubiously and from afar" at all the intimate details of life in past ages which help to throw some glimmer of light into the dark corners of history. "History is the essence of innumerable biographies." When, therefore, in our search for material about our printers, we find a document of human interest we may be pardoned for giving it a little more than ordinary attention. Of Adelkind, two letters have been rescued from oblivion, preserved by the care of Felix von Oefele, one time Royal Librarian at

Munich, and now given to the world by the scholarly Dr. Joseph Perles.* These letters, written in a peculiar idiom, in poor Italian betraying his German origin, were addressed by Cornelio to Andrea Masio.

Masio was a noted scholar, who after many years service as a diplomat had come to Rome for the purpose of studying Arabic Hebrew and Oriental literatures, with a coterie of scholars who had made Rome and Naples the great centres for these studies. It was customary for scholars to exchange letters, and among the correspondents of Masio were Daniel Bomberg the printer † and Elijah Levita the grammarian. The Bombergs had sent Masio a copy of a new Latin translation of Maimonides' "Guide of the Perplexed," and the latter in a letter to Elijah had given notice of his intention to visit Venice, an event that was hailed with delight by the printers. Then, as ever, men relied on personal intercourse with great men to enrich their minds and inspire them to higher efforts. Scholars scattered throughout the world were still finding rare and precious manuscripts and communicating the results of their studies of them in long letters or in literary conversations.

* "Beiträge" pp. 209–210.

† As a token of friendship, Bomberg sent Masio a shekel. "Et hoc verum Sicli argentei pondus esse, ostendunt vetustissimi Sicli, justissima trutina appensi, quorum unum mihi amicitiae gratia olim dono dedit vir, ob Hebraicam typographiam et ejus linguae non solum studium sed egregiam scientiam atque in primis ob singularem animi probitatem et candorem aeterna memoria dignissimus Daniel Bombergus." Masii Comm. in Josuam 7 : 20 cited by Perles "Beiträge" p. 212.

The advent of a great scholar was a matter of prime importance, and his opinion was taken with a respect that is rare in our more cynical age, when most men who have learned to read believe that they know as much about things in general as is worth knowing and look upon opinions of specialists with a certain half-contemptuous good humor. What the specialists say may be interesting but its importance must not be permitted to disturb the selfsatisfied judgment of the man of good common sense.

Let us read the letter of Cornelio to the Magnifico Messer Andrea Masio, at Rome:—

"Magnifico Maestro Andrea:

I saw your letter in the hands of Rabbi Elijah the Grammarian * and we spoke of you several times. When I heard of your intention of coming here to remain for some time in the house of my patrons the Bombergs, I was well pleased and both Rabbi Elijah and I look forward to your coming and hope for admirable things as the result of your visit. Our masters, the Bombergs, are sending you the 'Guide of the Perplexed,' in Latin, for your inspection for the purpose of obtaining your opinion on the corrections made by the Friar of Padua.† As to the translation I think that you

* The title by which the aged scholar was best known among his contemporaries, though among later generations he is known as Elijah Bahur, and Elijah Tishbi, from the titles of two of his works.

† An ignorant monk to whom for some reason this important work was entrusted. Perhaps the Church authorities had to be placated for reasons that now escape us. Rome was already very active in the affairs of Venice and heresy sniffing monks were everywhere in evidence.

will need the 'Guide of the Perplexed' in Hebrew. You will find at Rome a Jewish friend of the Bombergs and particularly of mine named Benjamin ben Joseph of Arigniano,* whom Messer Guglielmo† knows well. This Jew will find you the 'Guide' in Hebrew, and also any other book that you may need. I note that you want books of the Cabbalah which are easily found here. If you come here we will find them for you for copying without cost. I am sending you a sample of the 'Guide' as we think of making it and ask your opinion of the text as it stands; do not pay any attention to errors for you must know that it is a first impression that has not been corrected. Pardon me if I have been presumptuous in writing, never having seen or addressed you. My business is not writing, especially to a man like you; but I trust in your goodness to which I shall always recommend myself. Remain in good health.

From Venice May 21, '47.

Cornelio Adelkind."‡

* He had one of the largest Hebrew libraries of the time and was one of the founders of the second Hebrew press at Rome in that very year 1547.

† Masio's teacher of Arabic whom Cornelio met at Bomberg's in 1538.

‡ Mag'co M. Andrea. Altre volte ho visto vostre litere î man de Rabbi Eliyah Hamedakdek e pur assai volte avemo ragionato dela S. V. e a desso che io ho inteso che la V. S. dice venir qua a star alcun tempo î casa deli mei padroni bombergi tanto me son pur contento e Rabbi Eliyah e mi noi aspetemo lora che veniti e che fatti qualche bella cosa laudabil como spero. Li nostri siniori bombergi vi mandano el Moreh latino da veder ed intender la vostra opinion circa la corecion che a fatto fra paduano e cossi dela translatacio, io credo tanto sol vi

To this letter Masio promptly replied, and Cornelio's next letter is also preserved for us.
"Magnifico Messer Andrea:

For some days past I have had your most acceptable (letter) of May 28; I could not reply by the first courier because I did not have enough time, but it will now be part of my duty to reply as well as I can. First, know that I have given your dutiful greetings to Rabbi Elijah Levita who is anxious to see you before he is gathered to his fathers; know that he is very old, ill and failing mentally. That you have delayed your coming here, and are in doubt about coming at all is painful to me, for I had thought that you would bring fine fruit.

Be patient for in your honor and in all things pertaining to you I am your good servitor, and

bisogniasse el Moreh Nebukhim bileshon hakodesh, trovavile li in roma ebreo amico deli bombergi e mio in particolare che a nome binianim de iosef de ariniano el qual M. Gulielmo lo cogniosce bene, il qual ebreo vi trovava il more î ebreo e ancora qualche altro libro che vi bisogniasse; io so che seti desideroso de libri de Cabbalah, qui sene trova ben parte, si venerite quili troveremo per copiar senza spesa; io vi mando una mostra del Moreh in quel modo che pensamo de farlo e direti ancora voi la vostra opinion del sesto (testo?) quello che vi pare e non guardati sol ca (se?) fosse qualche erori, sapiati che el e la prima stampa senza esser corecta; perdonati me se son stato prosumtuoso a scrivervi e non anco mai vistovi no anche parlato; larte mia non e de saper scriver maxime a un tal homo como stati; ma me confido nela vostra bonta alaqual sempre me aricomando, stati sano. da vinezia adi 21, magio del 47.

Cornelio Adelkind.

(Addressed)
    Al Mag'co M. Andrea Masio
        Roma.
    Perles "Beiträge" p. 209.

[211]

whatever you command me, you will always find me ready to perform according to my strength. As to the Friar of Padua, he is so ignorant of Hebrew as hardly to recognize the letters. It will be necessary to retranslate the Guide of the Perplexed to do it well. Concerning the Hebrew text of the 'Guide' I have four very old manuscripts with the explanation of the foreign words, but it is necessary in order to do it well and make it useful to the world to print it with a commentary. There are four commentaries the best of which appears to be that of Narboni and I have several times written to my Master Daniel * to allow us to print it,—the Hebrew with only one commentary; but he would not consent, saying that these commentators have the habit of drawing out (meanings) not intended by the author, and so I do not know what we shall do now.†

I saw your list of books of Cabbalah; by my faith, it is a good one and contains many fine things. The books that we have are the following:—The Gate of Foundation, the Gate of Unity, the Book of Shining Light, the Book of Creation, the Reed, Illumination of the Eyes, Words of Pleasantness, Ten Numbers, Images and Secrets of the Law and the Secret of Secrets, Numbers,‡

* Bomberg seems to have retired from Venice perhaps to spend his last days in his native Antwerp, but still exercised control of his business and had to be consulted.

† In fact he did nothing and the death of Bomberg put an end to the entire plan.

‡ Not one of them printed but to be found in manuscript in Bomberg's library.

and furthermore there are others here among the
Jews which can be borrowed for copying.   I have.
recommended you to your friend and my Master
Messer Nicolo Stopio and your Rabbi Elijah
Levita.   My Master!   I think I shall not write
again without begging pardon for my presumption
being so awkward in writing.   My excuse is that
I am a German and you know well how 'delicate'
we are in writing* but the will is good.   We pray
God that he give you long life that you may be
able to do things pleasing to God and the world.
       From Venice June 11, 1547.

                     Your Cornelio Adil-Chind."†

  * A phrase wherein Cornelio characterizes the heaviness of his
countrymen of whom Joshua Soncino said that they are stammerers,
slow of speech and unable either by word or pen to express the deep
thoughts of their hearts.   Kore Hadorot ed. Cassel, 29 a.

  †Mag'co M. Andrea de questi giorni passati io ebe una vostra de
28 de magio ami molto gratissima, ala qual non poti dar risposta per el
primo curer per non aver tanto tempo comodo ala qual adesso furo
parte del mio debito de rispondervi meglio che sapero; e prima sapiati
che io ho fatto le debite salutacione de parte vostra a *Rabbi Elijah
Levi*, el qual vi videria volutiera inante che el vada apatrem; sapiati
che el e molto vecchio e non sta tropo î Cervello lui Zavaria spessi
volte.   E che ritardivesti la vostra venuta qua e anche stati î dubio de
venirce certo el mie rinchresce che io pensava che feriste gran frutto
melefede (?) paciencia la vostra volunta sia et î v̂ro honor e per tutto
onde sarite vi voglio esser bon servitore e quando me comandovite
sempre me trovarite pronto ali vostri comandi secondo la mia forza:
di fra paduano che el sea iniorante de *leshon hakodesh* lui apena cogniosce
le leteri ebraiche: el bisogniaria tradur questo *Moreh Nebukhim* de novo
afar bene: î quanto al more î *leshon hakodesh* io vene ho 4 pezi scritti
amano antigissimi co la dechiaracion deli *milat zarot* me el bisogniaria
a voler far bene e utile al mondo stampulo con un comento; el se trova
4 comentatori sopra deli quale se apar el meglior el *Narboni* e piu volte
ne ho scritto al mio signior daniel che voglia esser contento che lo
stampamo el ebreo solo con un comento, mai lui non sene contenento

There is but little more to record of the press of Bomberg. The last year of its activity was one of its most fruitful and ranks with the years 1521, 1522 and 1523 when the press reached its high water mark with the production of thirteen Talmudic treatises* a new (3d) edition of the Rabbinical Bible, Bahya's "Duties of the Heart", Gabirol's "Choice of Pearls", a Pentateuch, a volume of Penitential Prayers and two volumes of the legal works of Rabbi Jacob Weil.†

During Bomberg's life his types were sought for by the printers Dei Farri of Venice, and after his death most of his types came into the possession of Giovanni di Gara, a Venetian printer of note, from whose press many fine Hebrew books

digando che questi comentatori la tirano alor modo contra el voler del autor e cosi non so como lo faremo ancora.   Jo ho visto la vostra poliza deli libri de *Cabbalah*, per mia fe che stati bene e aveti de belle cose. Li libri che noi avemo sono questi, *Shaar Hayesod, Shaar Hayihud, Sefer Habahir, Sefer Yezirah, Hakanah, Meirat Enayim, Imre Shefer, Eser Sefirot, Temunot vesitre Torah vegam Sod Razai, Sefirot* e poi qui sene trova altro fra ebrei che se poderia aver per imprestido per copiar, io viho ricomandato al v͡ro amico e mio signior M. nic'o stopio e al vostro *Rabbi* elia levita; signior mio non so che scrivervi altro per ora se non pregavi che me perdonati se son presumtuoso ascrivervi essendomi cosi gofo nel scriver, la mia scusa sara che son todesco e voi sapetti bene como siamo gentile nel scriver, ma la volunta e bona: pregamo dio che vi dia vita longa e che posseti far cossa grata adio e al mondo, da Vinezia adi 11 da Gugnio 1547.

tutto vostro Cornelio adil chind.

(Addressed)

    date a. M. Andrea Masio patro honor'do in Roma.

    Perles "Beitraege" 210.

    * Rabb. "Maamar" 48.

    † Responsa and Shehitot ubedikot. These are dated 1549 all of the others 1548.

[214]

Title page of Pesikta Zutarta
Bomberg, Venice, 1546

were issued. In Antwerp, where Bomberg was born his fame was preserved through Christopher Plantin, whose printing office flourished for three hundred years, and whose Hebrew types, the "types and letters of Bomberghe" with which his "Bomberg" Bibles were printed, may now be seen in the Musee Plantin established by a grateful city in honor of his memory. Indeed, many a poor German printer was guilty of the pious fraud of stating on his title page that his books were printed with "Venetian types", a phrase that through the centuries testifies to the one-time fame of Daniel Bomberg.

Daniel Bomberg died in 1549* or 1550† and for his epitaph may be taken the words of the great bibliographer Wolf ‡

Daniel Bomberg
For the space of nearly forty years
First among all the craftsmen of his time
In his many editions of Hebrew and Rabbinical
works,
In the accuracy of their revision, in their beauty
of type and strength of paper.
Rewarded by Fame not less in Hebrew than Aldo
in Greek.¶

* Ersch & Gruber 43.
† Fumagalli 478.
‡ B. H. 4 : 449.
¶ Daniel Bombergus, Antwerpianus, multis Hebraeorum Rabbinicorumque voluminum editionibus, earundem accurata correctione, eleganti typorum forma, nitore solidae chartae purissimo, per annorum fere quadraginta spatium omnium iis temporibus artificum princeps; nec minus famae in Hebraicis, quam Aldus in Graecis, consecutus.

We, who know the work of Gerson Soncino, will always accord him equal honor with the famous Christian printer, but the world that knew Bomberg of Venice forgot the Jew, buried in far off Salonica.

BOOKS PRINTED BY DANIEL BOMBERG.*

1516	Pentateuch, Megillot & Haftarot
1517–18	Mikraot Gedolot (Great Rabbinical Bible)
	Bible
	Pentateuch & Megillot
1518	Psalms
1519	Commentary on Rashi by Isserlein
	Pesukim uketubim by Isserlein
	Likute Hapardes
	Terumat Hadeshen
	Responsa of Joseph Kolon
	Prayers (Roman rite)
	Mahzor (Spanish rite)
	Responsa of Solomon b. Adret
	Decisions of the Gaon of Liwa
	Talmud Babli Pessahim
1520	" " Berakhot
	" " Shabbat
	" " Yoma
	" " Kiddushin
	" " Sota

* See De Rossi "Ann. 1501–1540"; Schwab "les incunables &c." article " Bomberg " in Jew. Enc.; Freimann in Z. H. B. 10: 79.

1520	Talmud Babli Synhedrin	
	" "	Makkot
	" "	Aboda Zara
	" "	Niddah
After 1520	Mahzor Romaniya	
1521	Talmud Babli Bezah	
	" "	Hagigah
	" "	Moed Katon
	" "	Rosh Hashanah
	" "	Sukkah
	" "	Taanit
	" "	Megillah
	" "	Ketubot
	" "	Gittin
	" "	Baba Kamma
	" "	Baba Mezia
	" "	Baba Bathra
	" "	Shebuot
	" "	Horayot
	" "	Hullin

Mishnah Abot
" Eduyot
" Zeraim
Talmud Yerushalmi Shekalim
Bible
Psalms

1522	Alfasi
	Sefer Mizvot Gadol
	Turim
	Talmud Babli Erubin
	" " Yebamot

1522	Talmud Babli Nedarim
	" " Nazir
	" " Menahot
	" " Temura
	" " Zebahim
	" " Keritut
	" " Bekhorot
	" " Erakhin

Mishnah Kodashim
" Taharot
Hilkhot Ketannot
Mishnah Meila, Kinnim, Middot, Ta-
mid, Semahot, Kalla, Soferim
Megillat Setarim
Pentateuch
Rashi on Pentateuch and Megillot
Proverbs, Canticles & Ecclesiastes

Between 1518 and
1523   Nachmanides Responsa
1523   Mikne Abraham
Talmud Yerushalmi
Hiddushe Hullin, Berakhot, Gittin &
Baba Batra
Mishnah Taharot
Talm. Babli Nedarim
Recanati's commentary on the Penta-
teuch
Pentateuch with Megillot & Hoftarot
Sefer Haterumah
Sefer Hanokh
Zeror Hamor

1523	Meir Natib
	Hiddushe Berakhot of Solomon b. Adret
1524	Yad Hahazakah
	Pentateuch with commentaries
	Mahzor (Spanish rite)
	Psalms
	Proverbs, Canticles & Ecclesiastes
1255	Mikraot Gedolot 2d ed.
	Darke Hanikkud ve-haneginot
	Pentateuch
	Talm. Babli Pessahim (2d edition of Talmud)
1526	Talm. Babli Hullin
	" " Sukkah
	" " Gittin
	" " Shebuot
	Mishnah Abot
	Bible
	Mahzor (Roman rite)
1527	Mizrahi's commentary on Rashi
	Pentateuch
	Job and Daniel
	Talmud Babli Horayot
	" " Ketubot
	" Yerushalmi Shekalim
1528	" Babli Bekhorot
	" " Erakhin
	" " Temurah
	" " Meila, Kinnim, Middot, Tamid, Semahot, Soferim

1528	Talmud Babli Erubin
	" " Hagigah
	" " Yebamot
	" " Keritut
	Mishnah Kodashim
	" Taharot
	" Zeraim
1529	Karaite Prayer Book
	Prayers (German rite)
	Shorashim
	Talmud Babli Berakhot
	" " Kiddushin
	" " Nedarim
	" " Nazir
	" " Baba Batra
	" " Zebahim
	" " Menahot
1530	" " Ketubot
	" " Makkot
	" " Niddah
	" " Shabbat
	" " Beza
	" " Hilkhot Ketannot
	Seven rules of Asher b. Jehiel
	Mishnah Eduyot
1531	Talmud Babli Rosh Hashanah
	" " Yoma
	" " Baba Mezia
	" " Baba Kamma
1532	Arukh
1533	Pentateuch

1537	Psalms
1538	Massoret hamassoret
	Tub Taam
	Talmud Babli Baba Kamma
	" " Taanit
	" " Megilla
	Psalms
	Proverbs, Canticles, Ecclesiastes, Job & Daniel
	Rashi
1539	Responsa of Benjamin Zeeb
	Mishnah Abot
	" Moed Katon
	Talmud Babli Shebuot
	Shebile Tohu
1543	Pentateuch Megillot & Haftarot (several editions)
1544	Bible
	Pentateuch & Megillot
	Psalms, Job, Daniel
	Pentateuch
	Mahzor (Spanish rite)
1545	Mizrahi's commentary on Rashi
	Midrash Rabba
	" Tanhuma
	Seder Maamadot
	Psalms (Germ. trans.)
	Mekhilta
	Sifra
	Sifri
	Miklol

1545	Shorashim
1546	Petah Debarai
	Pirke Eliayahu Halevi
	Shebile Haleket
	Harkabah
	Zahut
	Mozne leshon hakodesh
	Sheiltot
	Pesikta
	Bahya on the Pentateuch
	Arama " " "
	Behinat Olam
	Marpe Lashon
	Midrash Shoher Tob
1547	Shaare Dura
	Gersonides on the Pentateuch
	Semag
	Hilkhot Ketannot
1548	Mikraot Gedolot (3rd ed.)
	Pentateuch Megillot & Haftarot
	Hobot Halebabot
	Selihot
	Mibhar Hapeninim
	Talmud Babli Berakhot
	" " Pessahim
	" " Yoma
	" " Megillah
	" " Aboda Zara
	" " Yebamot
	" " Taharot
	" " Sota

1548	Talmud Babli Taanit	
	"	" Nedarim
	"	" Nazir
	"	" Baba Kamma
	"	" Eduyot
	"	" Zebahim
	"	" Menahot
	"	" Zeraim
1549	Responsa of Jacob Weil	
	Jacob Weil, Shehitot ubedikot	
Date unknown.	Mahzor Minhag Aram Zoba (?)	
	Daily Prayers (German rite)	
	Pentateuch, Megillot & Targum	
	Haftarot	

CHAPTER X.

SOME MINOR PRESSES.

Influence of World Movements on Hebrew Typography—Bishop Agostino Giustiniani—The Polyglot Psalter of Genoa—Christopher Columbus—Trino—Jacob b. Abigedor of Padua—The Canons of St. Ambrose at Milan—The Jewish Silkweavers of Bologna—Printing Partnerships—Censorship before Publication—The Roman Ghetto—Leo X.—Cardinal Egidio of Viterbo—The First Hebrew Book at Rome—Elijah Levita—Later Roman Presses—The Church and the Press—The Duke of Parma—Antonio Blado.

A GREAT river sends down its flood to the sea; every pool and back water along its course feels, however slightly, the great onrush of the central current. A great world movement sweeps through the highways of society, and the humblest man is influenced and affected by it. In the history of even so comparatively unimportant a subject as Hebrew typography, the influence of the world movements of the Renaissance and the Reformation may be traced. Throughout the world non-Jews cultivated Hebrew learning, and even established Hebrew presses, and prelates and princes, professional scholars and craftsmen, sought entrance into the mysteries of the inner sanctuary of Hebrew literature. Among Biblical books the Psalms and the Prophets appealed most strongly to Churchmen. Here and there the prophets in their ecstasy uttered phrases, whose true meaning unknown to the historical criticism of the

time were easily interpreted into prophecies of
Jesus. Still truer was this of the Psalms, all of
them lyrical expressions of pure poetry with little
reference to the historical or personal events that
gave them birth. As illustrations we may consider Felice da Prato's translation of the Psalms
and another edition published at Genoa* by
Bishop Agostino Giustiniani, in 1516, the year
when Daniel Bomberg was preparing for his first
great work the Great Rabbinical Bible, and Gerson
Soncino was printing the Turim at Fano and entering into business relations with the printers of
Ancona. The Bishop was a member of the
patrician family of the Giustiniani of Genoa remote
kinfolk of the equally distinguished Giustiniani of
Venice, both branches of which gave some of its
sons to the press.†

The Bishop was a man of monastic type, who
sought peace in a Dominican monastery, where he
devoted himself to the study of Oriental languages,
but his scholarship and family connection soon
gained for him a bishopric at Nebbia in Corsica,‡
where he began his Bible. The book iteslf entitled "Psalterium hebraeum, graecum, arabicum
et chaldeum cum tribus latinis interpretationibus
et glossis"¶ is interesting as the first of those poly-

---

* De Rossi "Ann. 1501–1540" p. 11.

† Marc Antonio Giustiniani became a Hebrew printer at Venice
in 1545 and Michele Giustiniani founded a press at Avellino in 1627.
Fumagalli p. 22.

‡ Wolf B. H. 2 : 949.

¶ Schwab " les incunables &c." p. 20.

glot editions of the books of the Bible in which scholarship displayed itself in producing parallel versions of the texts in many languages. It contains the Hebrew text, the Greek Septuagint, the Latin Vulgate, the Chaldaic paraphrase, the Arabic translation, a Latin translation of the Chaldaic and a collection of notes by the editor. No Jew was permitted to participate in the publication of this edition of one of the greatest productions of the Hebrew genius, and indeed, although Hebrew letters were ardently cultivated by educated Genoese,* the Doge Ottaviano Fregoso at the very time of the publication of this book was decreeing the exile from Genoa of all its Jewish residents.† In the house of Nicolo Giustiniani Paulo the book was printed by Pietro Paolo Porro of Milan‡ after ten months labor by the scholarly Bishop.

He spared no expense in securing a perfect piece of typography, and in addition to paying for the entire edition of 2,000 copies, he had fifty copies especially printed on vellum for presentation to royalty. His notes to the text show that his love of learning was equalled by his love for his church for his not inconsiderable scholarship is

---

* The brother of the Doge the scholarly Fridericus Fulgosus, (Fregoso) was a Hebrew student. Perles "Beitraege" p. 182.

† Joseph Hacohen " Emek Habakha " ed. Letteris 94.

‡ Dibdin "An introduction to the knowledge of rare editions . . . with an account of Polyglot Bibles . . ." London 1827. Porro's bookmark is given by Kristeller "die Italienischen Buchdrucker und Verlegerzeichen." Strassburg 1893 p. 63.

marred by the manner of the ecclesiastical school-men, who in their study of the Hebrew classics sought prophecies of Christianity and authority for its dogma. The doctrine of the literary inspiration of Scripture and of the infallibility of its official interpretation led the greatest orthodox scholars into exegetical puerilities, which were the inevitable result of submitting reason and common sense to the dictates of what was believed to be an infallible tradition. What little there was of scientific historical investigation was cultivated by a small number of lay scholars whose attitude toward the church was more or less heretical. The trend of Catholic opinion is shown in the condemnation of Luther's heresy, which consisted in the perfectly simple and entirely reasonable proposition, that in order to understand the Bible we must study the Bible, instead of merely accepting the opinion of its official interpreters.

One of the bishop's notes (on folio 25) is especially interesting to us by reason of its allusion to the discovery of America. In commenting on the fifth verse of the nineteenth Psalm, "Their line has gone out through all the earth and their words to the end of the world," a text which he interprets in the manner of Paul in the tenth chapter of his Epistle to the Romans, the bishop says: "In our own times by his wonderful daring, Christopher Columbus, the Genoese, has discovered almost another world and a new congregation of Christians. In truth, as Columbus often maintained that God had chosen him as the instrument for the fulfill-ment of this prophecy, I deem it not improper here to refer to his life."

About 75 miles northwest of Genoa, between the cities of Turin and Milan, lies the little town of Trino, in its day a fine city, contended for by the Lords of Vercelli and the Marquises of Mont-ferrat. This town early became one of the chief centres of printing, producing some of the finest specimens of Italian incunabula and furnishing many printers to Venice. It is distinguished as the birthplace of Bernardino Stagnino and Gio-vanni Giolito, who established presses at Venice. Giolito had first printed at Trino 1518–23 but the disasters of war sent him to Venice* where he became the ancestor of a long line of famous printers. In the history of the Hebrew press it is represented by a single publication, a Hebrew prayer book, badly printed with poor type by Jacob, one of the sons of Abigedor, the butcher of Padua. Jacob, whose love for literature exceeded his scholarship, endeavored to promote the work of the press first at Rome when he and his brothers assisted in the establishment of the press which printed Elijah Levita's first book, and later at Trino, where he suddenly appears in the year 1525 and becomes the publisher of the only Hebrew book ever printed at that place, and indeed one of the few signs of the existence of the Jewish com-munity there. His prayer book may not satisfy

* Brown, "Studies" 2 : 90.

the requirements of higher scholarship, but the thing to be noted is not that an unlearned butcher's son produced a bad edition of the prayer book, but that he did it at all.*

For nearly a hundred years thereafter no Hebrew books were printed in this section of Italy. In 1620 a Hebrew press was established at Milan, at the Collegium Ambrosianum by the canons of Sant' Ambrogio, in charge of the famous Ambrosian library, and here were published the Commentaries of Rashi, Ibn Ezra and Gersonides.

Fifty years have passed since Abraham the Dyer printed in the old university town of Bologna at the house of Abraham Caravita; he and all of his generation have passed away. Francesco Griffo likewise of Bologna, who cut types for Aldo Manuzio and Gerson Soncino, is also gone, and now, after a long interval, the Hebrew press is re-established by a company of Jewish silkweavers. The Jewish silkweavers of Bologna, like other medieval craftsmen, probably organized a guild, one of those corporations that were organized for the purpose of protection against powerful princes. Jealous of their rights, proud of their privileges, devoted to their callings and imbued with high artistic ideals, they helped to cultivate an efficiency in workmanship and perfection in detail that powerfully affected the art, business and enterprise of the later Middle Ages. Unfortunately for

* The epigraph is given by Steinschneider, Ersch & Gruber 43 n. 25.

Jewish craftsmen, the recognition of Christianity was a necessary pre-requisite to admission into the guilds, and therefore the Jewish silkweavers of Bologna if they organized at all were probably

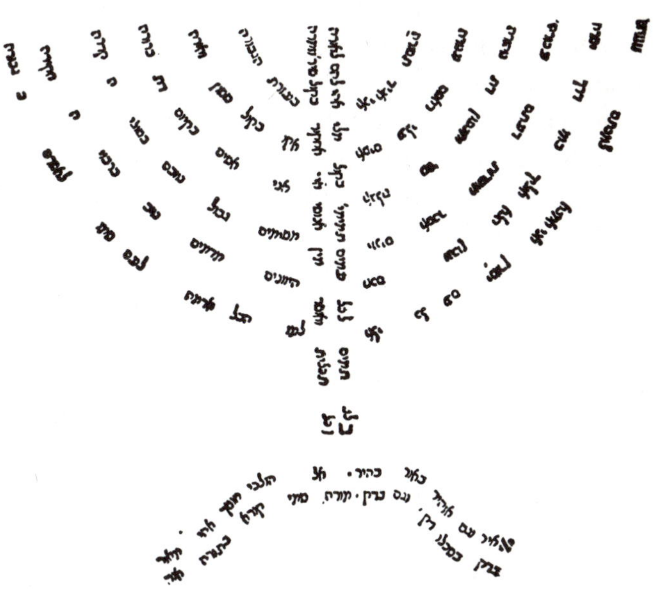

Introductory Poem in Torah Or (Law is Light)
The Silkweavers, Bologna. 1538

obliged to form a guild of their own. They are known as "the partners" and the "contracting partners" in the publication of their books. Although we shall meet such printing partnerships in other cities such as Sabbioneta and Venice we have

[231]

no information as to the terms of their contracts and the manner of their execution. We may however judge from the analogy of a similar association of five partners in Milan a record of which is preserved. One of the partners cut type and prepared ink and the other four supplied the funds. The rent of the shop was divided equally but of the profits one-third went to the active partner and the remaining two-thirds were divided among the four capitalists. The term of the partnership was three years. One of the capitalists acted as treasurer and was responsible for all the books, utensils, manuscripts etc. for which service he received one copy of every work issued. All the partners were obliged to agree before undertaking any business. Payment to the reader, copier and corrector was made in books and copies thus given were not to be put on the market below the regular selling price. The partners preserved secrecy, could have no connection with other presses, and might dissolve at the end of three years in which case the plant belonged to the active printing partner.*

The silkweavers established their press some time during the year 1536 and between 1537 and 1541 they published nine books, with the assistance of Isaac Immanuel de Lattes of Rome, a scholar of renown at that time sojourning in Bologna, who ten years thereafter in 1546 assisted in the establishment of the second Hebrew press

* Brown "Venet. Print. Press" 27.

at Rome. The nine books published by them are of varying degrees of importance, a volume of legal decisions, some rabinnical works, portions of the Bible and books of devotion. Among their prayer books was the first Italian translation of the Hebrew prayer book, published with Hebrew letters and known as the Tefillot Latini, which enabled women and unlearned men to follow the prayers understandingly. For at all times, as is well known, instruction in Hebrew and Jewish literature was almost exclusively confined to boys, and often, particularly in troublous times when communities were in deadly peril, even they learned only enough Hebrew to be able to read the prayers and follow the reading of the law. This prayer book shows the effect of the censorship before publication, established by the Pope twenty years before, for in the prayer beginning with the words: "It is incumbent upon us to praise the Master of all", this edition omits the sentence: "For they bow down to idols and vanities, and worship a god in whom there is no salvation," a sentence interpreted by the censors to be a scornful reference to the worship of saints and relics and to the adoration of the crucified son of God. And we read: "For they worship and bow down—" to what? Unfortunately for the Church, men's thoughts could not be controlled, and the pious readers were free to fill in the gap as they chose. The folly of censorship as an attempt to suppress knowledge is self-evident, yet for centuries, even to our times, the Church presumed to determine what men should think and say and print. When the censors deleted a passage of some text it was promptly memorized by all readers. If they ordered one word to be substituted for another, the original word was preserved by oral tradition, and the substituted word became a mere symbol, whereby its original was more keenly impressed on the memory. In many old books, the ink scrawls of the censors soon faded, and the marked passages were not only legible, but even made especially remarkable by the attempt to suppress them. Not to speak of the innumerable absurdities which the censor's ignorance of Hebrew produced, the whole system was a waste of thought, time and money.

Most of the printers at this press came from the Romagna to the jurisdiction of which Bologna belonged since 1512 and several of the printers at this press are known by name. Abraham b. Moses Cohen printed the Sefer Hasidim. The Mahzor of 1540 had four printers Jehiel b. Solomon of Ravenna, Menahem b. Abraham of Modena, Arye b. Solomon Hayyim of Monselice and Rafael Talmi of Forli.*

* Manzoni 1 : 99.

The following is a list of the books published by the "Silkweavers":—

1537 Or Ammim.
      Mahzor, Roman rite "by the hands of the contracting partners who also work in silk." Rafael Talmi, printer.
      Torah Or.

Near the Ponte Quattro Capi (Bridge of the Four Heads) at the southeastern entrance to the Ghetto of Rome, stands the little church of the Incannuciata, notable no doubt in its day for many a successful capture of stray Jewish souls, but distinguished in no wise today except for an inscription in Hebrew over its portal intended as a rebuke to the stiffnecked dwellers in the Ghetto. The Ghetto thanks to the government of the Kingdom of Italy is no more, and the inscription taken from the words of the great prophet of Israel now faces a broad open square where once stood the wretched houses. It is the crucified Jesus who from the church door cries in the words of Isaiah, "I have spread out my hands all the day unto a rebellious people which walketh in a way that was not good after their own thoughts; a people that provoketh me to anger continually to my face." Formerly this inscription adorned the doorway of another church at the opposite side of the Ghetto, the church of Santa Maria del Pianto (Holy Mary of Weeping). Why Santa Maria shed tears here is unknown, whether for the stiffnecked Jews who dwelling before the face of her church refused to worship at her shrine, or for the

1538   Piske Halakhot.
        Sefer Hasidim
        Tefillot Latini.
        Commentary on the Five Scrolls.
1539   Responsa of Solomon ben Adret.   Uncensored and complete; all later editons are incomplete. H. B. 1 : 48.
1540   Mahzor, Italian rite.

hard-heartedness and cruelty of her servants who made the lives of these Jews an endless nightmare. In the open square where once stood the Ghetto between the Incannuciata and Santa Maria del Pianto, the Jewish congregation in July 1904 dedicated a new synagogue, large, distinguished, shining in white and gold, in place of the old houses of worship that scarce dared rear their humble heads before the churches of the dominant faith. Well may Santa Maria weep at the revenge the centuries have taken, when even in her own city she must witness the eternal vigor now publicly manifest of that ancient worship which her priests had proclaimed dead and superseded.

In this very place, some four hundred years ago, there lived four Jews who had come from Padua after the disasters of the year 1509, when Padua was taken and plundered by the soldiers of the League of Cambrai. In the reign of Pope Julius III three of them, sons of a butcher named Abigedor Levi, and the fourth, a scholar and Hebrew grammarian, came down from the inhospitable north of Italy and settled in Rome under the shadow of the church of Santa Maria del Pianto. Some time after their advent in Rome Pope Julius III who desired to be "lord and master of this life's game" was gathered to his fathers and Pope Leo X who merely "desired to live" reigned in his stead.

We have often had occasion to mention this brilliant and liberal pontiff, who was friend and patron to the Jews the humanists the men of the arts and sciences. Through the influence of his private physician Bonet de Lattes, known to every denizen of the Jewish district, and without doubt well acquainted with Elijah Levita the Hebrew grammarian whose advent from Padua

Pope Leo X.

we have chronicled, the Pope in the first year of his pontificate granted a new trial to the noble defender of the Talmud Johannes Reuchlin, and thus auspiciously for the Jews inaugurated a reign which by contrast with their general condition seemed to the devoted people to be ushering in the advent of the Messiah.

During this comparatively happy period the Jews of Rome lived in peace and amity with their Christian fellows, not yet restricted to the narrow confines of the Ghetto and living freely in the district in which they were subsequently penned, and far beyond its confines. Within the purlieus of the Jewish quarter and within sight of the church where the pitiful inscription was later to invite the sons of persecution to the peace of the church, lay the Piazza Montanara. Here then as now, the Jews lived under the frowning walls of the fortress palace of the Orsini. Among them dwelt a Christian printer, one Giovanni Giacomo Fagiot da Montecchio, who was also to do his share in the press of 1518 toward producing the few books that were to mark an era in the history of the Jews at Rome. And now another figure appears upon the scene, one of the great ones of the earth Egidio of Viterbo the General of the Augustinians, raised to the Cardinalate in 1517 by Pope Leo, and distinguished by his oratory his general scholarship and his knowledge of Orientalia. In 1514 Elijah Levita not unknown even to the Pope himself, attracted by the prelate's well known reputation for Hebrew scholarship and great learning, presented himself at his palace gates and asked for an interview.* Egidio did not allow the grammarian to knock in vain. Elijah describes warmly how Egidio fell upon his neck and kissed him and took him and his family

* Vogelstein & Rieger 2 : 88.

into the palace, and they became teacher and pupil, exchanging knowledge and sharpening each other like iron upon iron. "And God enlightened the mind of this wise and learned man . . . and he called me Elijah the Levite the German unto him and he said unto me, 'What doest thou here Elijah? Arise and make a book expounding the grammar of the holy tongue for in all the writings of the grammarians that I have seen I find none to satisfy me.'" And thereupon Elijah composed his Sefer Harkabah and his Sefer Bahur.

Although Elijah Levita was about forty-seven years old and enjoyed an enviable reputation among scholars, he had printed nothing. But now that the time had come for the wider diffusion of his works, his friend and patron the Cardinal began to devise ways and means for obtaining the necessary permission to print. For the influence of the Dominicans was strong and showed itself in active opposition to even so innocent and harmless a thing as a Hebrew grammar. A concession had been made to them by the Pope, in his Bull published in 1516, which provided for the submission of every manuscript to a board of censors consisting in Rome of the Papal Vicar and the Master of the Sacred Palace. While plans were being formulated in the library of the Cardinal for the publication of Elijah's books, the sons of Abigedor generously undertook to finance the enterprise, and Giovanni Giacomo* da Montecchio

* Faciotto or Fazot or Fagiot.

was glad to have the work done at his shop in the Piazza Montanara. What arguments Cardinal Egidio used in his conference with the Pope is unknown, nor need we assume that much persuasion was required. The work was after the Pope's own heart, and the fact that it was properly financed by responsible men, protected the papal treasury from all responsibility. Therefore the Pope did under his papal seal permit a Hebrew press to be established in the house of Giovanni Giacomo Fagiot da Montecchio in the Piazza Montanara by Isaac, Yomtob and Jacob, the sons of Abigedor of Padua, and there on the first day of Ab 1518 after sixteen days' work appeared the Sefer Haharkabah* the first Hebrew book printed in Rome.† Three times daily the author and one whom he calls his friend superintended the work and read the proofs. It is possible that this friend was the Cardinal himself.‡ We shall see that the Bishop of Aleria the Pope's own librarian had assisted at the press of Schweinheim and Pannartz when they first set up their shop in Rome in 1407. And the enthusiasm which prompted the Cardinal to take Elijah and his family into his palace and sustain them for ten years, was surely at least in its inception sufficient to carry him through the ordeal of personally superintending

* De Rossi "Ann. 1501–1540" p. 17.
† The colophon of this book is reprinted in Vogelstein & Rieger 2 : 416.
‡ Vogelstein & Rieger.

the "holy work" of the press in the Piazza Montanara. "Grazia e privilegio" by grace and permission of the Papal Vicar, the book appeared, first of all Hebrew books to be subjected to Christian censorship before publication. With feverish haste the printers worked at the press as though they anticipated its early stoppage. Within three months two other books of Elijah Levita appeared, the Bahur,* which with the Harkabah, was the beginning of a long series of books with which this remarkable scholar enriched the science of Hebrew linguistics. But not at Rome were his other books to see the light, although he continued to live in the palace of Cardinal until in the sack of Rome in 1527 he lost his property and his books and was forced to flee for his life.† Suffice it to say that the three books of Elijah Levita were the first Hebrew books printed in Rome, and with the exception of a small pamphlet containing the 52d-53d chapters of Isaiah with a Latin translation, the last that were printed there until 1546.‡ Some scholars argue that as Rome had almost the earliest press in Italy it must also have had an earlier Hebrew press than the one that printed Levita's books and to this early press they have ascribed a dozen books printed without date or

---

* The approbation of the Bahur is reprinted by Perles "Beitraege," p. 202.

† Notwithstanding his ecclesiastical patronage his grammar was placed on the Louvain Index of 1550 & 1558. Reusch. p. 71.

‡ Vogelstein & Rieger 2 : 115.

place of publication but bearing evidence of having been issued before 1480.* Some of these contain the printers' names† but these have as yet thrown no light on the subject. There is no reason to believe that Pope Sixtus IV. who reigned from 1471 to 1484 or Alexander VI. (after 1492) would have refused an application of the Jews of Rome to permit Hebrew printing had such an application been accompanied by a sufficient sum of money. "Accipe, sume, cape, tria sunt gratissima papae" (accept, receive and take, three words most pleasing to the Pope.)‡ Bonet de

* The following list of these books is taken from Steinschneider's article in Ersch & Gruber p. 35; Sacchi p. 50; De Rossi "Ann. Sec. XV." 121–129; Freimann "Ueber hebr. Ink." p. 8; Jew. Enc. Art. " Incunabula."
    1. Maimonides "Moreh Nebuhim" (small folios).
    2. Moses de Coucy "Semag" (large folio).
    3. Nahmanides "comm. on Pentateuch" (large folio).
    4. Nathan ben Jehiel "Arukh" (folio).
    5. Rashi, "comm. on Pentateuch." (large quarto).
    6. Gersonides "comm. on Daniel" (quarto).
    7. Kimhi "Shorashim" (large folio).
    8. Solomon ben Adret "Responsa" (quarto).
    9. Maimonides "Yad " 2 vols. (large folio).
10. Psalms without points (duodecimo).
11. Psalms with index and grace after meals (duodecimo).
12. Kimhi, Isaiah and Jeremiah.
De Rossi thinks Nos. 1 and 2 belong to the same press and Nos. 3 to 7 have same types. No. 7 was printed after 1478 for its epigraph refers to an event of that year; Z. H. B. 7 : 25.
13. Maimonides "Yad."
14. Maimonides "Yad" a copy of which is in the possession of Dr. Gaster of London; apparently an Italian print.
† Nos. 3, 4, 5, Obadiah, Menasse and Benjamin of Rome. No. 9, Solomon b. Judah and Obadiah b. Moses. No. 13, Moses b. Shealtiel.
‡ Z. H. B. 10 : 62.

Lattes the physician of Alexander VI. could surely have accomplished as much with that easy going tyrant as Elijah Levita at a later date with Leo X. Bonet printed an astronomical treatise dedicated to Alexander VI. in 1493 and another one in 1498 at Christian presses.*   There were Jewish printers from Rome in various Italian cities† but no satisfactory proof that they or any one else printed Hebrew books at Rome.‡

We are not concerned with the disputes of the bibliographers, and until they agree we may safely assume that the burden of proof is upon those who allege that Hebrew books were produced in Rome before 1518.   The same arguments that point to Rome might be used for proof of an early Hebrew press at Florence or Venice.   Florence the home of the Muses had a flourishing press as early as 1471, yet no Hebrew book was published there until 1700; Venice freest of all the States of Italy printed upwards of 2,800 books before 1500, but none in Hebrew.   Hebrew printing began in the smaller States, in Mantua, Ferrara, Bologna, in

* Vogelstein & Rieger 2 : 81–82.

† Samuel b. Abi Samuel at Naples 1486, Israel Ashkenazi at Pesaro 1511–14.   Vogelstein & Rieger 2 : 114.

‡ The arguments for and against the existence of a Roman Hebrew press are given by

(pro)   Chwolson "Reshith Maase Hadefus "

         Schwab "les incunables " etc.

         Jewish Encyclopedia art. "Incunabula", "Rome"

         Simonsen "Hebraisk Bogtrygk "

(con)   Berliner "Gesch. der Juden in Rom"

         Seeligman "Z. H. B." 7: 25.

Freimann doubts existence of Roman press.   "Uebr. hebr. Ink."

the village of Pieve di Sacco, in the towns of Soncino and Reggio di Calabria and neither Venice nor Rome permitted Hebrew printing until after the beginning of the sixteenth century. In Venice after Bomberg's press started Hebrew books were printed continuously, with but rare intervals until our own days, but in Rome only an occasional and short-lived press arose. 1518, 1546, 1547, these three dates tell the whole story of the printing of Hebrew books by Jews in Rome. In 1563 the apostate Giulio Morosini published a book* for the Congregation de Propaganda Fide. From 1578 to 1581 Francesco Zanetti, with the assistance of Vittorio Eliano a grandson of Elijah Levita baptized and in good standing in the church, printed three of the Biblical books notably the Hebrew grammar of the Jesuit Cardinal Roberto Bellarmino.† Toward the end of the seventeenth century the Congregation de Propaganda Fide printed some books for missionary purposes, and thereafter until the year 1810 no Hebrew book left the press in Rome. During the short period of freedom in the days of the Roman Republic, the trustees of the Hebrew school had a Hebrew prayer book printed. Then came the period of reaction and again the presses were silent.

Well might Jewish literature have been forgotten under the century-long assaults of ecclesias-

---

* Derek Emunah.

† Institutiones linguae Hebraicae, Rome 1578. Assisted by Vittorio Eliano, he also printed a volume of Genesis in 1578, Megillot in 1580 and Psalms in 1581.—Vogelstein & Rieger 2 : 116.

tical intolerance. But in Italy they say "E ostinato come un Ebreo," and it was the determined obstinacy of the Jew that, despite threats and pains, blandishments and bribes, saved him and his literature from destruction. Even the non-Hebrew press had a thorny path in the Eternal City. Unlike the presses in the smaller principalities it had no noble patrons whose pride it was to support an enterprise which redounded to their glory. Its ecclesiastical patrons, intent with very few exceptions on using it as a means of furthering the glory of God, cared little for the welfare of the printers, and its history in the city of Rome is a record of bankruptcies. The magnificent folios of Schweinheim and Pannartz, printed on paper that rivals vellum in its beauty and durability, with types that imitate the calligraphy of the masters of the art, are to-day the admiration and delight of booklovers. The Pope's librarian the Bishop of Aleria gave himself up unreservedly to the work of furthering their splendid work; he ransacked the library of the Vatican for manuscripts to furnish them with "copy", he read proofs and himself stood at the press to superintend the work, but when the time came as it came to all the pioneers when the expenses of their undertakings could no longer be met by the income from their sales, they appealed in vain to the papal treasury for help. Peter's pence were needed for more important enterprises, the papal pensioners were many, the ambitions of papal nephews and satellites were gratified only at an expense that absorbed the stream of money which flowed into the treasury from the revenues of the papal states, from the offerings of the faithful and from the gifts of the princes of the world.

When we read of the neglect of the printer's art in the papal city, we see in the words of De Rossi, himself an ecclesiastic, a rebuke to the short-sightedness and unprogressiveness of the Holy See. He says: * "There is no art which carries men away into greater admiration than typography; none which even at its origin had gained greater renown. Scarcely had it been invented, scarcely had the first specimens been published, when it was esteemed by all, wonderful, portentous, divine. Kingdoms, provinces, States, princes, and private men† strove with one another in their eagerness to take hold of it, to cultivate it, to advance it to greater perfection, and, with equal zeal, authors learned in its origin and progress, are diligently investigating as to who introduced it into the world and developed it, as to which cities first took it up, as to which books were first produced in each province and state."

Pope Leo X had been succeeded by Clement VII, and now Paul III sat on the throne of St. Peter. He showed his favor toward the Jews in various ways. He made Jacob Mantino his private physician; he renewed all the privileges

* De typ-hebr-Ferrar. p. ix.
† Note how De Rossi omits all references to the church.

PAVLVS·III·PONT·OPT·MAX·

that his predecessors had granted; he permitted
the Jewish exiles from Naples to settle in his city;
he published a Bull condemning the blood-accusa-
tions in Hungary Bohemia and Poland; he abol-
ished the Passion Plays in the Colisseum, a source
of terror and suffering to the Jews, and finally he
permitted the re-establishment of the Hebrew
printing press.

By a mere accident Hebrew printing escaped
the notoriety of having the son of the Pope actively
engaged in its promotion.* Pier Luigi Farnese, the
son of Pope Paul III, applied for the privilege of
establishing a Hebrew press at Rome. For some
reason the Pope, who did not hesitate to confer
the highest honors and dignities and liberal grants
of territory upon his son, did not immediately
grant the privilege but referred the petition to a
commissioner, who reported favorably with the
proviso however that the press should only reprint
old Hebrew books. The plan was abandoned by
Pier Luigi whose appointment as Duke of Parma
and Piacenza by the Pope embroiled him in serious
political troubles with the aristocracy of his Duchy
whose privileges he had ruthlessly curtailed. Perhaps if he had confined his ambition to printing
Hebrew books instead of attempting to rule two
principalities that hated and despised him, his life
might have been more useful. It certainly would
have been longer, for he was assassinated by con-
spirators after a reign of only two years.

   * R. E. J. 27: 210, 233.

At the time when Pier Luigi Farnese was entering his new Duchy, Maestro Antonio Blado d'Asola, who had had some experience in printing Hebrew texts,* filed his petition in partnership with two of the leading Jews of Rome praying for leave to print Hebrew books in Rome. This was granted by the Papal Vicar, who was also one of the censors of the press, and on the 13th of Jan-

Title page of Rabbi Nissim's Responsa
Rome, 1546

ary, 1547, after five months' work, there was completed the Responsa† of Rabbi Nissim Gerondi. The partners of Maestro Antonio Blado were Isaac ben Immanuel de Lattes,‡ whose

* On July 25, 1524 he issued Canticles with translation and commentary of Guidacerius.

† Legal Opinions.

‡ Azulai "Shem Hagedolim" (ed. Frankf. 1844) 3 : 33. Vogelstein & Rieger 2 : 99; he helped to establish the press of the silk weavers of Bologna. Vogelstein & Rieger 2 : 100; Perles "Beitraege" 190.

father and grandfather had been court physicians to the Popes, and who was himself a scholar of renown and a member of the Rabbinical Court of Justice at Rome, and Benjamin ben Joseph d'Arignano, the scholar of whom Cornelio Adelkind wrote to Andrea Masio. Benjamin d'Arignano's large and noted library, was frequently used by Italian printers who found his splendid collection of manuscripts invaluable for correcting their "copy." The chief printer at this press was Solomon ben Isaac of Lisbon assisted by Samuel the Frenchman (Zarfati), who afterward in 1551 appeared at the head of a press at Ferrara. This partnership of Christian and Jew is by no means uncommon; the Christian obtained the official privileges and the Jew did the work of editing, proof reading, finding a market for the books, and often also the actual work of printing. The typesetters also were usually Jews, for the Christian craftsmen seem rarely to have acquired dexterity in handling and setting Hebrew type.

Antonio Blado was in his day the most distinguished printer in Italy, and was official printer to the Papal court for more than half a century from 1516 when Bomberg began his career at Venice to 1567 long after Bomberg's death.* From every part of Italy orders came to his press

* Fumagalli 19. His native Asola in the province of Brescia lies in the great Plain of Lombardy; here Andrea Torresano was born, the successor of Nicolas Jensen at Venice, the father-in-law of Aldo Manuzio and the successor of that great printer in 1515.

in the Campo di Fiore * and he was accustomed like many of the great printers of the time notably the great Hebrew printer Gerson Soncino to wander about carrying his presses with him. Unlike Gerson however he always came back again to his headquarters at Rome.†

The incense-laden atmosphere of Rome, however, was fatal to the production of Hebrew books,‡ and after issuing five books in 1547¶ the press so auspiciously begun came to an end. The Inquisition and its censors could not tolerate a Hebrew press under the very shadow of St. Peter's** and although some books were printed in 1578 they were merely Bible texts printed by a Christian and edited by an apostate none other than the grandson of Elijah Levita.

---

* Fumagalli 343; his book mark is reproduced by Kristeller "Die Ital. Buchdr. u. Verleg. Zeichen" p. 54.

† In 1549 he printed at Rieti; Fumagalli 326; in 1562 at Foligno in the palace of Cardinal Clemente Dolera; Fumagalli 159. In 1546 he declined an invitation of the authorities of Viterbo to establish his press there; Fumagalli 522.

‡ Prayer and school books for the Roman congregation of Jews were printed at Mantua and Venice.

¶ Responsa of Nissim b. Reuben.
  Iggeret Hakodesh of Nachmanides.
  Pesak.
  Yad Shearim of Samuel Zarfati; Ersch & Gruber 62.
  Also probably Grammar of David b. Joseph Yahya of Naples but see Schwab "les incunables" 125.

** Berliner, Gesch. der Juden in Rom 2 : 136.

CHAPTER XI.

THE QUARREL OF GIUSTINIANI AND BRAGADINI AND THE CONDEMNATION OF THE TALMUD.

Marco Antonio Giustiniani—His Talmud Edition—List of His Publications—Rabbi Meir of Padua and His Edition of Maimonides—The Foundation of the House of Bragadini—Giustiniani's Rival Edition of Maimonides—The Decision of Rabbi Moses Isserles—The Quarrel is Carried to Rome—The Roman Apostates—The Far-Reaching Effect of the Quarrel—The Cardinals Condemn the Talmud to Be Destroyed—The Protest of Andrea Masio—The Burning of the Talmud in the Campo di Fiori—The Decree of the Council of Ten at Venice—The Books of Judah di Lerma and the Heirs of Bomberg—The Papal Bull of 1554—The Death of Pope Julius III.

IN the year 1545 Marco Antonio Giustiniani of the family of Venetian patricians whose palaces still grace the Grand Canal, established a Hebrew press near the Bridge of the Rialto in the Calle delli Cinque alla Giustizia Vecchia.* His printer's mark bears a representation of the temple at Jerusalem and the words of Haggai the prophet, "Great shall be the glory of this house, saith the Lord of Hosts." "Greater perhaps than the glory of the house of Bomberg" may have been the thought of Giustiniani, for his wealth position and influence made him at once a formidable rival to the now aged Bomberg. But his glory was short-

* Brown "Venet. Printing Press" p. 106. See also Seder Tefillot German rite 1545.

lived, for although his press began with splendid prospects and showed great activity, his strength was not equal to the contest with the rising Bragadini, and after a short but fierce competition the glory of the house of Giustiniani departed and his proud printer's mark was supplanted by the three crowns of his successful rival. At the outset of his career he secured the services of the force of the Dei Farri press, including the master printer Cornelio Adelkind who after serving Giustiniani for a short time, apparently to help establish his press, resumed his work exclusively at the Bomberg press until Bomberg's death, when he returned to the service of Giustiniani remaining with him until the press came to a standstill in 1552. Cornelio's son Daniel now a printer of well established reputation also served at Giustiniani's press, dedicating one of his books Das Frauenbuechlein in 1552, to his father Cornelio as a gift from a devoted son. The partners Judah b. Isaac Halevi Ashkenazi of Frankfurt and Dr. Yehiel b. Yekutiel Ha-Cohen likewise joined the Giustiniani press and contributed to the success of the fine edition of the Babylonian Talmud published 1546–1551.* Giustiniani's types were cut by Michel Du Bois† and

---

* It was edited by Joshua Boaz and corrected by Meshullam b. Shemaiah, known as Kopman, evidently a German; Rabb. "Maamar," p. 43.

† Ceste grosse lettre est de la taille de Me Michel Du Bois qu'il tailla a Venise pour le magnifique Messer Marco Anthonio Justinian, gentil homme venitian, laquelle Me. Leon juif, me voulut fayre refayre. From marginal notes of Guillaume le Bé; Omont p. 7.

Guillaume le Bé * the Frenchman and by an engraver of the Venetian mint.† It was probably this edition that was the basis of the charge made by Bragadini that Giustiniani was attempting to ruin Bomberg by his competition. The edition of the Talmud was in fact based on the Bomberg editions just as these were based on the first editions of Soncino; ‡ and it in turn became the basis for subsequent editions.¶ It has almost completely disappeared** for it was published just before the decree of Pope Julius III. against the Talmud.

Of far greater importance than the productions of the Giustiniani press was the personal rivalry between Giustiniani and Bragadini, one incident of which totally unforeseen was of far-reaching consequences for the Jews of Italy. The innocent first cause of what was really a national Jewish disaster, was the man whose influence attracted Bragadini to Hebrew printing, the respected and learned Rabbi Meir of Padua, founder of the distinguished rabbinical family of Katzenellenbogen,

---

* Texte moyen que j'ay taillé à Venise pour le magnifique Marc Anthoine Justinian gentilhomme Venitian. Omont p. 4. And as late as 1556 after Giustiniani had ceased printing Hebrew books he had a law suit with Guillaume on account of types cut for one "Maggio." Perhaps Meir Parenzo, Omont p. 5.

† Ce petit texte est de Justinian, taillé par un graveur de monnoye et cachetz à Venise Omont. p. 7.

‡ H. B. 5 : 122.

¶ H. B. 5 : 122, Rabb. "Maamar" 48.

** Chwolson 23.

Title page of Rabbi Shem Tob's Homilies
Giustiniani, Venice, 1547

so called from the rabbi's birthplace in Hesse-Nassau.*

Among the rabbi's literary labors was an edition of Maimonides' Code of the Law, "The Strong Hand"† a book that was already well known in the Jewish book markets, for it had been printed four times, first at an unknown time and place again in 1490 at Soncino the third time in 1509 by the house of Nahmias at Constantinople and finally in 1524 by Bomberg. When Rabbi Meir concluded to seek a publisher, he naturally turned to Venice which harbored the only Hebrew press in Italy. The year 1549 was a period of extraordinary inactivity. Indeed there were but three houses in the world that were printing rabbinical books, Parnas at Constantinople the sons of Gershon Cohen at Prague and Giustiniani at Venice, and excluding Giustiniani's Talmud texts there were probably not half a dozen Hebrew books published in the world. For reasons unknown to us Giustiniani did not satisfy the rabbi and he determined to establish a new press, by associating himself with some enterprising and influential Christian. Such a man he found in Alvise Bragadini under whose name a press was established which in the year 1550 published Rabbi Meir's edition of "The Strong Hand." Scarcely had the book appeared when another edition of the full text of "The Strong Hand" was thrown

* Jew. Enc. 7 : 454.
† Yad hahazakah.

into the market by Giustiniani, of course without the notes of Rabbi Meir. Then there arose between the two houses a fierce contention that ultimately resulted in the confiscation and burning of all Hebrew books. Bragadini claimed perhaps with justice that Giustiniani's edition was published at this time for the malicious purpose of wrecking the new press, in pursuance of the policy through which he had endeavored to ruin the business of Bomberg. He charged him with the attempt "to prevent me from printing the Talmud on new paper of uniform quality—and not differing like his."* No doubt Giustiniani made appropriate reply, and the situation became acute. What was to be done? Wisdom and experience would have said, "Let the issue be decided by the rules of the open market. Let the Jewish reading public choose between the edition enriched with the notes of Rabbi Meir known throughout the Jewries of Europe, and the edition of Giustiniani containing only the text and the notes of the older commentators." But Bragadini and the rabbi, fearing the immediate consequence of this competition, determined to use positive measures to subdue their rival. Whereupon Rabbi Meir wrote to his disciple and kinsman Rabbi Moses Isserles, of Cracow, then just beginning the brilliant career that made him the greatest European authority on rabbinical law.

* Perles, "Beitraege" p. 230.

Censored page of Yalkut Shimeoni
Bragadini, Venice, 1566

We shall now be compelled to give some attention to a judicial opinion written by a sixteenth century rabbi and fortified by a goodly show of knowledge of Jewish law. Judicial opinions at best are dull reading except for lawyers, and even the giant intellect and literary style of a Mansfield or a Marshall can not successfully woo the wandering attention of the untrained reader. To expect patience with the technical lucubrations of Rabbi Moses Isserles of Cracow is probably asking too much. According to the opinion of Rabbi Moses* the matter presented the following difficulty: A Jew and non-Jew in partnership printed a book; a Christian rival printed another edition of the same book at the same time for the purpose of ruining the first printers. Although the dispute arose between two Christian printing houses the real sufferer was the Jew whose entire fortune was invested in this enterprise. He could obtain no redress against the Christian in the Venetian Courts, and the Jewish Courts could not assume jurisdiction. Here apparently was a wrong without a remedy. If the parties were both Jews the procedure would have been clear; for Jewish law does not permit this kind of business rivalry and malicious interference, and its mandate would have issued to restrain the second printer from printing his book, or if already printed from selling it until the edition of the first printer was exhausted. In this case the only remedy that could be applied by

* Responsa No. 10.

the rabbinical court of Rabbi Moses Isserles was the indirect one of enjoining all Jews under pain of excommunication (Herem), from purchasing the books of Giustiniani. Rabbi Moses seems to have given no thought to the danger of arousing the animosity and inviting the retaliation of the proud and powerful Giustiniani, but he did dwell on a possible danger to the spread of Jewish literature, by Giustiniani's withdrawal from the field. However he comforted himself with the reflection that after all the question was merely one of business, and that as the printers made and sold books just as others made and sold other merchandise, for their own profit, the defeated party would seek to make up in another enterprise what he might lose in this, and would continue to print Hebrew books as theretofore. Strongly convinced of the justice of Rabbi Meir's cause Rabbi Moses had regard only to the law, and gave no thought whatever to the real danger, the possibility of arousing the interest of the ever watchful ecclesiastical authorities and again directing their attention to Hebrew books, a danger that the experience of many generations should have made an ever present factor in the consideration of every question, and that might have suggested itself to an older and more experienced man.

The opinion of Rabbi Moses written August 16 1550 was the fire brand that started the conflagration that destroyed thousands of Hebrew books. Although it is quite possible that the papal decrees might have been issued even if the Venetian printers had not quarrelled, we must take our facts as we find them, and come to the conclusion that the ill-considered act of Rabbi Meir of Padua, in appealing to Rabbi Moses of Cracow to establish his monopoly in the sale of "The Strong Hand" of Maimonides was in great measure responsible for this far-reaching result. In those days as in all times the leaders of the Jewish communities were under sacred obligation to take heed of the ancient dictum, "Wise men be ye cautious with your words." The times were perilous. The devoted little groups of Jews scattered among the followers of a hostile faith, cowering in their Ghettos always scanning the political and ecclesiastical horizon for signs of storm, had need of wise leadership and a cautious crafty policy. Their very lives depended on the word, their property on the mood, of some potentate. The Pope's favor, like that of all princes, was never to be relied on. Ecclesiastical politics played with the sentiments of justice and mercy as the needs of the game of statecraft required. What one pope gave another might take away, and there was no assurance to the Jews that even the same pope would always be of the same mind. Their rights were guaranteed to them by long parchments with papal and royal seals, but where was the court of justice in which these rights could be enforced? Nothing but a sense of justice or considerations of policy could insure respect by the pope for privileges dearly purchased from some predecessor in the chair of St. Peter.

It seems strange that an Italian rabbi familiar with this system of statecraft, should have failed to foresee the result of antagonizing a Venetian patrician; or perhaps Rabbi Meir believed himself and the Jews protected by his Christian partner Bragadini from the suspicion of hurting the Christian. Perhaps he was lulled into a false sense of security by the disposition of the reigning pontiff Julius III, who began his career with strong marks of favor to the Jews and who seemed to promise a return of the good days of Leo X Clement VII and Paul III. Perhaps he was thinking only of his whole fortune invested in an enterprise threatened with ruin.

The publication of this opinion was a serious blow to the business of Giustiniani but his revenge was quick and sure. If Bragadini could obtain a rabbinical opinion against his books, why should he not obtain a papal opinion condemning those of his rival? As he himself had published "The Strong Hand" he could only hope to attack his rival through Rabbi Meir's notes which might be found to contain matter objectionable to godly churchmen. For this pious work of denunciation apostate Jews were always at hand, glad of an opportunity to use their knowledge of Hebrew to show their newly-born Christian zeal. What Giustiniani could do Bragadini could also do, and soon the cause of the Hebrew books was being represented at Rome by two sets of bribed apostates, working with fierce denunciation, heaping lie upon lie, calumny upon calumny, for the greater glory of God and the fees of their Venetian patrons. Joseph Ha-Cohen in his chronicle appropriately called the "Vale of Tears," has made known to us the names of the three Roman apostates * "of these slanderers who are among those who troubled us, Hananel di Foligno† Joseph Moro and Solomon Romano.‡ Oh, Lord, may their names be blotted out, and on the day of wrath deal Thou with them."

The case dragged through the official channels of the pontifical courts without reaching any decision. In the meantime Giustiniani's business fell off to such an extent that in 1552 his presses, which had been in operation since 1545, stopped entirely. Although one of the parties to the cause had thus practically withdrawn, the matter was far from being at an end and what had been merely a business quarrel between Venetian printers had, by the holy zeal of the apostates at Rome, developed into a general attack on the Talmud and the rabbinical writings. "The calumniator speaks in Rome and kills in Syria." The slanderers worked at Rome, and lo in a short time Hebrew books were consumed in the flames of a hundred fires in

* Emek Habacha. ed. Letteris p. 111.

† Supposed to be Rafaele Aquilino, author of several anti-Jewish books. Jew. Enc. 2 : 38.

‡ This Solomon Romano is said to be the same as Vittorio Eliano the grandson of Elijah Levita (Vogelstein & Rieger 2: 146) or, what seems to be the better opinion, his brother Giovannni Battista (Jew. Enc. 2 : 500; Berliner 2 : 107).

all the market places of Italy.   Both of the original parties to the quarrel went under in the fight, Giustiniani in 1552 * and Bragadini in 1554. When in that year the long expected blow fell, a general decree of confiscation of Hebrew books was enforced throughout the greater part of Italy and the Hebrew press at Venice was silenced for a period of nine years.†

None of the parties interested in the original dispute between the rival houses of Giustiniani and Bragadini had any intimation of its far-reaching effect.   The apostate calumniators of the Hebrew books had a free field at Rome, and the strong support of the Dominican monks, who were then as ever during the century-long battle for the emancipation of thought the strongest foes of all theological opinion other than their own.   They levelled against the Talmud the old old charges that had been made and refuted time and again. The Vatican archives contained many Bulls and Edicts that ought to have settled the question without further investigation, for Rome above all places should have respected the maxim "Stand by the decisions."   But the darkened intellect of the Dominicans was unable to see in the Talmud and its commentaries anything but literature inimical to their Christianity, and in response to their persistent agitation for its suppression a new

* In 1574 another Giustiniani, Antonio, was tried for press offenses by the Inquisition.   Brown "Ven. Print. Press" App. VII.

† All Venetian Hebrew presses stopped 1555–1563; Steinschneider Cat. Bodl. No. 174.

committee of Cardinals was appointed to conduct an examination of the evidence submitted by the Jewish apostates. The situation was practically controlled by the chairman of the committee the fierce reactionary Cardinal Caraffa, who was soon to ascend the throne as Pope Paul IV. In accord with his vigorous policy and his passion for inquisition, the committee reported in favor of the destruction of the Talmud, thus, in the bitter words of Andrea Masio the well-known Christian Hebraist, rendering "an opinion on the value of colors after their eyes had been blinded by perfidious calumny."

An independent judgment on the merits of the case was impossible to these Cardinals, for they were ignorant of the books they had condemned. There were some members of the Sacred College, notably Cardinals Pighinus and Marcellus (the latter subsequently pope) who voted against the decree of confiscation of the Talmud, but the great majority of them "gave too much credence to the baptized Jews." Let us hear the voice of the Christian scholar Masio.* In a letter to his friend Cardinal Pighinus he speaks his mind fully and without equivocation, and before the bar of his judgment the College of Cardinals stands convicted of ignorance and folly. "At the complaint of two men filled with zeal and greed (the printers Giustiniani and Bragadini) and acting upon the information of two Jewish Christians, if indeed

* Perles "Beitraege" p. 223. Vogelstein & Rieger 2 : 147.

PAVLVS · IV · PAPA · NEAPOLITANVS ·

they are worthy of the name, hired by these rival book sellers, you (the College of Cardinals) have to the eternal shame of the Apostolic See and to the detriment of Christianity rendered a hasty judgment. You are absolutely blind in this matter, for not one of you has ever read even a single word of these commentaries that you have condemned. I therefore deem it my duty toward you and toward the entire College of Cardinals to say that you ought not to give credence to the statements of baptized Jews concerning the affairs of the Jews, for there are no more jealous men nor any more intent upon unworthy gain than these. I dare take an oath that the two men, the apostates whom you have as I am told made judges over God knows what books, have accepted bribes not only from the one side but from both in payment of their false testimony." Words echoed by Cardinal Ganganelli in 1759, "Among such Jewish neophites there exists as a rule a certain vehemence against their own people which frequently leads them beyond the boundaries of truth."* But the protest of Masio was too late.

On August 12, 1553, the pope issued a Bull† directing the confiscation and burning of both

.* Berliner "Gutachten" p. 21.

† This Bull is no longer in existence. It is cited in another issued 29 May, 1554 "Cum sicut nuper accepimus licet alias fratres nostri haereticae pravitatis in universa republica christiana inquisitores generales certum Hebraicorum librorum volumen Ghemarot Thalmud nuncupatum, orthodoxae fidei offendentia continens de mandato nostro damnaverint et igne comburi fecerint nihilominus inter eos Hebraeos adhuc esse dicuntur diversi libri, etc." Graetz 9 : 346.

the Palestinian and the Babylonian Talmuds. All Jews were ordered on pain of confiscation of all their property to deliver up their copies of these books, and all Christians were forbidden to read them possess them or assist Jews in writing or printing them. Cardinal Caraffa stood behind this decree and hastened its execution. In all the streets inhabited by the Jews appeared the familiars of the Holy Office, the dread minions of the Inquisition. Along the Tiber in what was soon to become the Ghetto up toward the Campo di Fiori, through the Rione Campitelli lying at the foot of the Palatine hill, across the Tiber among the crooked streets and lanes of Trastevere, the black robed Inquisitors led their eager police amidst cries of horror and protest. Houses were searched property destroyed all privacy abused in the search for the hiding places for Talmudic works; and although many copies escaped the eyes of the Inquisitors, the plunder was very great.* On September 9, 1553, (Rosh Hashanah) all these printed books and manuscripts were carted to the Campo di Fiori and, on the very spot where forty-seven years later Giordano Bruno was to suffer at the stake for his heresy, they were burned "amidst the cries and applause of the populace" while the Jews of Rome in their synagogues on this New Year's Day wept "for the burning which the enemies of the Lord had caused."†

* Popper p. 31.

† Berliner "Censur" p. 3; Reusch "Index" 1 : 47. See also Zemah David, ad an. 1554; Shalshelet Hakkabalah, end.

Now that the work had been so well done in Rome, Cardinal Caraffa and his committee turned their attention to other cities. The decree spread like wildfire through Italy, and within a month the blaze of burning books ascended from the public squares of Bologna Ravenna Mantua, Ferrara and the entire Romagna. In Venice which had sown the seeds from which this universal disaster sprung the fruit was most bitter. Here the execution of the decree was left to the Executors against Blasphemy (essecutori contra la Biastema). On October 21 the Council of Ten, that "evasive dark inscrutable body" that controlled the destinies of Venice, published a decree that in the opinion of Masio exceeded even the harshness of the original papal edict. It ordered the confiscation and burning within ten days of all copies of the Talmud, as well as "all compendiums summaries or other books depending on said Talmud;" and the severest penalties were threatened for any disobedience to this order or evasion of its strict execution. Then arose the question what books could be considered compendiums summaries and books depending on the Talmud.* Another apostate, Eleazar ben Raphael maintained that these several heads practically included the entire Jewish literature, and that the decree could be properly executed only by destroying all Hebrew books in existence, and "they stretched forth their hands to the very Scrolls of the Law in

* Popper p. 34, 35.

the Ark, but the leaders of the congregation arose and stood in the breach and saved them from their hands." The zeal of the apostate carried him too far. The pleadings of the Jewish congregation raised doubts in the minds of the "Executors against Blasphemy" as to the correctness of the apostate's opinion. The men who sat in judgment in this case were Venetian patricians whose self-respect compelled them to assume an attitude of fairness, and the arguments and reasons urged against Eleazar's opinion finally bore fruit. The "Executors against Blasphemy" in order to secure additional expert information appointed a committee of three, who defined the terms "compendiums summaries and books depending on the Talmud," in a manner that betrayed no desire to extend the terms beyond their proper meaning, whereupon the decree was promptly carried into execution.*

Among the sufferers in Venice was Rabbi Judah di Lerma who in the second edition of his "Bread of Judah" (Lehem Yehudah) says: "I printed my book in Venice and in the beginning of the year 5314 (1553) the powers at Rome decreed that throughout Christendom the Talmud and its commentaries should be burned. In the month of Marheshvan (October) they decreed at Venice that on a Sabbath day the Talmud together with its commentaries the codes of Alfasi and the books of the Mishnah should be burned together.

* Popper p. 35.

Among these they burned the entire edition that I had printed fifteen hundred books, and thus I lost all that I had in Venice and there remained unto me not even a single leaf as a memorial. I proceeded to rewrite the book from memory, but after I had written three chapters I found one copy of the edition in the hands of some Christians who had plucked it from the fire, and I bought it from them for much money." *

Andrea Masio also suffered from this confiscation. While living in Rome he had purchased from Daniel Bomberg at Venice a set of his edition of the Talmud, which he had left in Bomberg's possession until he should return to Germany. In the meantime Bomberg died, and the books which had come into the hands of his agent and executor Johannes Remalinus were seized and ordered to be burned together with the books taken from the Jews. Through the intercession of influential friends and upon the just plea that it was against all morals and law to destroy them since Bomberg had printed these books with the express sanction of the Pope the Emperor and the Signoria, Remalinus succeeded in gaining a respite, and the books were ordered into custody until a final decision could be rendered at Rome. When the news of this seizure reached Masio in his retreat at Kloster Weingarten, he wrote appealing letters to his friends Cardinal Pighinus at Rome the Venetian Ambassador at the Imperial Court

* Emek Habacha ed. Wiener p. 208.

and the Elector Palatine Frederick II * but all in vain; his books seem to have met the common fate. In a subsequent letter to a prelate at Rome he says that the mere loss of money although great was of much less importance to him, than the shame of "this most godless sacrilege that was performed by the leading men of our faith to our eternal disgrace in the eyes of posterity." As to the Signoria of Venice this body of practical gentlemen from whose commercial instinct and cosmopolitanism better things might have been expected, Masio says in another letter, "Your wise Senate who ought rather to have laughed at that stupid contemptible decree than to have countenanced it, did immediately after the receipt of this papal decree exceed even this Roman impiety, for that is the proper name for it."

In spite of great influence brought to bear by scholars and liberal men the decree could not be averted. The Jews themselves made herculean efforts to save their books; the leaders of their community at Rome appeared before the pope and despite the opposition of Caraffa himself and his apostate advisers defended their books so well that on May 29 1554 the pope probably induced by Cardinal Sacristo who as a Hebrew scholar was opposed to the destruction of the Hebrew books, issued a Bull which was intended to modify the severity of his earlier edict.† This Bull directed

* Perles "Beitraege" 223.
† Popper p. 38.

that within four months all Hebrew books should be delivered up for examination to ascertain which of them contained attacks on Christianity. The Jewish communities felt the danger that lurked in this new decree, for it was now possible for the enemies of the Jews to argue that the pope intended to condemn not merely the Talmud and its commentaries, but all Hebrew books in which anti-Christian sentiments might be found, for every Hebrew book expresses or implies the unity of God, and is anti-Christian because anti-Trinitarian. Their feeling towards Pope Julius III who had begun his pontificate with sentiments that led the Jewish communities to compare him with his milder predecessors, is reflected in this outburst of Joseph Ha-Cohen, "Break out in joy, oh ye mountains, for Pope Julius di Monte who wished to lead us to apostasy and who ordered our glorious books to be burned died on the 21st day of March in the year 5315 (1555). Oh God Lord of the spirit of all flesh, may his worm never die and his fire never be quenched and may he be an abhorrence unto all mankind." This violent outburst of hatred was the legitimate reflex of such Christian love as was extended to the people of Israel.

No attempt can now be made to tell the whole story of the confiscation of Hebrew books in Italy. In every city similar scenes were enacted with variations depending upon the temper the good nature or the cupidity of local administrators and ecclesiastical officials. While priests in their official robes marched in procession, holding up to the people boxes of dry bones as things worthy of their worship, the fires kindled by their followers were consuming the precious distillation of two thousand years of living imperishable intellect.*

BOOKS PRINTED AT PRESS OF MARC ANTONIO GIUSTINIANI.†

1545   Piske Recanati
Zebah Pesah
Seder Olam
Nahmanides, Comm. on Pentateuch
Iggerot Rambam
Abodat Halevi
Responsa of Solomon b. Adret
Halakhot Gedolot
Seder Tefillot (German rite)
    "   "   (Roman rite)

1546   Terumat Hadeshen
Shulhan Arba
En Yaakob
Zeror Hamor
Otiot di Rabbi Akiba
Midrash Rabba
Agur

---

* Dr. Berliner states that at his first visit to Rome in 1873 he did not find a single copy of a Talmudic treatise of early editions among the people. But splendid specimens were preserved in the Vatican and Casanate libraries. "Censur" p. 8 note.

† See Ersch & Gruber 44; Z. H. B. 9 : 152, 61; Jew. Enc. 1 : 190; Rabb. "Maamar" 41–42.

1546 Talmud Babli Berakhot
      Mishnah Zeraim
         "   Taharot
         "   Abot
         "   Kodashim
1547 Derashot of Shem Tob
      Kolbo
      Tefillot (Roman rite)
      Abudarham
      Pentateuch & commentaries
      Talmud Babli Eduyot
      Mishnah Moed
         "   Nezikin
         "   Nashim
      Talmud Babli Bezah
1548   "   "   Rosh Hashana
         "   "   Taanit
         "   "   Ketubot
         "   "   Baba Kamma
         "   "   Baba Mezia
         "   "   Baba Batra

      Ohel Moed
1549 . Talmud Babli Hagigah
         "   "   Moed Katon
         "   "   Sukkah
         "   "   Megillah
         "   "   Yebamot
         "   "   Sanhedrin
         "   "   Shebuot
1550   "   "   Shabbat
         "   "   Erubin

1550   Talmud Babli Pessahim
          "   "   Yoma
          "   "   Shekalim
          "   "   Kiddushin
          "   "   Gittin
          "   "   Sotah
          "   "   Makkot
          "   "   Aboda Zara
          "   "   Hullin
          "   "   Bekhorot
          "   "   Erakhin
          "   "   Keritut
          "   "   Temurah
          "   "   Meila
          "   "   Kinnin
          "   "   Tamid
          "   "   Middot
          "   "   Semahot, Kalla, Sofer-
                          im Derekh Erez
                          Rabba ve Zutta
                          Abot d'Rabbi Na-
                          than
        Millat Hahigayon
        Yad Hahazakah
1551   Talmud Babli Nedarim
          "   "   Nazir
          "   "   Horayot
          "   "   Zebahim
          "   "   Menahot
          "   "   Niddah
        Orah Hayyim

1551   Pentateuch with Latin translation
        Bedikot of Jacob Weil
        Degel Ahabah
1552   Bible 4to.
        Bible 16mo.
        Later Prophets
        Megillat Sefer
        Lakol Hefez
        Frauenbuechlein

CHAPTER XII.

FERRARA, SABBIONETA AND RIVA DI TRENTO.

The Jews of Ferrara—The Abrabanelli—Samuel ibn Askarah—The Family of the Usque—Abraham Usque and the " Ferrara Bible"—Samuel Usque the Poet—The Jewish Congress at Ferrara, and Its Decree Concerning the Hebrew Press—Tobia Foa of Sabbioneta—The Personnel of His Press—An Attempt to Reprint the Talmud—The Fame of the Sabbioneta Press—Rabbi Joseph Ottolenghi, Dr. Jacob Marcaria and Cardinal Madrucci at Riva di Trento— Renaissance and Reaction—The Cardinal's Patronage of the Hebrew Press—His Reputed Heresy.

WHILE events were leading to Pope Julius III's decree there was a sudden outburst of activity in Hebrew typography in Northern Italy, and when the presses of Venice came to a standstill, the presses of Mantua Ferrara Sabbioneta Cremona and Riva di Trento nullified the decrees of Pope and Signoria.

Seventy-five years had passed since Abraham the Dyer had printed at Ferrara in the days of Ercole I. Now another Ercole was reigning, who preserved the traditional policy of heeding the interests of his State more than the wishes of the Pope. A record of a hundred years of commercial expansion and artistic development had made Ferrara famous, and its liberal policy had attracted wandering Jews from Spain and Portugal as well as from less hospitable Italian States.* Strong

---

* Ducal decree of 23 December 1555 permitting settlement of Spanish and Portuguese Jews in Ferrara printed by Sacchi p. 65.

rich and comparatively free from oppression, the Jews of Ferrara were at this time probably the leading Jewish community in Italy. When in 1543 Rabbi Isaac Gunzburg conceived the plan of reprinting the Talmud it was in Ferrara that he attempted it, and when in 1554 a Rabbinical Congress was held to take counsel and action upon the state of the Jews of Italy it met in Ferrara. The community was headed by many noble old families of Italy, among them the sons and grandsons of the noblest of them all Don Isaac Abrabanel that scholarly sad-faced wanderer who passes in tragic stateliness across the tear-stained pages of the history of the time. From Portugal to Spain across the sea to Naples again grasping the wanderer's staff upon the fall of that city he traverses Italy and settles at Venice, and is finally called to his eternal rest in the city of Padua. The Jewish cemetery without the walls containing his grave has now disappeared, trampled into the common dust in the many wars that were fought around Padua.*

In the year 1551 Samuel ibn Askarah Zarfati (the Frenchman), perhaps the same Samuel who

---

* Of all the ancient houses of the Jews of Italy, that of the Abrabanelli boasted most ancient descent, even from the house of King David. "His children", says Mr. Howells, speaking of Don Isaac, in his entertaining "Italian Journeys," "still abide in Ferrara; and it may have been one of his kingly line that kept the tempting antiquarian shop on the corner from which you turn up toward the library. I should think such a man would find a sort of melancholy solace in such a place; filled with broken and fragmentary glories of every kind, it would serve him for that chamber of desolation set apart in the houses

assisted at the second press at Rome in 1546, began to print Hebrew books at Ferrara. Perhaps Abraham Zarfati then professor at the University of Ferrara was a kinsman of this Samuel, and this holding of a professorship by a Jew may be another indication of the tolerance that made possible the establishment of a Hebrew press. Samuel printed six books among them a work on medicine another on the interpretation of dreams two on the laws of kosher slaughtering and two philosophical works, one of which entitled "Fountains of Salvation" by Don Isaac Abrabanel was the first book of this press, printed January 22 1551. The taste of Jewish readers was then as ever a broad one. Medical science was not always freed from transcendentalism and dream books furnished contributions to therapeutics. Kosher food and philosophy were not deemed incompatible, and the good people of those days lived their lives without much regard for the opinion of their Christian neighbors, upon whom they looked with some justice as a race of oppressors among whom there occasionally appeared a generous king or duke, who lightened a little the yoke of the ever-enslaved Jew.

At that time there were in Ferrara three men

of Oriental Hebrews as a place to bewail themselves in; and, indeed, this idea may go far to explain the universal Israelitish fondness for dealing in relics and ruins." Mr. Howells, always charming and picturesque, need not be taken too seriously in his reflections upon the house of Abrabanel, in his excursus into Jewish psychology, and in his suggestion of that wretched, absurd, yet all too commonly believed "old clothes theory" of Jewish history.

bearing the name of Usque,* distinguished in three fields,—Abraham ibn Usque as printer, Samuel ibn Usque as chronicler and moralist, and Solomon ibn Usque as poet. It is with Abraham that we have specially to do, for he succeeded Samuel the Frenchman and carried on the press of Ferrara until the year 1558. Indeed it is not unlikely that he was the founder of the press that was carried on for a year or two in the name of Samuel ibn Askarah just as the press of Bomberg was for a time carried on by Cornelio Adelkind. Whether this be so or not, Abraham ibn Usque took over the types and Samuel Zarfati acted as his editor after 1552.

Some time before 1550 Duarte Pinel a Catholic gentleman, found that his residence in Portugal was no longer possible, for he was suspected by some of his neighbors of being a Jew. The lives of suspected persons were never safe and no mere profession of faith nor even observance of all the ceremonies of the Catholic Church could save them from the hands of the priests and monks of the Inquisition. Duarte Pinel probably had a guilty conscience, and while taking communion as a good Catholic was made aware of watchful eyes under hood and cowl noting his manner and his actions. He finally concluded that life under the sword of Damocles was not worth living, and leaving his native place he sailed for Italy, where in the city of Ferrara he assumed his Jewish name of Abraham, openly attended the synagogue of his

* Taken from the town of Huesca, in Spain, whence the family originally came.

Title page of "Honor of God"
Usque, Ferrara, 1556

fathers and devoted himself to the spread of the literature of his ancient people which had long been proscribed in the land of his nativity.

The motto that is entwined around his printer's mark taken from the 130th Psalm might well express his thought when he was abiding in Portugal, waiting for the happy day when he might publicly avow the faith of his fathers: "I wait for the Lord; my soul doth wait, and in His word do I hope." His press produced many valuable books, especially works of philosophy and theology. He seems to have cared little for the sterner rabbinical and liturgical literature, or perhaps the times were happily so changed that his patrons could devote themselves to Jewish philosophy and belles lettres, instead of confining themselves as in more hopeless days to the liturgy of the synagogue and the special synagogal poetry of lamentation. His fine books are today much sought for and the title pages that decorate many of them testify to the artistic atmosphere in which they were produced. He preserved the memory of the seafaring prowess of his native Portugal in his printer's mark, where a globe encircled by the ecliptic and zodiacal marks is supported by an anchor. His initials A. U. defiantly seem to proclaim his release from the tyranny of the personality of the Duarte Pinel, whom he had shaken off. Once only does he use his old name, in the Spanish translation of the Pentateuch published in 1553 and dedicated to the Duke of Ferrara.

The influence of the double life led by the Marranos, may be seen in a striking peculiarity of this edition of the Pentateuch. It is known as the Ferrara Bible and was published in one edition but in two differing forms, with different title pages and epigraphs and some variations in the text, the one apparently intended for Jewish and the other for Christian readers. The volumes intended for Christians were dedicated to the Duke of Ferrara, printed by Duarte Pinel the Portuguese, and published by Geronimo de Vargas the Spaniard; those intended for Jews were dedicated to the illustrious Donna Gracia Mendesia Nasi and the printer becomes Abraham Usque the Portuguese, the publisher, Yomtob the son of Levi Athias the Spaniard.* This Donna Gracia is the famous kinswoman of Don Joseph Nasi, Duke of Naxos, and a member of that illustrious family whose picturesque career may be followed in Portugal Italy and the Orient. It was the eternal wandering of the landless nation pursued by the fury of an ever-watchful Church, that made the lives of the Jews so rich in experience so replete with incident so affecting in its pathos and sorrow.

Abraham's kinsman Samuel ibn Usque, expressed their sorrow in a book entitled "Consolation for the Tribulations of Israel"† which was printed at the press of Abraham in the same year as

---

* Kayserling "Sephardim" 138; Graetz 9 : 333.
† Consolaçam, as tribulaçoens de Ysrael.

the Ferrara Bible.* This chronicle and martyrology
was written in Spanish and takes its place beside
the "Rod of Judah" of Solomon ibn Verga, and
the "Vale of Tears" of Joseph Hacohen. It was
dedicated to that noble Donna Gracia, whose life
epitomized the woes of the exiles. She had given up
wealth and noble station in Portugal in order to
seek the liberty to be herself. Her wanderings
from Portugal to the Netherlands thence to Venice
and finally to Constantinople, always helping and
protecting her weaker co-religionists, inspired the
learned Solomon Usque. In considering her misfortunes and those of her people, the author found
some consolation in the fact that the worst was
over. "Memory," he says, "of past misfortunes
eases the burden of present ones for oppressed
souls, especially if the past misfortunes were more
painful than those which must now be borne;
and although one misfortune is a poor cure for
another, nevertheless those excellent men who
through their great wisdom have left us remedies
for the trials of the soul, have recommended such
remedies. . . . Therefore Socrates was accustomed to say that he 'who finds himself oppressed
should compare the misfortunes that have passed
with the present ones.'" And so the author introduces the Patriarch Jacob and the prophets
Nahum and Zachariah under the names of Icabo
Numeo and Zicareo, Jacob speaking for the en-

* J. Steinschneider "Zur Geschichte judischer Martyrologien"
in Festschrift zum X Stiftungsfest d. Akad. Ver. f. jud. Gesch. u. Lit.

tire people of Israel, the others offering him consolation.

When this book left the press of Abraham Usque on September 27 1553 the decree of confiscation of Hebrew books had already gone forth and the Talmud had already been burned in Rome. From all over Italy went up prayers and cries, and many were the fast days when the people prostrated themselves in their houses of prayer and called upon God to help them in their affliction. Even in Ferrara notwithstanding the liberality of its Duke the outburst of fanaticism following the ecclesiastical agitation bore fruit but the press of Abraham Usque was not interfered with and he continued apparently undisturbed until 1558 to print many Hebrew books.

On June 21 1554 the leaders of the Jewish communities of Italy roused by the dangers of the decree of confiscation met in congress at Ferrara. Under the presidency of Rabbi Meir Katzenellenbogen of Padua, delegates from Rome Mantua Ferrara the Romagna Bologna Reggio Modena Padua and Venice met in the city of Ercole to take counsel concerning the welfare of the Jews of Italy. Among the many important matters discussed and agreed upon was the question of the publication of Hebrew books. It was the consensus of opinion that while as a rule the vindictiveness of the persecutor could not be shaken by argument or proof, it was necessary to avoid every possible appearance of offense to the dominant religion, so that at least milder Christians would be won over to the Jewish side by proof that no harm was intended to their faith. A great danger existed in the action of irresponsible Jews who in the happy freedom of authorship said and printed things for which the entire community was called to account. All Jews were indeed then as now sureties for one another's good conduct; all had to suffer the consequences of the acts of each, and it was felt that some central authority should protect the community against its members. The congress at Ferrara therefore decreed * "Printers shall not print any book not before printed without the license and approbation of three Rabbis ordained by three Rabbis, nor without the approbation of the heads of the congregation near to the place of publication, if the press be in a small town. If it be in a larger city then the approbation of the heads of the congregation of this city together with the said three ordained Rabbis shall suffice. The names of the Rabbis and heads of the congregations shall be stated in the preface of the book and without this no Jew shall buy such book under penalty of 25 scudi; the said 25 scudi gold to go to the charity fund of the domicile of the misdemeanant."

The danger of attracting the attention of the Church was not exaggerated. Even the Bible was not safe from destruction at the hands of the min-

* Tekanot Hakhamim ed. Isaac Baru'h Ha Levi of Ferrara Brody 1879.

ions of the Inquisition. Of the edition of the Pentateuch of 1555 printed by Abraham Usque only a few copies survive. One might have supposed that the book upon which the gospels of Christ were founded would have been respected by his worshippers, but ancient Inquisitors like modern "higher anti-Semites" destroyed the Old Testament while professing to uphold the New. The Inquisition knew everything, read everything stretched forth its hand to the confines of Christendom. When in 1556 Abraham Usque published a poem by Jacob ben Elia di Fano, containing satirical verses against women, it was soon brought to the attention of Cardinal Michele Ghislieri, who in a letter to the Duke of Ferrara ordered the punishment of the author and the printer and the burning of all copies of the book by the Vicar of the Archbishop of Ferrara.* Fortunately for Abraham Usque he had by that time given up his press, and we cannot tell whether the order of the Vatican was obeyed. The temper of the duke would probably have saved the printer from too great punishment, for in those days the house of Este took orders from no one and more than once defied the Pope himself.

Duke Ercole's fame as an independent sovereign went far and wide and when about ten years before these events (1543) Rabbi Isaac Gunzburg, of the distinguished Suabian family of that name, conceived the plan of publishing a Talmud, he

* J. Q. R. 10: 447.

determined to send his printers down to Ferrara where the liberality of the duke promised success to his undertaking.* Following the general practice of having a Jew and a Christian working together at the press, Rabbi Isaac brought together the printers Paulus Emilius of Augsburg and Hayyim Schwarz of Prague. But after losing eight months' time and seventy gulden in money, Paulus withdrew from the undertaking, for the time was not yet ripe for a new edition of the Talmud in Italy. The forces of fanaticism and reaction were now dominant and even liberal Ferrara had to bow to the power of a militant Church.

"The Hebrew Press at Sabbioneta," says De Rossi,† "an illustrious press established and flourishing under the patronage of Vespasian Gonzaga, added to his glory and gave unequivocal proof of the favor he accorded to the sciences and the arts." The town of Sabbioneta is, if the Jewish Encyclopedia is accurate, undistinguished in Jewish history except for a Hebrew press that flourished there between the years 1551 and 1559. The map of Italy published in the Jewish Encyclopedia and supposed to contain the names of all the cities of Italy that had Jewish communities does not show the name of Sabbioneta, and the guide books are silent as to this little town. However, it has

* Perles "Beitraege" 172.
† Annali Ebreo-Tipografici Di Sabb. sotto Vespasiano Gonzaga. Parma 1780 p. 3.

Title page of the Book of the Grievous Vision
"The Partners," Sabbioneta, 1552

always had a more or less prosperous community of Jews, most distinguished among whom is the family of Foa, whose latest distinguished representative is the great Italian pathologist, Pio Foa. In the same year in which Abraham Usque established his press at Ferrara "on the new-moon of Sivan 5311 (May 6, 1551) the Lord stirred up the spirit of one of the leaders among the people of the God of Abraham, . . . Rabbi Tobia Foa, Tobia was his name and good (tobim) his deeds, for he established the press at Sabbioneta,"* associated with Joseph ben Jacob Ashkenazi of Padua and others; and as at the press of Ferrara the first production was a book written by the distinguished Don Isaac Abrabanel. This book Merkebet Hamishneh bore in itself the seeds of the dissolution of the press, for Abrabanel partly as a result of his philosophical and theological views and partly as a result of his own persecution and suffering at the hands of Christians, had conceived profound contempt for the dogmas as well as the practices of Christianity. And here and there in his books may be found broad passages expressing his impatience with the theological absurdities and his hatred of the political pretensions of the dominant church.

It must be remembered that the controversy raised by the contending claims of Giustiniani and Bragadini was then raging at Venice and Rome, and while the apostate hirelings of the quarreling

* "Chronicles" of Joseph Ha Cohen ad an. 1551.

printers were doing their best to secure the condemnation of all Hebrew books by Papal decree, the publication of any book reflecting even remotely upon the doctrines and dogmas of Christianity was fraught with unusual danger. Although the presses at Sabbioneta published many books never before published in which certain aspects of Christianity were treated with considerable freedom, the decree of Pope Paul III. in 1553 passed over this city without apparent effect. It is certainly a tribute to the liberality and culture of the ruling prince that the press flourished for a decade and then yielded only to irresistible pressure from Rome.

No Hebrew press of the century was more fortunate in the number and quality of its workmen. The burden of the typographical work was borne by Cornelio Adelkind who was recognized as the most distinguished Hebrew printer in the world; Jacob of Gazolo whose work contributed much to the renown of the press at Mantua; Vicenzo Conti of Verona who subsequently established a notable press in the city of Cremona;* and Israel Zifroni one of those travelling workmen who not only worked at Mantua and Venice, but appears likewise as a printer at the press in Switzerland; the Rabbi of Ferrara Raphael ben Yohanan Treves acted as editor and proof-reader. Most of

* Forty books were produced at the press of Conti with the assistance of many good craftsmen driven from their homes in other Italian cities, among them Hiyyah Meir b. David of Venice, Hayyim b. Samuel Gatinio and Abraham b. Kalonymos Pescarol.

the books that appeared at this press are published as the work of "the partners" and it is not unlikely that these were Foa, Adelkind, Joseph Ashkenazi of Padua and perhaps one or two patrons who assisted in furnishing the funds to carry on the work. Their printers' mark consisted of a peacock standing on a rock, a not unworthy emblem of their just pride in the excellence of their work. One of the earliest books published at this press was the "Guide of the Perplexed" by Maimonides, the finest and most perfect edition of this notable book, with three commentaries. Cornelio Adelkind was the printer and probably this was the very edition which he had unsuccessfully attempted to induce his former patron Daniel Bomberg to print at Venice.

It was to Sabbioneta that Judah di Lerma came in 1554 to print his "Bread of Judah" the first edition of which had been confiscated and burned at Venice, and it was here that the famous Chronicle of Joseph Ha-Cohen "The Chronicles of the Kings of France and of Turkey" was first published about the year 1553.

In the same year the proprietors of this press attempted the hazardous work of republishing the Talmud, and one Treatise saw the light; but the papal decree of that year made the further publication of the Talmud in Italy an impossibility. The end of this press came in the year 1559 due as De Rossi intimates * to anti-Christian state-

* Ann. Sabb. p. 7.

ments in some of their publications, which finally brought down upon them the wrath of the church. A hint is given in a letter of one Marani, addressed to the reigning prince Vespasian Gonzaga and dated October 16 1574.* "I also wrote to you that Signor Ercole, (meaning the Duke of Ferrara), in his letter of the 24th ultimo from Rome charged me to inspect with diligence and secrecy the houses of the Jews of his dominion, to see whether they

Printer's mark of " the partners " at Sabbioneta

had prohibited books or presses, and to make a proper report sending it to Signor Alfonso his brother, because the report had to go subsequently into the hands of the cardinals and also of his Holiness. I do not know of the origin or final cause of this order, and therefore am proceeding

* This letter was in the possession of padre Ireneo Affo by whom it was shown to De Rossi, as stated by him in his Ann. Sabb. p. 6 and 7, where a portion of the letter is reproduced.

cautiously." * Before its final cessation this press had contributed somewhat too the spread of Hebrew literature and the promotion of intercourse between Jews living in different parts of the world. Some of its books were published for export only,† notably a prayer-book intended primarily for German Jews living in the Turkish Empire, but also used by German Jews living in Italy. During the 15th and 16th centuries the influx of German Jews into Italy was very great and was one phase of the constant migration from land to land that has continued down to our day. Vicenzo Conti who had in the meantime established himself at Cremona,‡ came back to Sabbioneta in 1567 eight years after Foa had ceased printing, and published two or perhaps three books with which the press at Sabbioneta ends its labors in the cause of Hebrew letters. The eagerness with which Conti and Joseph ben Jacob of Mantua secured the types of Foa after the cessation of his press and the pride taken by the house of Bragadini in Venice fifty years later,

* "Le scrissi anche, che il Sig. Hercole per sue di 24. del passato da Roma mi commisse, che con diligenza e secretezza dovesse veder per casa di questi hebrei del Stato si haveano o libri prohibiti, o instromenti da stampare libri, e del tutto in bona forma farni una rellatione inviandola al Signor Alphonso suo fratello, perchè dovea poi andar in mano de' Cardinali e anche di Sua Santità. Io non intendo l'origine, e causa finale di questo motto, però si procederà oculatamente "

De Rossi "Sabb." pp. 6–7.

For further reference to the breaking up of this press see Ersch & Gruber, 46, note 93.

† Berliner "Aus meiner Bibliothek," p. 67.

‡ From which city he was ultimately obliged to depart.

in advertising the fact that they published books "with letters of Sabbioneta,"* indicate the esteem in which these publications of the press were held, and the value of its name and good will. Its title pages were used by Di Gara in Venice and

צדיק כתמר יפרח

Printer's mark of Tobia Foa
of Sabbioneta

by Turkish publishers in Salonica. The printer's mark which Foa adopted for himself, a spreading palm tree bearing the shield of David with two rampant lions as supporters, all under a text from the Psalms, "The righteous shall flourish like a palm tree," was unfortunately in no sense prophetic of the fate of his press.

* Bible 1615.

Among the German immigrants into Italy during the end of the fifteenth or beginning of the sixteenth century was a family which came from the town of Ettlingen, who after a short residence in Italy modified their name into Ottolenghi. The last and most distinguished member of the family was General Joseph Ottolenghi, late Minister of War and Commander-in-Chief of the Italian armies * whose namesake and ancestor, Rabbi Joseph Ottolenghi of Cremona enters into the history of the Hebrew printing press as the associate of Cardinal Christofolo Madrucci and Dr. Joseph Marcaria of Riva di Trento. The cardinal as patron,† the rabbi as editor and the physician as printer, established a notable press which in an active period of five years produced upwards of thirty books of value and importance. The rabbi was head of the rabbinical academy at Cremona and not only edited many of the books of the Riva press at the request of the cardinal but contributed a considerable part of his fortune toward the expense of their publication.‡ Dr. Jacob Marcaria the active member of the partnership, was a practicing physician at Riva who like so many of his profession was inspired by loyalty to his people and a deep-seated love for its literature. Himself an author of some ability, he wrote

* He was born in the little town of Sabbioneta.

† The cardinal was not the printer as stated by Steinschneider, Ersch & Gruber 64; see H. B. 1 : 112.

‡ Emek (ed. Wiener) p. 90; (ed. Letteris) p. 112; Nepi & Ghirondi p. 164.

prefaces to many of the books published at his press, and made himself so invaluable that with his death in 1562 the press of Riva came to a standstill.* He seems also to have published Hebrew books and we know one of them, on the Council of Trent, written by Vincenzo Zannelli and dedicated to Cardinal Madrucci.†

The most interesting personage connected with this press was the distinguished prince of the church whose coat of arms adorns many of the title pages of its books. Cardinal Madrucci was born of the noble Tyrolean family of Madruz, and after becoming Bishop of Trent and Prince Bishop of Brescia was created cardinal in 1542 by Pope Paul III. The seat of his diocese was the city of Trent lying about twenty miles northeast of Riva, which had contained a flourishing Jewish community for upwards of one hundred years until in 1475 the horrible charge of ritual murder was brought against it by the monk Bernadino da Feltre, and after an orgy of robbery and massacre in which the insulted Christian sentiment of the community expressed itself, the Jews of Trent were forever exiled from the city. How shall we account for the fact that so many eminent Catholic churchmen were deeply interested in the spread

* See Carmoly "Riva" passim.

† Full title as follows:—

"De Concilio Tridentino et omnibus patribus in eo congregatis ad illustrissimum & reverendiss. principem & cardinalem Ludovicum Madrutium Vincentii Zannelli–Thausignani Archipresbyteri Sylva. Ripae Tridentini: Apud Jacobum Marcoriae, 1563." Z. H. B. 10 : 94.

of Hebrew literature, notwithstanding that the Inquisition was constantly and consistently plotting and legislating for its destruction?

With the accession of Pope Paul IV the Inquisition which had been gradually gaining in strength since the end of the fifteenth century, was established upon a firm and permanent basis in Italy.* No one was safe from its investigations; knowledge science culture and the joys of life were put under its ban, and gloomy monasticism was made the ideal of human life. The beautiful gods of ancient Greece that had charmed the minds and elevated the tastes of men during the Renaissance, were now supplanted by images of the tortured Christ and his saints resurrected from the darkness of the Middle Ages. The Talmud and Hebrew books were proscribed and burned, and Christian printing presses were placed under a censorship that practically reduced them to the publication of only a single class of books.

Under these conditions we find Cardinal Christofolo Madrucci in 1558 founding and patronizing a Hebrew press at Riva di Trento. Among the Jews this fact must have been looked upon as nothing short of miraculous and when they saw the title pages of their law books and books of philosophy and devotion ornamented with the cardinal's coat-of-arms they must have believed that the universal redemption of the Jews was imminent and that the Messiah was about to appear.

* For Paul IV. see Graetz 9: 347 &c.

Although Cardinal Madrucci was not the fore-runner of the Messiah he was a scholar and a gentleman. He was free from the prejudices of his more churchly brethren and belonged to that class of men who cultivated a philosophy of life

Arms of Cardinal Madrucci
on title page of "Turim",
Marcaria, Riva di Trento, 1560

that enabled them to preserve their serenity amidst scenes that must have shaken their very inmost being with pity and regret. The condition of the states of the Church in the middle of the sixteenth century was wretched beyond belief. Wherever the hand of the Church fell ruin followed; prosperous cities like Ferrara passing from the rule of their own dukes and princes into the hands of the Pope withered away as though a blight had struck them. Their inhabitants deserted them; commerce and art disappeared, and the remnants of their communities consisted of priests monks diseased beggars and prostitutes. Amid such evidence of ecclesiastical misrule, gentlemen like Cardinal Madrucci occupied themselves with such pursuits as suited their tastes and inclinations not through any indifference nor lack of sympathy, but because of the impossibility of making any change that would improve the condition of society and at the same time continue the rule of the church. It was not until a much later period when the cup of misery and degradation was filled to overflowing, that forces arose that broke the iron rod that ruled in Italy and elsewhere and made of the head of the greatest of all world powers a recluse in the gardens of the Vatican. During the reign of Pope Paul IV, the difference between the princes of the church and its real rulers the monks of the so-called Holy Office, the dreaded Inquisition, was so wide that in a list of heretics prepared at this time appear the names of thirteen cardinals and eleven bishops and archbishops. The heretic cardinals were Bembo, Badia, Contarini, Cortese, Di Fano, Fregoso, Pole, Simonetta, Sadoleto, Sacripante, Sfrondato, Madrucci and Morone.* It appears that no practical attempt was made to bring Madrucci to account and he died in 1578 in an odor of sanctity

* Lanciani " Golden Days of the Renaissance at Rome " p. 208.

at the age of sixty-six.* Although this prince of
the Church had publicly sanctioned the publication of Hebrew books at Riva, the Inquisition
which had suspected him of heresy naturally declined to recognize his imprimatur. There lies
before me a copy of the "Toaliot" of Rabbi Levi
ben Gerson, bearing the cardinal's name on the
title page; here and there through its pages may

ברוך מוריד נשיאים שזכנו להשלים תועליות הר'לבג
על הנביאים ' שנת שך לפ'ק פהרי:וא דטרינטו '

Censors' signatures on last page of Toaliyot of Ralbag
Marcaria, Riva di Trento, 1560

be seen the ink scrawls of the censors and on the
last page are the signatures and dates showing
that not only were the inquisitors dissatisfied with
the cardinal's imprimatur, but so jealous of each
other's orthodoxy that the book had to undergo
four examinations to satisfy the theological idio-

* Madrucci's intimate association with Sadoleto, Contarini and
Pole justifies the thought that he understood the meaning of the
Lutheran movement and was prepared to seek a via media between
its heterodoxy and the policy of the church. (Brown "Studies" 2 : 111).
A Tyrolese by birth, his knowledge of what was going on beyond the
Alps might have saved the unity of the church had it not been for
the blindness of the Italian and Spanish cardinals.

syncrasies of four servants of the Inquisition of equal standing, presumably of equal faith, and certainly of equal ignorance.

BOOKS PRINTED AT FERRARA.*

By Samuel Zarfati:—

1551　Ma'yene Hayeshuah

1552　Behinat Olam
　　　Refuot Geviah
　　　Pitron Halomot
　　　Hilkhot Shehitah
　　　Hilkhot Hareah

By Samuel Usque:—

1553　Hosha'ot Lesuccot

1554　Maamar Haahdut
　　　Yesod Haemunah
　　　Or Hahayim
　　　Hibbur Maasiyot
　　　Zedah Laderekh
　　　Meah Berakot
　　　Seder Maamadot †

1555　Sefer Hazikkaron
　　　Pentateuch, Megillot & Haftarot
　　　Or Adonai

1556　Sefer Naftulim
　　　Shaar Hagemul
　　　Sefer Ha-Emunot
　　　Kebod Elohim
　　　Shilte Hagibborim

* See De Rossi "De typ. Hebr. Ferrariensi comm. Hist."
† Ersch & Gruber 45.

1556   Masaot of Benjamin of Tudela
       Likute Shikha
       Issur Vehetter
       Amarot Tehorot*
1557   Hibbur Yafe Mehayeshuah
       Ben Hamelekh Vehanazir
       Hashagot of Moses Alaskar
1558   Maarekhet Haelohut
       Mea Berakhot.†

BOOKS PRINTED AT SABBIONETA.‡

1551   Merkebet Hamishneh
       Commentary on Ruth by Isaac b.
          Joseph Ha-Cohen
1552   Hazut Kashah
1553   Moreh Nebukhim
       Talmud Babli Kiddushin
       Arba Turim
1553(?)Dibre Hayamim lemalke Zarfat umalke
          bet Ottoman hatogar
1554   Alfasi
       Simane kol shemoneh binyanim
       Shehitah ubedikah
       Lehem Yehudah
       Pardes Rimonim
       Responsa of Moses Alaskar

* ? See Ersch & Gruber 45.
† Z. H. B. 9: 152.
‡ Some of the books unfinished at Sabbioneta were subsequently
published at Mantua and Cremona. Cohn: Chron. Beitr. p. 8; Zunz
Z. G. p. 255.

1553–1555 Bible
    1556 Psalms
          Minhagim
    1557 Pentateuch and Megillot
          Ateret Zekenim
          Rashi on the Pentateuch
          Mahzor (German rite)
    1558 Pentateuch and Megillot
          Canticles
          Psalms
    1559 Mishnah
    1567 Pirke d'Rabbi Eliezer
          Halikot Olam
          Zedah laderek

BOOKS PRINTED AT RIVA DI TRENTO.*

1558 Alfasi
      Toledot Yizhak
      Shaare Shebuot
      Shebile Emunah
      Minhagim
      Mordecai
      Hiddushim of R. Nissim (two editions)
      Berakhot of Meir of Rothenburg
      Simane vekizzure Ha Mordecai (two edi-
          tions)
1559 Bahya on the Pentateuch
      Sefer Bar Sheshet
      Mishnah (two editions)

* Carmoly "Annalen"; H. B. 7 : 113; 4 : 57.

1559   Iggeret Hamussar le Aristoteles
       Kizzure Ibn Roshd
       Kol Malakot Higayon
1560   Toaliyot of Levi b. Gerson
       Massa Ge Hizayon
       Commentary on Megillot by Levi b. Gerson
       Dikduke Rashi
       Sefer Ibronot
       Milhamot Hashem
1561   Haggadah shel Pesah
       Arba Turim
       Pentateuch (two editions)
       Shaare Orah
       Shaare Zedek
       Masseket Derek Erez upirke Ben Azai
1562   Biurim of Isserlein
       Goren Nakon
       Meir Iyyob (?)

CHAPTER XIII.

CREMONA AND MANTUA.

IN the middle of the sixteenth century Cremona was the centre of Jewish learning in Northern Italy. Lying in the heart of Lombardy the city was topographically as it was spiritually the centre of a large number of Jewish communities within a radius of fifty miles. Eastward lay Mantua and Verona; northward Brescia Bergamo and Milan; westward Pavia and Piacenza; southward Reggio and Parma, while scattered within this region were many smaller towns distinguished as the dwelling places of Jews of renown—the towns of Guastalla Colorno Rivarolo Pizzighettone Pescarolo Codogno Marcaria and Castiglione. Somewhat to the north of Cremona lay the City of Soncino the birthplace of the most distinguished of Jewish printers and the cradle of his press.

While everywhere the Jews were hiding their heads in fear of the Inquisition Cremona saw the establishment of a new centre for the spread of

Jewish learning the famous rabbinical academy of Joseph Ottolenghi*—and through the growth of her book-trade, took the place of Venice as the chief distributing centre for Hebrew books to all the world.

From the windows of the municipal palace of Cremona one may see the great cathedral and its bell tower, beyond which lay the ancient Jewish quarter the Ghetto for several centuries the innocent cause of much turmoil and alarm. For many years the Jews had lived in happy obscurity in their Via Giudecca, ignored by the mitred prelates and black robed friars who passed and repassed in endless processions to the great cathedral. Occasional riots instigated by rogues intent on plunder or monks zealous in saving souls were promptly suppressed by the strong hand of the civil authorities, and until the middle of the sixteenth century the Jews of this city had comparatively little to complain of.

The city of Cremona at that time lay under the jurisdiction of the Senate of Milan and the entire ancient Duchy of Milan was an appanage of the Spanish crown, ruled by a royal governor the appointee of Philip II, that king whose cruel and bloodthirsty religious fanaticism exceeded that of any European monarch. In the Senate of Milan however and even among the Episcopal Vicars a milder religious sentiment prevailed, and it may very well be that herein was manifest the

* Graetz 9 : 367; H. B. 5 : 125.

influence of the sometime Governor of Milan Cardinal Christofolo Madrucci. But a change came in 1553. For four years Pope Paul IV had been rigidly enforcing his predecessor's decree against the Talmud and everywhere the officials of the Inquisition had confiscated and burned Hebrew books by the thousands. In Cremona however the final blow was for a short time delayed by a conflict of authority between the civil and ecclesiastical officials. The attention of the authorities at Rome was attracted by the reasonable and at times even lenient interpretation of the rules of the Inquisition, and in a letter addressed to the Senate of Milan the Inquisitor General Cardinal Michele Ghislieri * complained that "in the city of Cremona there are some who have treated the authority of the Holy Apostolical Throne with contempt and have printed certain works commentaries etc. . . . called Talmud, although such works have been condemned by the Venerable College of Cardinals . . . and burned in Rome Venice and other places." And the Cardinal demanded that the Senate of Milan refer the matter to the Chief Inquisitor of Cremona in order that the decrees of the Inquisition might be strictly enforced.† The Senate directed the podestà, the chief civil magistrate of the community,

* Popper " Censorship" p. 43.

† What had been done in former ages by the self-sacrificing zeal of the followers of the new religion of Christianity (Acts 19 : 19), had now become the established policy of the Christian Church in its efforts to bend the minds of men to its yoke.

to make the investigation, and in obedience to his summons Vicenzo Conti and Vittorio Eliano awaited his pleasure in the municipal palace. No two men in Cremona could better answer the question about to be propounded to them: "Is the Talmud of the Jews being printed at Cremona?" for the one was the master of the Hebrew press established in 1556 at Cremona * and the other a learned Jewish apostate in his employ who was also reviser of Hebrew books for the Inquisition.† Vittorio Eliano's connection with the press of Conti no doubt induced him to give his employer the benefit of every reasonable doubt, and it was probably this laxity in the interpretation of the rules of the Inquisition that provoked the wrath of the Inquisitor General. Conti and Vittorio quickly satisfied the podestà that the Talmud was not being printed at Cremona, and that the copies in use among the Jews of that city were principally those of the Venice edition from the press of the late Daniel Bomberg, which had until now escaped the general confiscation. Acting upon the report

---

* Conti was born at Verona. Ersch & Gruber, 45. De Rossi Ann. p. 4, says that he was a native of Cremona. Fumagalli, p. 302 says that Conti was a Jew. This does not seem to have been suspected by the bibliographers. Conti served his apprenticeship at the press of Foa in Sabbioneta, De Rossi "Ann. ebr. tip. di Cremona." He learned printing there in the style of Bomberg through association with Adelkind; see his Mibhar Hapeninim.

† Every book had, of course, to be submitted to the authorities for examination and approval. Eben Bohen issued 1558 with privilege of the Episcopal Vicar Decio Alberio and the Vicar of the Inquisition Girolamo de Vercelli.

of the podestà, the Senate of Milan notified the Inquisition at Rome that the charges made by the Inquisitor General were unfounded, and showed their independence by refusing to obey his order to confiscate and destroy the copies of the Talmud in use among the Jews of Cremona sustaining the objection made by the Jews to his order upon the ground that the decree of Julius III did not require the destruction of the books, but merely the elimination of passages that were deemed offensive to the Christian religion. It was therefore with a lighter heart that Vicenzo Conti and Vittorio Eliano went back to their shop to continue for a time undisturbed in their work.

Ghislieri owed his position as Cardinal and Inquisitor General to Pope Paul IV, and as a member of the Sacred College, and subsequently when he was elevated to the throne as Pope Pius V, he proved himself the spiritual brother of that gloomy zealot in his policy of suppressing heresy by the iron hand of the Inquisition. In English history he will best be remembered as the Pope who aided and abetted Mary Stuart in her treasonable designs upon the crown of England and who excommunicated Queen Elizabeth. The story of his interference with the peace and happiness of the Jews of Cremona is a short, but significant chapter of his life's history.

In the beginning of the year 1559, Pope Paul IV published the first index of prohibited books, "Index of authors and books against which each

ספר כריתות

להרב רבינו שמשון מקינון

בן עטרת חכמים

Title page of Sefer Keritut
Conti, Cremona, 1558

and every one in the whole Christian world is warned by the Holy and Universal Inquisition, together with the punishment decreed against those who read or possess books prohibited in the Bull 'In Coena Dominis,' and other punishments contained in various decrees of the Holy Office." A copy of the index was sent to Milan, but the Senate of that Duchy again exhibiting the extraordinary independence that had marked its action in other cases sent an address to the Royal Governor protesting against the injustice of permitting any individual—for thus the Senate spoke of Cardinal Ghislieri—to confiscate books that had been passed by the censor and permitted by the Inquisitors, especially such books as contained nothing against Christianity, indeed referred in no way to religion, and had been approved everywhere by churchmen as furthering the spiritual welfare of mankind. This appeal evoked no immediate reply, but when the Jews of Cremona protested to him that the demand of the Inquisitor for surrender of all copies of the Talmud was a clear violation of the law, the Governor ordered the podestà of Cremona to take possession of all the surrendered copies of the Talmud but to return all other Hebrew books to their owners and to prevent any further annoyance to the Jews. The Inquisitor answered boldness with boldness and refused to obey the order, and a serious clash between Church and State seemed imminent. But the wily officers of the Inquisition, determined to convert the Governor to their view, called to their aid the Dominican friars, who thereupon became, as the Chronicler Joseph Ha-Cohen pathetically says, "as thorns in the side of the Jews of Cremona." But the Governor was not moved by the appearance of pasquils demanding the death of the Jews * nor by charges of Talmudic blasphemies against Jesus and he repeated his order to return to the Jews all books not included in the Index. The Dominicans then seized upon this order as a pretext for the appointment of a new commission to determine which books were included in the Index, and the apostates, Vittorio Eliano and Joshua dei Cantori, were appointed on this commission.† As a result of their decision a number of books were seized and stored in the Dominican monastery and in token of apparent submission to the will of the constituted authorities, the keys of the monastery were delivered to the podesta. What other methods were used for the purpose of weakening the opposition of the Governor are not known, but he suddenly yielded to the importunities of the Dominicans and directed the local authorities of Cremona, including the commander of the Spanish troops quartered in that city, to assist the Inquisitors in the search for forbidden books. When we consider that even the priests themselves were unable to read Hebrew, the bitter irony of the situation is made manifest, for to the

* H. B. 1 : 131.
† H. B. 1 : 131.

brutal and ignorant Spanish soldiers was left the task of assisting in the determination whether or not Hebrew books were among the classes forbidden by the Index. Under the zealous leadership of Sixtus of Siena the soldiers tore the books from the houses of their owners; they broke into the shop of Conti and took all of his books, including a freshly printed edition of the Zohar, which had been edited by Vittorio Eliano himself. But here the religious zeal of Sixtus interfered and saved from the flames the Zohar, whose mystic pages were believed to hold confirmation of the dogmas of Christianity.* Another book, an edition of one thousand copies of a commentary on the Pentateuch, known as the Ziyuni, after its author, Rabbi Menahem Ziyuni was seized and burned by the very Inquisitors who had just authorized its publication. In all upwards of ten thousand Hebrew books were burned in the faithful city of Cremona. The very next year, the new Pope Pius IV, who had been Cardinal of Milan and was opposed to the ruthless policy of extermination inaugurated by the Jesuits and Dominicans, attempted to recompense Conti for his loss by permitting him to print a second edition of the Ziyuni.†

Following this wholesale confiscation and destruction a further search was made and every Hebrew volume submitted to the rigid censorship.

---

* H. B. 1 : 112; Ersch & Gruber 46.

† This book is notable for the first reference to Norway in Jewish literature page 66c. H. B. 11 : 137.

It is impossible to speak of all of the absurdities committed by the censors in the expurgation of Hebrew books. In the Sefer Keritut, published by Conti, the word Talmud was deleted wherever it appeared, but time laughs at the Inquisition, and in the copies of this book now extant the censor's ink has faded and all of the deleted words are clearly legible. It can well be imagined that during this reign of inquisitorial terror at Cremona the life of the printer was scarcely a happy one, but with undiminished courage Conti continued his work for eight years. When in 1567 he abandoned his work at Cremona * and returned to the town of Sabbioneta where he had long before served his apprenticeship, he found there under Prince Vespasian Gonzaga Colonna, an atmosphere free from persecution and misrule. Exultingly the printer writes in one of his colophons, "From Sionetta shall go forth the law," and on his title page appears as a printer's mark a picture of Hercules strangling the dragon with the motto "At virtus superavit," emblematic of the historical fact, in his day a mere shadowy hope, of the destruction of the all devouring Inquisition by the unconquerable strength of enlightenment. At Sabbioneta he produced three books in 1567 and he then became a licensed printer at Piacenza.† Dying in 1570 he bequeathed his press to his sons

---

* In 1597 there were only two Jewish families at Cremona, J. E. 1 : 340.

† Fumagalli 302.

על יד וויצינצו קונטי ובביתו

Printer's mark of Vicenzo Conti

who continued printing for many years but never entered the field of Hebrew typography, unless the Responsa of Nissim of Gerona published in 1586 issued from their press.* An attempt was made by another Cremonese, Cristoforo Draconin to print Hebrew books, but after the publication of a single book with the aid of the Jewish printer Solomon ben Jacob Bueno † he desisted.‡

LIST OF BOOKS PUBLISHED AT CREMONA. ¶

1556 Toldot Adam
Tashbatz
Maalot Hamiddot
Amude Golah
Responsa of Jacob Levita
1557 Rokeah
Kizzur Mordecai
Zebah Pesah
Rosh Emunah
Ateret Zekenim
Responsa of Meir of Rothenburg
Maamar Haskel
Zori Hegon
Or Enayim
Responsa of Nissim of Gerona
Responsa of Joseph Kolon

* Fumagalli ibid.
† Yosef Lekah 1567.
‡ For Draconin see Fumagalli p. 107.
¶ De Rossi "Ann. ebr. tip. di Cremona."

1558	Arba Turim
	Minhagim
	Keritut
	Mibhar Hapeninim
	Eben Bohen
	Orah Hayim
1559	Hizkuni
	Mehir Yayin
1560	Zohar
	Ziyuni
	Pentateuch & Megillot
1561	Mahzor
	Psalms with commentary of Kimhi
1565	Tanya
1566	Torat Habayit
	Imre No'am
	Minhagim
	Rua'h 'Hen
	Milot Higayon
	Horban Bet Hamikdash
	Megillat Sefer
1567	Pentateuch & Megillot
	Yosef Lekah
1586	Responsa of Nissim of Gerona
Without date	Sefer Hasidim
	Sefer Hamussar

Since the days of Abraham Conat and Samuel Latif no Hebrew books had been published at Mantua. Toward the middle of the sixteenth

סוף כל הדורות • כמו שמציין באברה' אבימ שגא' כי ידעתי למען אשר יצוה את בניו ואת
אחריו אחריו ושמרו דרך ה' לעשות צדקה ומשפט למען הביא ה' על אברהם אשר דבר עליו :
ואשרי הבנים חנוכחים ומזורזים לשמע למצות אבותיהם'המוכיחים ומייכרים ומלמדים אותם
ליראה את ה' ולהתעסק בתורה ובמצות עליהן ועל כירצא בהן נאמ' תחת
אבותיך יהיו בניך תשיתמו לשרים בכל הארץ :

ק   מצות הבן על האב

כשם שהאב חייב בבנו כה' דברים שכתבנו כן חבן פתחייב באביו ואמ' כה' דברים
ואילו הן כיבוד ומורא חכאה וקללת' שתים מהן מצוה ושהם ועשה מהן סצות
לא תעשה • על ארבעתן הוא מתחייב בהן בחייו והחמישית היא קללה שלאחר
מיתה • המקלל אביו לאחר מיתח חייב ועליהן שנה הכתו' הקללה ולא שנה בהכאה רכה' וכבת
אביו ואמו מות יומת וכתיב • ומקלל אביו ואמו מות יומת וכתיב כי איש איש אשר יקלל את אביו
ואת אמו מות יומת אין לי אלא בחייו לאחר מיתה מגין תל' אביו ואמו קלל רמזו בו לרבות לאחר
מיתה • הרי ה' דברים שהבן זוכה בהן כאביו ואמו • ושני חכמי' איזהו מורא ואיזהו כיבור : מורא
לא יעמוד במקומו ולא ישב במקומו ולא סותר דבריו ולא מכריעו • ואיזהו כבוד מאכיל ומשקה
מרבין ומרחיץ וכן מלביש ומנעיל ומכניס ומוציא • ושני חכבי' מכבד בחייו מכבד במיתתו :
בחייו כיצר הרי שנשלח בדבר אביו למקם לא יאמ' שלחוני בשביל עצמי מהרוני בשביל עצמי
פטרוני בשביל עצמי אלא אמ' בולחו בשביל אבא • במותו כיצר היה אומ' דבר שמעת מפיו לא
יאמר כך אמ' אבא אלא כך אמר אבא מרי הריני כפרת משכבו • והם' בתוך י"ב חדש מכן ואילך
אומ' זכרוט לחיי העולם הבא : ושני חכמי' תמכבד את אביו ואת אמו במיתתן כאלו כבדן בחייהן
שהמבזרן בחייהן אינו מכבדן אלא מיראה והמכבנן במיתתן אינו מכבדן אלא מפני המקום •
אשרי הבן המכבד תמקום ומכבד אב' אביו ואמו במעשיו הטובים שהרבים אומ' עליו אשרי
שזח ילד אשרי שזח גדל תדע שהשהה הכתו' כיבור אב ואם ומוראם לכבוחו ומוראו : ולא אילו
חדברים בלבד שחוזכרט יש בכיבור ומורא אלא כל דבר החוכה לכיבוד צריך אדם ליזהר בהן חן
יוח על השאר • ישמע חכם ויוסיף לקח ובבת תחבולות יקנה ובכן אוכל אדם פירות בעולם הזח
וקרן קיימ' לו לעולם הבאו בכן הוא אומ' כבד את אביך ואת אמך למען יאריכן יאריבן יסיך בעול' שכולו
אריך ולמען ייטב לך בעולם שכולו טוב •

נשלם מנהג אבות כפר ותגיא בחדש סיון
שנת חמשת אלפים ושבעים וארבע
לבריאת עולם ה' יזכנו בביאת
משיחנו ככתוב בתורתך
ושב ה' אלקיך את שבותך
ורחמך
ושבו וקבצך מכל העמים אשר חפיצך ה' אלהיך שמה : אמן
על יד הצעיר שמואל לטיף פה מנטובה

century this city had become a place of refuge for many victims of ecclesiastical persecution. The reigning Duke, Guglielmo Gonzaga, was, like many of the Italian princes, educated by masters who were inspired by the spirit of free inquiry and thought that was one of the noblest fruits of the Renaissance of literature and learning. His intercourse with scholarly and high-minded Jews, who were freely received at his court, tempered his judgment toward "the people of affliction." Duke Guglielmo's decrees concerning the Jews well illustrated the conflict of forces in a community whose ideal was not justice but faith, for while on the one hand, under the influence of his churchly advisers, he forbade the Jews from tilling the soil and renting real estate,* he on the other hand decreed that "we desire that the Jews shall be as free and secure as the Christians in pursuing their business and professions in our city and our duchy." † Yet in the very year of this decree he permitted the monks to take possession of the Jewish cemetery under the right of eminent domain claimed by the Church, in order to enlarge their already capacious monastery.‡ Thus by concessions to the spirit of the time the Duke kept his peace with the Church and on the whole gave his people as good a government as was possible under the system of petty tyranny and ecclesiasti-

* R. E. J. 11 : 274.
† J. E. 8 : 299.
‡ J. E. 8 : 300.

cal interference then in vogue throughout Italy and the world—a system under which the farmer the laborer the petty mechanic and the Jew suffered equally, a system that was only beginning to recognize the merchant and that had since time immemorial enthroned the soldier and pampered the priest.

In the fifth decade of the fifteenth century, as the presses of Venice came to rest, a number of active presses sprang up in Lombardy. In Mantua the enterprising initiative of two descendants of Paduan Jews, Joseph ben Jacob Shalit and Meir ben Ephraim the Scribe again set the Hebrew presses in motion. The first of these, Joseph ben Jacob whose surname Ashkenazi indicates his descent from German Jews, who had settled in Padua to escape persecution, was not only a craftsman but a scholar and linguist, and entered the republic of letters in 1550 with an Italian translation of a Hebrew dissertation written by Rabbi Moses ben Abraham of Provence, on the mathematical problem of two lines constantly approaching each other but never meeting.* After the appearance in 1550 of his first Hebrew book the Passover Haggadah,† Joseph Shalit removed to

* Zunz Z. G. 251. He was one of the six judges and leaders of the German Jewish community at Mantua. Zunz. Z. G. 252. He wrote introduction to Abrabanel's commentary on Deuteronomy, 1551, Isaac Arama's "Hazut Kasha" 1552 published at Sabbioneta and dedicated to Aaron Habib of Pesaro. Also introduction to Tikkun Middot Hanefesh and Goren Nakon published at Riva 1562.

† Not at Venice as Zunz Z. G. 251 has it, but at Mantua Wiener " Oster Haggadah" No. 9.

Sabbioneta where for several years he was associated with the press of Tobia Foa and whence he brought with him the right to use the printer's mark of "the partners" of Sabbioneta, the peacock on the rock which appears in some of his books at Mantua. In 1556 he resumed his work as a printer at Mantua and during 1556–1558 issued at least five books.* His importance as a printer was completely overshadowed by his contemporaries Meir the Scribe and Jacob of Gazolo, who sometimes alone and sometimes in partnership and assisted by many competent craftsmen, produced the books that gave Mantua a notable place in the history of Hebrew typography. Most of these books were printed at the press of Venturin Ruffinello, a Christian printer who came to Mantua from Venice in 1545. We know that at Venice the Hebrew printers were obliged to do their work at the presses of the Christian printers, who had secured a monopoly of the right to issue Hebrew books. It is not unlikely that a similar state of affairs existed at Mantua; for although both Venice and Mantua were comparatively liberal in their treatment of the Jews, they were in many ways influenced by the prevailing Christian sentiment. Ruffinello secured many privileges from the Cardi-

---

* 1556   Hatehiyah vehapedut
             Hapedut vehapurkan
   1557   Iggeret baale hayyim
             Ben hamelekh vehanazir
   1558   Mishle Shualim
  Zunz. Z. G. 249.

nal Archbishop Ercole Gonzaga for there had been no press of any kind in Mantua for twenty years. At his death in 1558 he was succeeded by his son Giacomo who in 1576 was followed by his son Tommaso.* The rival house of Fillipono, established by Francesco Fillipono who was succeeded by his sons Filotarsi and Calidono Fillipono,† does not seem to have seriously contested for supremacy with the Ruffinelli.

Jacob ben Naftali Cohen of Gazolo after having served at the press of Foa in Sabbioneta as one of "the partners" came to Mantua in 1556 and during the following eight years established a splendid record for good typographical work.‡ His first work appears to have been a new edition of Elijah Levita's grammatical work the "Bahur" which he printed at the press of Venturin Ruffinello for Meir b. Ephraim the Scribe. The relations thus established between Jacob and Meir continued until 1563 when Jacob either died or retired or removed from Mantua.¶ Of all the books printed at Mantua the most important is the Zohar preparations for which were made as early as 1556. The Zohar, "the Shining", seems to have been named upon the principle by which in polite and

* Fumagalli 202.

† Filotarsi and Calidono were probably the sons of Francesco and the same as the printers of the Haggadot of 1568 known as "the sons of Fillipono."

‡ J. E. 7 : 40.

¶ His last book seems to have been the Mishnah printed in the house of Francesco Fillipono. Zunz. Z. G. 255.

tender Hebrew phraseology a blind man is called "full of light", for its mission seems to have been to add little light, but much darkness, to the Jewish mind. The original stimulus for the printing of this book seems to have come from Moses Bassola of Pesaro a son of that Mordecai Bassola who was proof reader at the press of Soncino. At his solicitation his disciple Immanuel of Benevento who promoted the publication of two other mystical works * undertook to publish it,† by bearing the expense and assisting at the press. Its publication was further favored by Isaac b. Immanuel de Lattes of Rome ‡ and by the Cardinal Archbishop of Mantua who issued a statement in its favor.

The long series of persecutions to which the Jewish people and their literature had been subjected had somewhat affected the thought and hopes of many of them, and in the mysticism of the Zohar they found adequate literary expression of their revived hopes for a Messianic time that should redeem them from their unbearable misery. Their once political Messianism had been refined into a Messianism of subtler type, which projected redemption into a more distant future and longed for something more than a restored Jewish com-

---

* 1557   Tikkune Zohar
     1558   Maarekhet Elohut
           Conforte, Kore Hadorot 40 a.

† Immanuel was *not* the printer but the patron of the work. Jew. Enc. Article "Basilea," Graetz 9: 369.

‡ Vogelstein & Rieger 2 : 99.

monwealth. It had now become a mad dream of miracle-workers who considered themselves fore-runners of a miraculous redeemer. The trinitarian elements in this jumble of mysticism, philosophy and theology attracted many of the leading men of the Church who, deceived by the apparent antiquity of the Zohar, looked with favor on what seemed to them to be confirmation of the funda-mental dogmas of Catholicism.* After three years of work the Zohar appeared in 1559 in three quarto volumes.† While it was in press Vicenzo Conti of Cremona, anticipating the printers of Mantua ‡ issued another edition which through judicious advertising and the patronage of Vittorio Eliano and of the Inquisitor General, threatened to wreck the newly established press at Mantua.¶ The obvious superiority of the Mantua edition, Buxtorf to the contrary notwithstanding,** gained for it success in the open book market, and defeated Conti's attempt to overreach his rivals.

Although the activity of the press at Mantua was temporarily stimulated by the cessation of the press at Ferrara in 1558 and at Sabbioneta in 1560 and by the acquisition of the types of the latter, it soon succumbed at the renewed competition of the presses of Venice, which resumed work in 1564. Mantua like all the other Italian cities suffered to

* Graetz 9 : 369; Jew. Enc. Art. "Zohar."

† Abraham b. Meshullam of Modena, corrector.

‡ Graetz 9 : 370.

¶ It was a state of affairs similar to that which brought such mis-fortune to the houses of Giustiniani and Bragadini of Venice.

** De Rossi "Cremona" p. 12.

such an extent, that she seems to have been unable to make use of even so valuable a concession as that given in 1562 when the Council of Trent, probably under the influence of its president the Cardinal Archbishop Ercole Gonzaga of Mantua, granted the Jewish community of Mantua permission to print Hebrew books. Cardinal Gonzaga died in the same year at about the time when the Inquisition, having at last discovered that the Zohar and the Kabbalistic literature were of no help to Catholicism, decreed their condemnation. This reversal of the policy of the Church caused the greatest alarm everywhere, especially in Mantua. The Jews there believing that a reversal of this decree could be obtained through the intercession of the new Pope Pius IV, a man of milder manner and temper than his predecessor Pope Paul IV. sent a committee to Trent and succeeded in having the matter referred to him, at Rome. The Jews of that city, aided by their brethren elsewhere, brought all their influence to bear and succeeded so well that when the new Index was published in March 1564, it was found that although the old phrase against "the Talmud its glosses annotations interpretations and expositions" had been retained, it had been modified by the clause "but if they shall be published without the title 'Talmud' and without calumnies and insults to the Christian religion they shall be tolerated."* This was almost equivalent to per-

* Popper, 52.

Title page of " Generations of Isaac "
Meir of Padua and Jacob of Gazolo, Mantua 1558

mission to establish a free Hebrew press. But although this privilege was conceded in 1564, eight years elapsed before the printers of Mantua took advantage of it. It may well be that they were restrained by their knowledge born of long and bitter experience that it is easy for a Pope to take away that which his predecessor has granted, and that the minions of the Inquisition were ever ready to pounce upon and misinterpret any innocent phrase or word appearing in a Hebrew book and use it as a pretext for extortion and persecution.

In 1572 Meir the Scribe took courage and began to reprint the great Code of the Law of Maimonides, which some twenty years before had been the bone of contention between the printers of Venice. Nor did he venture upon this step until after he had obtained a special license from the Inquisitor of Mantua Giovanni Battista di Milano issued to the Jew Mirra di Crescino of Padua (none other than our Meir the Scribe) and his partner.

Soon after the publication of the first part of this great work the plague broke out and the ghetto of Mantua rendered its quota of victims. The printer Meir lost his daughter and daughter-in-law, and Jews as well as Christians paid a fearful penalty for the unhygienic conditions that prevailed in most of their habitations. Following the plague came the edict of Duke Guglielmo introducing the hated yellow badge to distinguish the Jews of his city from their Christian fellow subjects.* The persecuting mania once aroused grew stronger with every victim and it was the fate of the printer Meir in his extreme old age to feel the heavy hand of persecution. A short entry in his diary records that without notice or trial he was suddenly arrested and imprisoned immediately after the Jewish New Year, kept in solitary confinement and released for want of evidence against him a few days after the Day of Atonement. The cruel injustice of the whole proceeding against the helpless and innocent old man broke down his health, and he died after a lingering illness.

PUBLICATIONS OF MEIR THE SCRIBE AND JACOB OF GAZOLO.†

1556	Habahur
	Behinat olam
	Shehitot
1557	Mahzor
	Megillat Antiochus
	Haggadah (Roman Rite)‡
	Tikkune Zohar
	Livyat Hen
1558	Sefer Hamussar
	Maarekhet Elohut
	Toledot Yizhak

---

* A badge originally invented by a Mohammedan ruler and borrowed for the benefit of the Christian world by Pope Innocent III.

† Zunz. Z. G. 249.

‡ Z. H. B. 9 : 152.

1559 Mekor Hayim
      Hobob Halebabot
      Zohar
1560 Mishnah Abot with commentaries
      Bedikot
      Haggadah
1561 Shaare Orah
      Orah Hayim
      Marpe lenefesh
      Seah Solet
      Hamiznefet
      Mishnah Nashim
          "   Nezikin
      Yihus Buch
1562 Sefer Yezirah
      Mishnah Kodashim
      Prayers with Judaeo-German transla-
          tion
      Psalms
1563 Mishnah Taharot

Jacob of Gazolo has no part in the following
publications:—

      Mahalakh
      Midrash Tanhuma, Meir the Scribe &
          Ezra b. Isaac of Fano
      Menorat Hamaor, Meir the Scribe,
          Ephraim b. Isaac and Meir b.
          Moses Heilprun.
1564 Judges
1566 Ele Hadebarim*

* Divorce proceedings.

```
     1568   Haggadah
     1570   Bedikot*
     1571   Psalms
     1572   3 books of Mishneh Torah
  1574–76   Meor Enayim
Sine anno   Samuel
            Prophets
            Hebrew letter writer.
```

After the death of Meir the Scribe, his nephew and son-in-law Ephraim ben David inherited his types and toward the end of the century printed a few books at the press of the Ruffinelli.† He was followed by Moses Elishama of the family of Zifroni who printed at the press of Tomasso Ruffinelli for the brothers Isaac and Solomon Norzi members of an old and distinguished family of Mantuan Jews.‡

* Ersch & Gruber 46 note 107.

† 1588 Abot (in Italian)
  1589 Pentateuch with Targum, etc.
  1590 Abot with Rashi.

‡ 1593 Halikot Olam
        Shearit Yosef
        Shearit Yisrael
        Darke Hagemara
  1597 Responsa of the Geonim.

Moses Elishama was the son of the well-known printer, Israel Zifroni of Guastalla, who lived at Gazolo whence came that other excellent printer, Jacob ben Naftali, who printed with Meir the Scribe. Israel Zifroni conducted the new press at Basel where, among other works, he printed the Talmud in 1581. He had also printed at Sabbioneta and Venice before his son Moses Elishama came to Mantua to attempt to revive the dying Hebrew press of the Ruffinelli. Zunz "Zur Geschichte und Literatur" p. 258.

In 1594 Moses b. Katriel Weiss of Prague printed Mishnayot at the press of Tomasso Ruffinelli.

But neither the skill of the printer nor the devotion of his patrons the Norzi could stay the decay of this enterprise. The insidious work of the Inquisition and the ruthless censorship made Hebrew printing a thankless task and Moses Elishama Zifroni sadly withdrew to Venice to join his father, and for fifteen years no Hebrew books appeared at Mantua.

In 1612 another attempt was made to re-establish the press. Eliezer d'Italia first of the printers to print in the Mantuan ghetto which had been established in 1610 * called Moses Elishama Zifroni back from Venice and with his aid and the patronage of Dr. Abraham Portaleone printed the work of the latter, the "Shields of the Mighty." † Eliezer d'Italia fondly called his press, "one such as we had here in former days," but the times had changed and after printing two books besides that of Dr. Portaleone,‡ Eliezer d'Italia and his press disappear.

After an interval an attempt to re-establish the press was made in 1619 by the sons of Israel Conian. But all that appeared was a Purim song

* Carnevali "il ghetto di Mantova" p. 33.

† 1612 Shilte Hagibborim. The author hardly survived the publication of his book. This Dr. Abraham Portaleone, whom Graetz, "Gesch. der Juden" 9 : 486, calls "a half-crazy physician and tiresome writer," was a fine scholar, a distinguished physician and a patron of the Hebrew press to the day of his death. Fürst, Jahrbuch für Gesch. d. Juden 2 : 346 calls his Shilte Hagibborim "a book of wonderful riches and scientific value" and quotes Wagenseil who calls it "librum aureum" and Menasse ben Israel "ingeniosum opus.

‡ Ayelet Hashahar, Yashir Mosheh. Zunz, Zur Gesch. p. 259.

צורך אחר וז״ל אבכרהס הכינו דכר כוה
הספר כנסתר על אופן הנכיאיס
שמדכרוכ בכתר על בד החידה שהרי
הכרהס אכונו אחר כפירות מעניו
ספיריס וכמו שהספיר מקכל המרחיס
כלכ כן יכאר כוה קכול כל הנורות וכל
הכריכותוהאנוליו וכל וה לאות שהשם
ות׳הנוא אחד ומדת רחמיס מתלכשת
למדת סדין וימדתסדין מתלכשתלמדת
רחמיכ וזהוסוד ס׳איס מלחמה ה׳ אחו:
נלחכן מוו דזל כאמרכ ויעבר ה׳ על כניו

ואהריס הוכנא כרסיעיס זה מזה נעין
עטרה עגוליס זס נתיך זה ונסתר
כאמנעיתס כוור לטוט דמות העד
ודמות הרן הפחיס וקולן כפירות
להיותס זכיס ונהיריס כמראה לכן
ספיר דמות ככא ·   והנה מכאן יש
לך להכין וכל מה שפידשׁ לעיל העניו
המקיקות אשר כחכמה כולה ככוי רן
ונמקק· ככלרק׳ע ורקיע מלו הכפירות
והנה ככל אחק מהכ כתינות ושמות
ואותנית וספריך וזהו נזרן:

From "Book of the Creation"
Jacob of Gazolo, Mantua, 1562

in Italian.* In 1622 Judah Samuel of Perugia founded a press apparently under the patronage of Duke Ferdinando Gonzaga and "con licenza dei superiori," with his son Joshua as foreman and Hananiah Marun b. Mordecai as chief printer and although they used old and battered types of the Mantuan and Venetian printers, some of their books are not ill-looking especially in comparison with other productions of those days of the decline of the art. They printed until the death of the Duke in 1626,† and while they were printing their last book, the first of the productions of the press of Amsterdam was being made ready, and the leadership in printing passed from Italy to Holland.

During the interval from the death of the Duke in 1626 until after the Thirty Years War, the Jews of Mantua suffered greatly from mob persecution plagues and military invaders. After the close of that long series of wars in which religious antagonism fused with dynastic policies embroiled Europe until the Treaty of Westphalia, Lombardy which had been the scene of many conflicts began

* Zunz. Zur Gesch. p. 259.
† 1621   Tikkune Bakashot Anshe Maamad
  1622   Massoret haberit
         Ben Shemuel
  1623   Tomer Deborah
         Korban Todah
          Assis Rimmonim
         Tapuhe Zahab
  1624   Yemin Mosheh
         Meire Shahar
  1626   Maabor Yabbok

to revive and the very year of the signing of the
Treaty of Peace marks the revival of the Mantuan
Hebrew press under the direction of Joshua the
son of Judah Samuel of Perugia who had been associated with his father at the press which ended
in 1626, and whose sons in turn carried on the
work intermittently until the seventh decade of
the century,* printing a few books of devotion
and prayer but nothing of any importance.†

   * 1648   Mekiz Nirdamim
      1653   Siddur Miberakah
      1657   Magen Hayim
      1661   Commentary on Perek Shirah
      1662   Prayers
      1664   Mafaresh Hataim
      1667   Seder Nahon
      1670   Shehitah
      1672   Selihot
      1673   Seder Tahanunim
      1678   Mantua Tekanot
      1695   Statutes of the Congregation
† Zunz. Zur. Gesch. u. Lit. 259–261.

CHAPTER XIV.

THE RESUMPTION OF THE PRESS AT VENICE.

The Press at Padua—The New Presses at Venice—The Hebrew Press Exempt from the General Decline of Printing —The Zanetti Family—Giorgio di Cavalli—The Popularity of the Law Codes—Giovanni Grifio—Giovanni di Gara the "Heir of Bomberg"—The Fame of the di Gara Press— Printing Then and Now—The Law of 1571 Forbidding Jews to Print—The Blunders of Christian Compositors—Isaac Gerson and His Opinion on Index and Table of Contents— New Regulations Concerning License—Sixtus V—Alvise Bragadini and Meir Parenzo—The Types of Guillaume le Be.

IN 1563 the ban that seems to have been on Hebrew typography in Venice was removed, and the resumption of Hebrew printing began at Padua which had been under the dominion of Venice since 1405 and had never had a Hebrew press. This press did not survive its second book, for after Lorenzo Pasquato and his associates published the "Way of Faith" by Meir b. Gabbai * for Messer Sidro del Portel Vecchio in 1563 and the Homilies of Shemtob b. Shemtob in 1567 † for Messer Piero del Portel Vecchio, we hear no more of Hebrew printing in Padua until 1622.

The Jews were not favored in Padua and were being gradually enmeshed by the restrictions under

* Derekh Emunah finished 27 Tebet 5323, corrector Samuel Boehm who fled to Italy from Bohemia where his father Isaac Boehm had suffered martyrdom for his faith. See introduction to the Derekh Emunah.

† Derashot Hatorah.

Title page of " The Way of Faith "
Pasquato, Padua, 1563

which they suffered in Venice. In 1602, after a half century of clerical agitation that began the very year in which the first of the five books of Padua appeared, she introduced the ghetto, that characteristic institution of the later middle ages which owes its formal establishment to Venice. The University of Padua, however, was in some respects well disposed toward the Jews; it permitted them to register in its faculty of medicine and it supported their efforts to join the guild of booksellers, for the students were thereby enabled to buy their text books more cheaply. It seems that the Christian booksellers successfully excluded the Jews for the reason so often assigned then and even now that the Jews undersold their Christian competitors; and the economic absurdity of maintaining high prices by establishing monopolies prevailed to the regret and chagrin of the University authorities and students.* Although the Hebrew press at Padua contributed very little to Jewish literature, we in America may well remember this city, for at a much later date there lived and died there Giuseppe Almanzi, scholar and bibliophile, whose great collection of Hebrew books came into possession of Columbia University through the munificence of the Temple Emanuel of New York.

At Venice the presses were soon extraordinarily active. Five independent Christian printers took up Hebrew printing at about the same time and

* Putnam 1 : 193–4.

soon Bragadini, Di Gara, Zanetti, Grifio and Cavalli were in active competition for the Hebrew book trade. In non-Hebrew printing it was this competition, this zealous bidding for the favor of an ever expanding market that compelled the printers to cheapen their wares, and of course produce works of inferior workmanship. Venetian books were threatened with official exclusion from Rome on account of their inaccuracy and general inferiority and copyists and caligraphers were again in demand to prepare texts for those who cared for artistic excellence and scholarly accuracy.* It is remarkable that this general condition of decline did not affect Hebrew texts, probably because the editors and correctors employed were pious men to whom the preparation of Hebrew texts was still as of old, a "holy work"; and also because the printers who undertook their publication belonged to that class of craftsmen who were not yet prepared to sacrifice everything for the sake of mere gain. Cristoforo Zanetti was one of those who cultivated Greek and for whom Guillaume le Bé cut Greek type in 1548, the same Guillaume who cut Hebrew type for Giustiniani, Meir Parenzo and others.†

Zanetti was classed with Giolito, the Aldine family, Gardoni, who printed the Shulhan Arukh in 1577–78, and others who still maintained the ancient reputation of the Venetian press.‡ He

* Brown "Venet. Printing Press" 99.
† Brown "Venet. Printing Press" 104.
‡ Brown "Venet. Printing Press" 100.

first printed Hebrew in 1564 at the order of Di Gara and in the following two years produced on his own account several Hebrew books of good quality.*

In 1593–96 Matteo Zanetti associated with Comino Presigno† published a few books and Matteo's heirs continued the press under the superintendence of Daniel Zanetti who at the same time was printing in his own house in the Calle de Dogan. Finally in 1606 Zanetto or Zuan Zanetti took charge and printed Hebrew until 1608 after which no Hebrew books appear at this press.

A PARTIAL LIST OF BOOKS OF THE ZANETTI PRESS

    1593   Biure Rashi
    1595   Seder Hanikkud
    1596   Dibre Shalom
    1597   Vayakhel Mosheh
           Ho'il Mosheh
    1598   Tanna de Be Eliyahu
    1599   Leshon Zabah
           Tiferet Israel
    1601   Keter Shem tob
    1602   Responsa of Asher ben Yehiel

* 1565   Darke Hatalmud
  1566   Pentateuch
         Midrash Hane'elam
  1567   Rashi on Pentateuch & Megillot (Ersch & Gruber
            59)
† Ersch & Gruber 59.

1602   Hekhal Adonai
          Responsa of Menahem Azariah
          Commentary on Malachi
1603   Urim vethummim
          Magen Abraham
1604   Bet Hauzieli
1605   Mili d'aboth
1606   Lehem Mishneh
          Lehem Dim'a
          Imre Shefer
          Responsa of Joseph ibn Leb
          Abodat Hakodesh
          Bedek Habayit
          Mashbit Milhamot
          Mishnah in Spanish
1608   Pirke d'Rabbi Eliezer
          Apiryon Shelomoh

Daniel Zanetti's most interesting publication is a volume of translations from the Hebrew, by Deborah Ascarelli a poetess of renown far beyond her native city who wrote equally well in Hebrew, Latin and Italian. Her most notable work is her Italian version of the Hebrew text of "The Temple of the Supplicants," part of a larger work written by Moses of Rieti, who was Rabbi in Rome in the second half of the fifteenth century and private physician to Pope Pius II.* "The Temple of the

* Although, according to Graetz, Moses of Rieti's work lacks style and depth as well as poetic imagination, it has long been known as a Jewish Divina Commedia; it is notable in that it successfully introduced the terza rima into Hebrew poetry.

Title page of Responsa
Zanetti, Venice, 1602

Supplicants" was first translated by Lazaro da Viterbo, whose text was printed by Giovanni di Gara in 1585; then followed the translation of Deborah Ascarelli, which was edited for the aged poetess by David della Rocca a distinguished Talmudic scholar who also wrote the introduction.* Giorgio or Zorzo di Cavalli, a new comer in the field was assisted by the veteran Vittorio Eliano, "grandson of the greatest of the grammarians Eliah Bahur",† Abraham Ayllon one of the Rabbis of Venice and Samuel Boehm who had helped Pasquato print his first Hebrew book at Padua.‡ Upwards of a dozen books appeared at his press ¶ among them several of the great codes and com-

* Vogelstein & Rieger 2 : 264.

† See Meir Iyob 1567.

‡ The Cavalli were an ancient Veronese family who had been made Venetian patricians for services rendered to the State by Giacomo Cavalli at Candia (Moreri, Dict.). It is not improbable that Marinus de Caballi, a Paduan knight who licensed the publication of the Derekh Emunah at Padua, was a kinsman of Giorgio di Cavalli.

¶ 1565   Tur Eben Haezer

1566   Mishle Hahamim

En Yaakob

Midrash Rabba

Bahya on the Pentateuch

Yesod Mora

1567   Meir Iyob

Abkab Rohel

Nahlat Abot

Zeror Hamor

Kolbo

Shulhan Arukh

1568   Mahzor (Polish rite)

Mahzor (German rite)

Ele Hadebarim (record of a divorce case)

Sine dato Parshiyot for Monday and Thursday etc. Ersch & Gruber 59.

Title page of the record of the Divorce Proceeding of
Samuel Ventorozo
Cavalli, Venice, 1566

pendia of the law. These were the favorite books of the time, a time of no great legal originality or development but of painstaking examination of the law as it had survived from past ages and of overwrought zeal in preserving it unchanged. The Jewish authorities had to a certain extent taken color from their Christian environment, and the exponents of orthodox tradition were never more fiercely insistent upon its sanctity and immobility than in the sixteenth and seventeenth centuries. Here and there a scholar of originality ventured to suggest departures from the beaten paths, but the time was not favorable to such free flights and their attempts were of little avail. The results of the labor of the great men of former days who were unhampered by the restrictions that the Church had laid upon later generations, seemed in the eyes of their successors, immured in dark ghettos and hemmed about by inhuman legislation, to be the fruit of such extraordinary genius that it was akin to impiety to even venture to criticise them. In the Christian world the efforts of the Inquisition to suppress free thought were still successful, although the increase of heresy indicated that a new time was approaching. The printer's mark of Cavalli, the elephant bearing a castle, and its significant motto may be interpreted to indicate how the times were changed. The elephant marches "tarde sed tuto," slowly but surely, like the march of enlightenment that led men out of the darkness of the Middle Ages.

A third Venetian printer who entered the field of Hebrew typography at this time was Giovanni Grifio * probably related to the Gryphos of Lyons and having like them the mark of the griffin holding a stone in its claws from which a winged globe is suspended.†   Although he had excellent assistants, notably Samuel Boehm, Meshullam Kaufman, Solomon Luzatto and Samuel Archevolti, and published five books in 1567,‡ a notable achievement in view of the magnitude of several of them and the care required in their editing, he seems to have given up Hebrew printing after this year.   Perhaps like Zanetti and Cavalli of Venice and Pasquato of Padua he realized in his attempt to compete with Di Gara and Bragadini, that, as he expressed it in his various printer's mottos, "wisdom without good luck accomplishes little." ¶

Of all the printers who resumed after 1563, the only ones who survived for any length of time were the houses of Di Gara and Bragadini.   Since Aldo Manuzio had made Venetian typography

---

* This form of the name seems more correct than Grypho as Stein-schneider gives it.

† Fumagalli 492.

‡ Turim

Shulhan Arukh

Sforno's commentary on Pentateuch

Abodat Hakodesh

Genesis Rabba

Ersch & Gruber 59.

¶ "Virtute duce, comite fortuna."

"Poco val la vertù senza fortuna."

"Beli hashpiat tob hamazalot, me'at mo'ilot hamuskilot."

synonymous with inimitable excellence and Daniel Bomberg, following in his footsteps, had produced models of typographical perfection, Venice had maintained her hegemony among the book producing cities of the world and had preserved the traditions of these masters. The types of Bomberg or imitations of them found their way into the printing houses of Northern Europe, but most of his fonts eventually came into the possession of Giovanni di Gara who proud of his assumed title as "heir of Bomberg," * emulated his predecessor and produced a great number of books, many of them worthy to take their place with the best productions of Bomberg. The activity of Daniel Bomberg and Giovanni di Gara practically spans the entire sixteenth century, and the combined output of their presses is an enduring monument to Hebrew printing in Venice. It seems that the heirs of Bomberg kept up some sort of an establishment long after the founder's death, for Di Gara printed some of his early books "in the house of Bomberg" † and used the press of Cristoforo Zanetti ‡ for the production of others before printing Hebrew at his own press.

At the beginning of his career as a Hebrew printer, Di Gara used the very type that printed the books of Bomberg and advertised the fact in

* Seder Maamadot 1564, Servus Bombergii a pueritia, Rabb. Bible 1568.

† Tur Eben Haezer 1565

‡ Seder Maamadot 1564.

many of his publications until "with letters of Bomberg" became a mere form and simply meant in the Bomberg style. There was a good deal of "borrowing" among the printers, and title pages and style of types are often no indication of the place of publications. The characteristic title page of Di Gara, a Roman arch whose pillars are garlanded with flowers and fruits, was copied in books issuing from the presses of Lublin,* Cracow † and Bistrowitz ‡ in Poland. So on the other hand, Di Gara imitated the title pages of Meir the Scribe of Mantua,¶ and then of Foa of Sabbioneta ** though not until after these presses had ceased publication. For many years the presses of Di Gara and Bragadini seem to have been on terms of close business relations for Bragadini's foreman Asher Parenzo superintended work done for his master at Di Gara's press,†† and we find not only the three crowns of the Bragadini printers' mark on the title pages of Di Gara's books,‡‡ but the three crowns and the small single crown of Di Gara on the same page.¶¶

In considering the productivity of the Hebrew press we must not allow our judgment to be in-

* Maharil 1590.
† Tolaat Yaakob 1581.
‡ Zebah Pesah 1592.
¶ Yesha Elohim & Marpe lenefesh 1595.
** Arugat Habosem and Hamekah vehamemkar 1602.
†† Nefuzot Yehudah 1589.
‡‡ Nefuzot Yehudah 1589; Torat Haadam 1595; Mahzor 1600.
¶¶ Kol Bokhim 1591.

באור על התורה

אשר חבר אזן וחקר

הגאון השלם האלהי כמהר"ר

עובדיה ספורנו

אביר הרופאים

זלה"ה ·

נדפס פה ויניציאה

בבית מי' זואן גריפו שנת שב"ז לפ"ק

Title Page of Sforno's Commentary on the Pentateuch
Grifio, Venice, 1567

fluenced by what we know of the possibilities of the modern press. In those days there were no regular lists of subscribers; Jewish communities were neither numerous nor large, methods of transportation were primitive, and communication was possible only along highways whose passage was beset with dangers unknown to modern travelers. The printers worked from hand to mouth, risking their enterprises on the uncertain seas of public demand and trimming their sails continually to meet the shifting winds of ecclesiastical whims and prejudices. To-day printers need fear neither edict nor decree; no censor passes upon their manuscripts or mutilates the productions of their press. When Di Gara sought to employ Jewish compositors he was met by a decree of the Venetian Senate that "no Jew may work at the press or print books under penalty of confiscation of the property and payment of a fine of one hundred ducats." *

Giovanni di Gara's enforced use of Christian typesetters † makes clear the complaint of Rabbi Isaac Gerson, di Gara's editor-in-chief, who regretted the errors that crept into the texts of his books because, as he put it, "Everybody knows ‡

* "In the year 1571, 18th December, the Senate made a general order forbidding Jews to print at all: non possa alcun hebreo lavorar di stampa ne far stampare libri, et contrafacendo incorrino in pena di perder la robba, et pagar ducati cento. Et quelli che facessero stampar sotto nome de Christiani incorrino nell istessa pena et li libri stampati si intendano esser et siano di colui in nome de chi fussero stati stampati." Brown, "Venetian Printing Press" 106.

† Ersch & Gruber 58.

‡ Epigraph to Reshit Hokhmah, 1578; see also Bine Sefer Kohelet, 1577.

how the taskmasters drive in the press-room crying 'hurry up your work and finish the quota of the press,' for it is the rule to turn out a certain number every day and they do not give the correctors any rest. As to this book there is to be added that the greater part of it was printed by Christians during the month of Tishri, the greater part of which is taken up with Sabbaths and holy days, and a third trouble was that the editor was deceived and confused and there was no one to assist him. From this time, it is quite common to find such complaints in the epigraph against the ignorance and carelessness of the workmen,* whose errors Isaac Gerson likened to the fabled evil spirits born at twilight on Friday evening when the call of the Sabbath summoned the corrector, and the workmen were left to do their will.

Di Gara would have been glad to save himself the cost of correcting the many errors made by his Christian compositors and, whenever possible, he employed Jews at his Hebrew press as proof readers and editors and in any other capacity permitted by the law. Among his assistants were such men as Asher Parenzo † brother of the more famous Meir Parenzo, and one of the family of printers well known and esteemed in Italy; Samuel Archevolti, a scholar who published some of his own books at di Gara's press,‡ Israel, the

* H. B. 18: 113, 114; epigraph to Khozari 1594.

† Asher was born in a printing house.

‡ Among them a well known Hebrew grammar, characteristically called "The Bed of Spices."

son of Daniel Zifroni * and his son Elishama members of a well known family of Hebrew printers; Leon da Modena, distinguished as a rabbi in Venice and one of the most brilliant scholars of his time, and lastly Isaac Gerson who in the employ of the various printing houses for upwards of thirty years, according to the statement of David Conforte the historian, "corrected all of the books printed in Venice." Gerson deserves the gratitude of posterity, for he was one of the first among Jewish scholars to recognize the importance of a good index and table of contents. Without them he never permitted a book to pass his hands, for he deemed them "as important for a book as eyes for a man." †

The great problem of the publishers and printers was to conform to the rules of the Inquisition. The sleepless vigilance of the guardians of the faith allowed nothing to escape their vision. Toward the end of the sixteenth century examination and expurgation of books before printing had been pretty well established throughout Italy, and a license to print had to appear next to the title page of each publication. Thus, in a book of Norzi ‡ you may find the following: "The three works above named by the same author have been revised and expurgated by the Rev. Father Don

---

* Ersch & Gruber 58, note 9.

† Zifroni also appreciated the importance of indexes.   See colophon of Seder Hayom 1604.

‡ Marpe le-Nefesh, 1579.

Title page of "Health to the Soul"
Di Gara, Venice, 1584

Marco Marino da Brescia and printed by Giovanni di Gara in Venice with the permission of the authorities." "Con licentia dei superiori" is found on every book issuing from this and the other Venetian presses of the time, and represented the right of the State to refuse to sanction publication of a book even though the Ecclesiastical censors had passed it.*

The hope entertained by the Jews that the reign of Pope Sixtus V would inaugurate a new and better era was justified, for within half a year after he ascended the throne he issued a bill repealing all previous restrictions against the Jews, allowing them to live openly in Italy and to keep their Hebrew books, provided they had been expurgated in accordance with the rules of the Council of Trent. The Jews were so elated that they even entertained the thought of petitioning for the privilege of issuing a new edition of the Talmud, an act that would have been sheer madness during the reign of any one of the predecessors of Sixtus since the time of Paul IV. For the purpose of properly undertaking a censorship of the Talmud and all its "glosses, notes, interpretations and expositions" the Congregation of the Index

* Manzoni, p. 108, states that he is of opinion that Di Gara's editors first introduced a significant change in the text of the Khozari published 1594 with commentary by Judah Moscato. The author says, "I have been asked what arguments or replies I had to those who disagree with us, among publishers and men of other faiths," to which in Di Gara's edition there were added the words "except Christians."

had directed the translation of the entire work into Latin, inasmuch as most of the members of the Congregation did not understand Hebrew. This enormous difficulty was removed, however, by the brief of the Pope, who authorized the revision of the Talmud by those members of the Congregation who understood Hebrew. A further indication of the change of sentiment on the part of the ecclesiastical authorities was the invitation extended by the Cardinals in charge of the revision to seven representatives of the Jews of Italy to meet them to decide upon rules to govern the censorship. This meeting was in fact held, the rules agreed upon and a committee appointed by the Cardinals for the purpose of undertaking the revision, which had as its final object the re-publication of the Talmud. But within two weeks after the appointment of the revisers Pope Sixtus V died, his successor Pope Urban VII died within a month after his election, and with the accession of Pope Gregory XIV all hope for the re-publication of the Talmud with the consent of the Pope was abandoned.

Sixtus V was no fanatical zealot like some of his predecessors, but rather a wily diplomat who had secured his election by feigning insignificance and mildness and showed extraordinary powers as a statesman and ruler after he had attained the summit of his ambition. In him was again exemplified the fact often illustrated in the history of the Papacy, that the Jews had much less to fear from a Pope who was given to politics than from one who took himself seriously as the head of the Church and laid stress upon the importance of its function in the spread and maintenance of religion. As though to emphasize the difference between Pope and Church, de Pomis' dictionary printed with the Pope's consent dedicated to him and bearing his arms was like the books bearing the imprimatur of Cardinal Madrucci of Riva di Trento, impudently but piously "revised" by the censors, and the copy lying before me bears the marks of their disfiguring hand and the fading yellow signatures with which they finally approved the "purified" book.

No attempt is here made to give a complete list of the publications of di Gara, but the entire Jewish literature was drawn on,—law and philosophy, natural science and mysticism, grammar and lexicography, in fact all of the known branches of learning were enriched by some specimen of his press.

BOOKS PRINTED BY DI GARA.*

1565   Tur Eben Haezer
        Responsa of Levi ibn Habib
1568   Rabbinical Bible
1574   Responsa of Saul Cohen & Isaac Abrabanel
        Tur Yore Deah
1576   Mizmor Letodah

* The list represents about one-half of the output of his presses.

SIXTO V. PONT·MAX
ATQVE BEATISSIMO.

ÆLICISSIMVS ille dies, (Beatiſſime, atq; San
ctiſſime pontifex) orbi terarum illuxit, in quo
te Deus ad pontificatus culmen euexit. Salutaré
vniuerſis, & optabilem principatum, præclaro
initio auſpicatus es. Nulla vnquàm mortaliụm
memoria in Pont. Maximo eligendo concor-
dia maior, nulla præclarior; nulla ſalubrior electio. ingenti profe-
ctò ſtudio, maximo affectu, tuę huius ad principatum aſſumptionis
gloria, ab omnibus excepta conſtantiſſimè eſt; quinimmo hac oc-
caſione, atq; hòc ipſo tempore, nil optatius, ardentiuſue, expectari
poterat. Animum erectum, & ſublimen, ſemper habuiſti; Nihil
ex ore tuo fictum, nihil vanum, omnia ingenuæ rectitudinis plena,
integræq; veritatis, à te prodire comperta ſunt. Quæ & multa alia
Cœlitus tibi ſortita dona, te ſicuti in Præclariſſimo Reuerendiſſi-
morum, & Illuſtriſſ. Cardinalium ſenatu collocarunt, ſic eam ſemper de te ſpem ſpoponderunt, quàm hoc duntaxat ſolio preſtare
potes; in quo te tandem Diuina prouidentia conſtituto, (veluti ſpe
rabamus) tua Beatitudo ventorum noſtrorum rabiem vnius tuæ
iuſſionis momento compeſcuit. Hoc tuæ gloriæ reſeruatú, vt poſt
noſtrā difficillimā oppreſſionē, tuæ Beatitudinis clementię, ęqui-
tatiſq; corona, preclarior, maiorq; reddatur. Hęc vera Principis
laus exiſtit, vt quamcunq; in partem vertat oculos, omnia manſue-

A 2   tiora

Dedication of De Pomis' Hebrew Dictionary to Pope
Sixtus V. showing Papal Arms
Di Gara, Venice, 1587

1577 Gallico's Commentary on Ecclesiastes
1578 Reshit Hokhmah
1579 Seah Solet
     Marpe Lenefesh
     Orah Hayim
1585 Menot Halevi (Comm. on Esther)
     Maon Hashoalim
     Hamon's Commentary on Ruth
1586 Hazon Lamoed
1587 Shalshelet Hakabbalah
     Perush Seder Abodat Yom Hakippurim
     Psalms
     Zemah David
     Or Neerab
1588 Heshek Shelomo
     Maamez Ruah
     Debek Tob
1589 Yoreh Hataim
     Nefuzot Yehudah
     Shaare Gan Eden
1590 Oheb Mishpat
1591 Habazelet Hasharon
     Kol Bokhim
     Haftarot
1593 Reshit Hokhmah
     Shulhan Arukh
1594 Khozari
1595 Yesha Elohim
     Marpe Lenefesh
     Torat Haadam
     Tur Hoshen Mishpat

1595	Menorat Hamaor
	Bible
1597	Yeriot Izim
	Asarah Maamarot
1598	Iggeret Dofi Hazeman
1600	Mahzor
1601	Sefer Hahinnukh
	Arze Lebanon
1602	Arugat Habosem
	Hamekah Vehamemkar
1603	Maase Adonai
	Marot Hazobot
1604	Seder Hayom
1605	Responsa of Alshekh
	Commentary on Semag by Joseph of Crementz
	Torah Or
	Bet Moed
	Hibbur Maasiyot
1607	Massorot
	Mikveh Israel
1608	Lehem Setarim
1609	Toldot Yaakob
	Sifra
	Mishnah *

The Hebrew Press of Venice from the middle of the sixteenth well into the eighteenth century was dominated by the House of Bragadini con-

*After 1609 we hear no more of Di Gara though as late as 1616 a mahzor is printed "in his house."

nected with many a family whose name is inscribed in the Golden Book from Alvise the founder of the house, down to Alvise III the last known member. Alvise, Giovanni, Pietro, Lorenzo, Alvise II, Girolamo, Giacomo, Vicenzo, Nicolo, Vicenzo II, Alvise III,—these are the generations of the Bragadini, proprietors of the Stamperia Bragadina whose books went out to all corners of the earth, to the depths of Poland and Russia to the North Sea to Holland and France to the Barbary Coast and to the recesses of the land of the Crescent.* Even their political and social influence as members of a family who together with the Giustiniani Cornaro and Bembo families were known as the four evangelists—the oldest families of Venice,† could not withstand the zeal of the dominant elements in the Church and in 1551 they suffered with the other Hebrew presses at Venice.

After the "Strong Hand" of Maimonides published in 1551 which provoked the quarrel with the house of Giustiniani, Alvise Bragadini printed a number of books until the interdict in 1554,‡ and

---

* The later chiefs of the House of Bragadini farmed out some of their work to the presses of Lorenzo Pradotto, Domenico Vedelago, the Calleoni, Cristoforo Ambrosio, Giovanni dei Ragazzi and Giovanni dei Pauli.

† Moreri "le grand dictionnaire historique" art. "Bragadini."

‡ 1551   Yad Hahazakah
        Kiryat Sefer
        More Nebukhim
        Yore Deah
  1552   Alfasi
        Birkat Abraham
        Responsa of Asher b. Yehiel

Title page of Cordovero's " Sweet Light "
Di Gara, Venice, 1587

upon the resumption of Hebrew printing in 1563 he printed until his death in 1575.*

Bragadini was fortunate in having as his foreman so able and skilled a printer as Meir ben Jacob Parenzo. His forefathers had come from the Dalmatian coast and settled in the capital † and some time before the year 1545 Meir Parenzo learned his craft in the shop of the prince of printers Daniel Bomberg, where he was associated with Cornelio Adelkind.

Meir's father was also a member of the craft and his death in 1546 is piously commemorated by his son in these words published in the colophon of a Yalkut issued in that year, "And now while I was in the midst of this work, alas the light of my eyes and the crown of my head was taken away, the pious one who was sought in the Court of Heaven, behold it was my father my master the distinguished Rabbi Jacob ibn Parenzo may his memory be a blessing. These are the words of

1553 Mesharim
      Responsa of Meir of Padua
      Arukh
      Mayan Gannim
      Iggeret Derekh Adonai
1554 Megillat Setarim

* Some of his books were:—
    1563 Tur Orah Hayyim
    1564 Meir Natib
    1565 Akedat Yizhak
  1574–75 Mishne Torah

† Manzoni thought he was a Frenchman and that his name should be read Franzoni. In the Kozari 1547 he says in colophon "I am the printer known as Meir of Parenzo as that is the name of my city."

him who is engaged in this work of God, Meir ibn Parenzo who mourns his father." *   After a short term of service at the press of Giustiniani he entered the employ of the House of Bragadini with whom he remained until his death, bearing to them the same relation as that of Adelkind to the house of Bomberg.† It is noteworthy that the Bragadini employed members of the family of Parenzo until far into the seventeenth century. The books published by Meir Parenzo are many of them quite as handsome as those published by Adelkind and show no sign of the approaching decline of the Venetian press.   Although our records of Meir's activity are exceedingly meagre his training in the shops of Bomberg and Giustiniani where he met the artists and skilled craftsmen of his time, his association with the distinguished French engraver and typecutter Guillaume le Be,‡ his printer's

* Meir attempted to print on his own account, probably at the Bomberg press in 1548–49, Yalkut, Meshal Hakadmoni, Khozari, Issur vehetter, during which time he is recorded as an independent printer in Cicogna's list as Mazo de Parenzo.   Brown "Venet. Print. Press." In 1549 he printed part of the Mishnah in the house of Carlo Quirino. Cat. Bodl. 9496.

† Meir and Cornelio collaborated, see p. 187.

‡ The way in which the type was produced was as follows:—The artist, first of all, cut upon a punch of hard metal a raised form of each letter.   The excellence of his fount depended on the skill with which he executed this part of his business; his whole artistic resources were expended to render the form on the punch as perfect as possible.   Impressions were taken from these punches in soft metal, and these were called the matrices (matres) or moulds, from which the actual type was founded.   The type, by use, might become blunt; the moulds, by use, might lose their clearness of line; but as long as the hard metal punches retained their form intact, the typographer could always renew

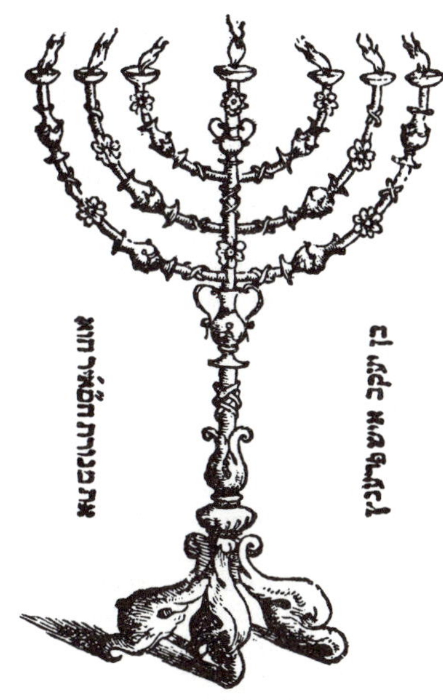

Title page of Mashal Hakadmoni
Meir Parenzo, Venice, 1546

mark the beautiful candelabrum, the illustrations published in his Mashal Hakadmoni, all indicate that Meir Parenzo was not only a skillful but an artistic printer.

There is some suggestion that Guillaume le Be had a law suit with Giustiniani arising out of a font of type, which was cut for Meir by Guillaume

his fount. Punches lasted a long time. Jenson employed his one set during his eleven years of copious work, and they were worth bequeathing to his compeer Ugelleymer in 1480. And the punches for the type from which Aldus printed Bembo's Aetna, in 1495, lasted sixty years from that date. Brown, "Venet. Print. Press" page 18. Guillaume cut type for Giustiniani as well as Parenzo. M. Omont, in his monograph on the types of Guillaume Le Be, shows that Le Be, who was a pupil of Robert Etienne, came to Venice in 1545, and there cut Hebrew type for Marc' Antonio Giustinian, a Venetian noble who owned a Hebrew press at the Rialto, in the Calle delli Cinque alla Justizia Vecchia. Le Be talks of this type as la premiere de mes ouvrages, aage lors de 20 ans et huict moys. Le Be stayed in Venice till the year 1550, when he went to Rome for the jubilee of Pope Julius III. During his five years sojourn in Venice he cut two kinds of Hebrew type for Giustinian and six kinds of Hebrew type for Mazo da Parenza. The fourth and fifth of Le Be's Hebrew types were cut coubz l'adveu de magnifique bout d'une ruelle regardant sur le quay de la Madona de l'Orto. The sixth character was cut aussy en acier, faicte a Venize pour le dit May de Parensa, en une chambre que je tenoye a loyage a un ducat par moys, ayant veue sur le Camp de St. Lio, a coste de l'eglise. Le Be was in the habit of cutting his own name and that of Venice on the punches which he made there. His seventh Hebrew type was cast while he was at Rome for the papal jubilee, and his eighth was cut before the preceding character. But while Le Be was absent from Venice celui a qui je laissay mesdits poinsons en garde on a fait des frappa et tout mange, ayant vendue et poinsons et matrices a un Allemant, ainsy que de Dansi m'ont mande. While in Venice Le Be made drawings and designs for various characters, which he preserved, and used in Paris as patterns for his fifteenth Hebrew type. The name of Mazo da Parenza does not occur in the copyrights; the name of Marc' Antonio Giustinian is recorded in Cicogna's list of Venetian printers. Brown, "Venet. Print. Press," pp. 105–106.

le Bé, but the reason for the suit is unknown and we can only guess at its cause. Another engraver Jacob of Mantua seems to have cut type for Meir Parenzo while he was in the employ of Giustiniani.*

Meir Parenzo, somewhat more than his contemporaries, made a pathetic bid for immortality by elaborately spreading his name on title page, introduction and colophon. But the trumpet of fame sounds no very loud note, and even the great brazen instruments that herald the deeds of the chosen ones sound but a faint echo when heard through the long corridors of the centuries. Meir Parenzo, notwithstanding his hope for immortality, is completely forgotten except by a small circle of Hebrew bibliographers who, although conscious that the individual contributions of the men they commemorate are negligible in the great current of human affairs as it flows majestically down through the ages, nevertheless hand down the names of those who sleep in the dust and preserve knowledge of the existence of so many faithful men who have contributed their share to the enlightenment of the world.

* R. E. J. 16 : 308; Omont p. 7.

CHAPTER XV.

THE SEVENTEENTH CENTURY AND AFTER.

The Press of the Vendramini—The Succession of the Bragadini—The Tribulations of Jewish Bookmen—The Story of Leon da Modena—The Decline of Italy and Rise of the Netherlands—The Perpetual Interference of the Venetian Authorities and its Effect—The New Presses in Northern Europe Rise at the Expense of Venice—The Paltry Output of Other Italian Presses—Padua and Verona—The Story of Rabbi Abraham Saba—The Decline of Hebrew Printing— Chieri and Asti—The Humility of the Bookmen—The Polacco Family and the Foa—Sporadic Presses at Pisa, Mantua—The Rise and Progress of the Press at Leghorn— Florence—Modern Conditions in Italy.

THE last of the important presses of Venice was established in 1631 by Giovanni Vendramin and conducted in his name until 1640, after which it was known as the Commissaria Vendramina and the Stamperia Vendramina and after its union with the Bragadini press, it continued until well into the eighteenth century. The old flourishing press of the Di Gara and the less important one of Zanetti had come to a standstill in 1608–1609, unable to compete with the more powerful house of Bragadini, and oppressed by the persecuting mania that had finally attacked the presses of Venice, as well as all the rest of Italy. Of all of these noted presses there remained only the inconspicuous press at Leghorn, which although established in 1650 did not really flourish until 1740.

The House of Bragadini continued to enjoy a monopoly of Hebrew printing in Venice under Giovanni son of Alvise Bragadini who succeeded his father about 1579 and who in turn in 1614 passed it on to his sons Pietro and Lorenzo. Giovanni's chief printer was Asher Parenzo, the brother of Meir Parenzo who had held a similar position at the press of his father.* After his

פה ווניציאה

Printer's mark of Alvise Bragadini

brother's death Asher seemed at a loss for a time and finally to use his own phrase, after turning this way and that and seeing no one assisting in the work of the press, he sat at the crossroads and watched for good books to help their publication.†

* See p. 368.

† See Mikrae Kodesh 1586; among the books printed by him are:—

1583	Reshith Daat
1586	Mikrae Kodesh
1589	Nefuzot Yehudah
1591	Pentateuch
1594	Shenem Asar Derashat

In 1614 the press passed into the hands of Pietro and Lorenzo Bragadini who joined by Alvise II in 1624 and Vicenzo, Nicolo, Giacomo and Girolamo in 1639 remained in possession until 1650 after which Girolamo Bragadini appears to have continued alone. During the time of Pietro and Lorenzo the principal printer at their press was Giovanni Cajun * and the owners had become "clarissimi" and "illustrissimi signori" who no longer took any personal interest in their press but enjoyed an income from it without soiling their hands. Another printer who probably printed at their press was Giacomo Sarzino who printed several books of Leon Modena † and who was probably the same person as Jacob Sorzinah of Castellaz corrector of the press of Zanetti. Giacomo also was troubled by the compositors, that reckless class of workmen that has disturbed the happiness of publishers and authors even to our own days, for he says ‡ "a very beautiful and divine invention would printing be if it were not subject to fall into errors, and indeed, without exaggerating, it turns out very few books that are well done." ¶

* Some of his books are:—
    1617   Heshek Shelomoh
    1618   Shete Yadot and Responsa of Meir Lublin
    1619   Commentary on Canticles and Ez Shatul
† 1612   Galut Yehudah
  1617   Leb Yehudah
‡ Colophon of Galut Yehudah.
¶ Troppo bella e divina inventione sarebbe la stampa de libri, se non fosse sottoposta ad incorrervi errori e ben che dove piu dove meno, pochissime pero sono quelle opere di essa, che ne escano nette a fatto.

Following Cajun came Giovanni Caleoni as the chief printer at this press * some of the books being printed in his house, Antonio Calleoni,† and Lorenzo Pradotto.‡ From 1667 to the end of the century, the press seems to have been known as the Stamparia Bragadina and not connected specially with names of any of that family and during this time, among its printers, were Cristofolo Ambrosini,¶ Giovanni Doriguzzi,** and Domenico Bona.††

A Typical Bragadini ornament

*	1623	Orhoth Hayim
	1625	Bet Lehem Yehudah
	1626	Kenaf Renanim
		Mahzor
	1628	Hibbur Havoth Yair
	1640	Pi Aryeh
	1641	Midrash hehadush
†	1644	Pentateuch
	1655	Mishnah
‡	1659	Nahlat Zebi
	1667	Zibhe Zedek
¶	1671	Prayers
	1672	Mahzor and Emet veemunah
**	1670	Kevanat Shelomoh
††	1687	Siddur (Spanish rite).

MASTER PRINTERS AND PUBLISHERS AT
VENDRAMIN PRESS.

1633	Giovanni Caleoni
1636–61	Giovanni Martinelli
1643–51	Francesco Vieceri
1651–56	Giovanni Imberti
1657–65	Antonio Rizzini
1663–64	Domenico Vedelago

CORRECTORS AND FACTORS.

1647	Samuel b. Shemaya
1648–63	Moses Zacut
1653	Jacob b. Naftali Gnesen
1654	Isaac Bingen b. Samuel

PRINTERS, COMPOSITORS, ETC.

1651–64	Venturin b. David
1651	Meir b. Zekhariah of Mestre
1651	Jacob Hayim b. Abraham Flores
1687	Solomon b. Isaiah Nizza
1690	Jacob b. Isaac Levi
1695	Isaac b. Jacob Levi
1690	David b. Solomon Altaras
	Joseph b. Solomon Israel

PARTIAL LIST OF BOOKS OF THE VENDRAMIN
PRESS.

1651	Maase Haya?
1653	Yeven Mezulah?
1654	Maarekhet Elijahu
1655	Tub Haarez

1656 Zophenat Paaneah
1657 Shemen Hatob
     Yefe Toar
1662 Mizbah Yaakob
1663 Mazzil Nefashat
1665 Letters of Maimonides

PARTIAL LIST OF LATER BRAGADINI BOOKS.

1695 Meziz Umeliz
1698 Birkhat Abraham
1704 Hilkhot Ketannot
1706 Tefillot
1712 Bat Melekh & Zera Kodesh
1713 Hobot Halebabot
1720 Ashmoret Haboker
     Hemed Elohim
1728 Tikkun Lel Hoshaanah Rabbah
1730 Tikkun Lel Shabuot
1735 Selihot
1736 Arba Taaniyot
1737 Parshiyot
1739 Bible
1740 Parts of Mishneh Torah
1760 Ozar Nehmad
     Mehadesh Hadashim
1778 Amud di Rashi
1795 Maamadot veshir hayihud

PARTIAL LIST OF BOOKS OF STAMPERIA
BRAGADINA E VENDRAMINA

1700 Yad Haruzim
1703 Or Kadmon

1704   Ez hadaat
1744   Mussar Melakhim
1746   Kore Hadorot
1753   Tikkun for Hoshaana Rabbah
1762   Sekhiyot Hahemda
1772   Mahzor

At the end of the sixteenth century the Jews of Venice had adopted a self-censorship that had rendered them freer from the restrictions of official censorship than in any other Italian state.*

Perhaps nothing will better illustrate the condition of the Hebrew book business and the tribulation of Jewish authors than some biographical extracts from the books of Rabbi Yehuda Aryeh known as Leon of Modena who was rabbi at Venice and who died in 1684. About 1616 he wrote a book in Italian entitled "History of Hebrew Rites", at the request of an English nobleman who desired to present it to the learned King James I of England who was notably interested in theological matters. Knowing that the work was to remain in manuscript and was intended for Protestant readers, Leon da Modena wrote many things that the censors of the Inquisition could not have passed. About twenty years thereafter he showed the manuscript to a noted French scholar Gaffarelli who, after having read it, begged the privilege of printing it in Paris and Leon consented. Two years later on the second day of the Passover

* Popper p. 94.

From Yalkut Shimeoni
Bragadini, Venice, 1566

in 1637 Leon received a letter from Gaffarelli at Paris announcing that the book was printed, whereupon Leon writes: "I became very anxious and hurried to look at the copy of the manuscript which I had kept. I then noticed four or five forcible expressions which the Inquisition had forbidden to be uttered, not to say written or printed. I cried aloud in my terror because I thought that if this work became known in Rome it would become a pitfall for all the Jews, and it would be said, How impudent are these Jews for not only do they instruct Christians in their laws in the vernacular but they even write against our religion and decrees. For myself I expected the most terrible consequences. I exaggerated the danger because, after all, the things that I had said were not so very offensive. As a matter of precaution I entered a preliminary notice at the office of Inquisition stating that a book of mine had appeared through another person without my knowledge and without my revision. I was received in a friendly manner and I finally consoled myself. Shortly thereafter Gaffarelli traveled to Rome and from there sent me a printed copy, and I then saw to my great satisfaction that he himself had been careful enough to strike out the passages that I had feared. He wrote a preface to the book in which he covered me with praise, and dedicated the book to the French Ambassador at Venice who sent me a letter of thanks. Although I was now relieved of my anxiety I was still afraid that much in the book might displease Christians, and this consideration, together with the other that in this Paris edition there were many typographical errors, induced me to prepare a second edition from which I omitted and to which I added whatever I found necessary." *

We shall better understand his fear when we read of the persecution to which he was subjected as related by him in another book "The House of Judah." He says: "In Adar 1634 I began to print my book 'The House of Judah' and I longed for nothing so much as to see it finished and spread throughout Israel, for I felt satisfied that through it I would obtain honor and an immortal name. A long time passed however before it was finished in Heshvan 1635 for in Ellul 1634 informers had slandered the book before the Cattaveri, and as a result the press was closed for six months. Thereafter the work went on again under the direction of my grandson Isaac the Levite who had been engaged in printing for about two years. On the 28th day of Iyyar 1635 my grandson and his two assistants were suddenly arrested at the printing house put into a dark dungeon and the house sealed up and I was much grieved because I was unable to secure their release. However after fifteen days of effort they were permitted to go out from darkness into light, but kept in the prison where they remained for sixty-six days, and I came and went daily in great distress and incurring

* Geiger "Leon Modena."

[382]

great expense. Finally by the mercy of God, the Criminal Court acquitted them on Tammuz the 28th 1635."* Such attacks upon printers were quite common. The officers of the Inquisition without notice to their victims seized them put them away into dark prisons, perhaps the famous dungeons of the ducal castle to which not a ray

צורת החחה גבהל ורוה   ולפני המלך ישתחוה »

From Mashal Hakadmoni
Meir Parenzo, Venice, 1546

of daylight could penetrate, sometimes subjecting them to torture always to a severe inquisitorial investigation. If the prisoners were fortunate enough to be released from such long and merciless incarceration, they were usually broken in health and spirit and unfitted to carry on their work.

The seventeenth century witnessed the gradual decline of the power of Venice. When Vasco da

* Geiger, ibid.

Gama rounded the Cape of Good Hope he struck her maritime supremacy a blow from which she never recovered, for weakened in the very heart of her power she was unable to survive the political catastrophies that followed each other in rapid succession. The Netherlands quick to take advantage of the opportunities offered by trade with the Indies began to develop and prosper, and Antwerp and Amsterdam took the place in the commercial world so long held by Venice.

Contemporaneously with the decline of political and commercial supremacy, Venice together with the rest of Italy suffered from the gradual encroachment of the militant Church. The Papacy which had for several centuries flourished as a political power had gradually undermined the liberties of the Italian States and by its policy of suppression deprived them not only of political initiative, but of all those instrumentalities of progress and civilization necessary to the prosperity of a free State. Education instead of being controlled by learned laymen was relegated to the charge of various monastic orders, and freedom of inquiry and intellectual liberty yielded to ignorance and intolerance, which degraded Italy from her once high estate and inflicted wounds that the efforts of the last half century have not yet been able to heal.

The self-censorship established by the Jews of Venice resulted in the practice of requiring a rabbinical approbation printed after the title page of the books, as a certificate of the orthodoxy of the book and its freedom from passages that might prove offensive to Christians. But this regulation by no means supplanted censorship and there were at least three bodies established by law to check the multiplication of Hebrew books. The Council of Ten in addition to its political and administrative concerns found time to meddle with Hebrew books; the "Essecutori contra la Biastema" were specially created to prevent all sorts of blasphemies, including blasphemies expressed or implied in Hebrew books; the "Reformatori della studio in Padoa" were the university authorities whose approval was required before publication, and finally there were the Cattaveri, a Council or License Board, consisting of three noblemen whose rights were after the beginning of the seventeenth century transferred to the Reformatori.

This board was in charge of many other matters concerning the Jews, and in connection with the supervision of books and the issuance of licenses for publication they particularly exercised the function of raising revenue for State purposes. After the book had run the gauntlet of criticism a license was issued by the Council of Ten, in form substantially like the following one which appears in the edition of Leon da Modena's "Heart of the Lion"—

"The undersigned, the most excellent Signori, Chiefs of the Excellent Council of Ten, having faith in the Signori, the Supervisors of Study at

Padua, namely, in the report made by two of them delegated for that purpose, to wit, the Rev. Father Inquisitor and the Secretary of the Senate, Giovanni Maraviglia, who have made oath that in the book entitled 'Lev,' i.e., 'Heart of the Lion,' they found nothing against the law and that it is worthy to be printed—grant a license that it may be printed in this city.

Given the 5th day of May, 1612.

(Signed) D. ZUANE DANDOLO,
D. AND. CONTARINI,
D. GIUST. ANTO. BELEGNO,
Chiefs of the Exc. Council of X.
BARTH. COMINUS,
Secretary of the Illust. Council of X.

Registered, etc.

ANT. LAURED,
Notary of the Office Against Blasphemy."

We are not surprised to learn that toward the end of the seventeenth century Hebrew books had become quite rare in Venice, for the history of the Hebrew press indicates the history of the larger movement that affected all Europe. With the decline of Italy under the yoke of the Church came the rise of the free States of Northern Europe which had won their religious and political independence.

When Cardinal Richelieu was engaged in building up the Bibliotheque Nationale at Paris a correspondent of his special agent sent to collect Hebrew books reported that there was not a single

Jewish library in Venice, and that the only things published there were prayer books and rituals.* The Hebrew printers had been driven from their ancient home to seek an asylum elsewhere. The presses established at Constantinople in 1503 and Salonica in 1515 flourished under the liberal and humane regime of Mohammedan rulers. The presses that had been established in the Slavonic lands, at Prague in 1518, Cracow 1534, Lublin 1559, did as well as was possible in the midst of barbarism. At Amsterdam an important press was established in 1627 under the direction of the distinguished Menasseh ben Israel, and it was to this press above all others that the presses of Italy yielded their importance. Amsterdam was a typical Northern community of free men on a free soil, where Jews driven from Southern Europe by the intolerant followers of the Church were free to contribute their share to the intellectual, mercantile and industrial life of the community. The city of Frankfurt am Main although not specially distinguished for its press became the great Hebrew book market for its fairs brought together in large numbers the Jews of Germany and the Slavonic States. Notwithstanding the rivalry of other cities, it has maintained a respectable position in this field even to this day.

The conditions that prostrated the press at Venice affected the whole Italian peninsula. Padua and Verona which in 1405 had come under the

* Perles "Beitraege" p. 231.

dominion of Venice were completely dependent on the policy of that great city. In neither of these cities were Hebrew books printed until 1563 when Lorenzo Pasquato printed the "Way of Faith"—the first of the five books printed in Padua during the 16th and 17th centuries, a paltry number for the ancient city whose University was one of the great institutions of learning of the world. As Steinschneider puts it, there were in Padua nearly as many Hebrew printers as Hebrew books, for following the "Way of Faith" we have record of the Homilies of Rabbi Shemtob printed in 1567, the "Inheritance of Jacob" and a volume of Lamentations printed by Gaspare Crivellari in 1622–3 and a lexicon by Leon da Modena printed by Giulio Crivellari in 1640.*

The record of Verona is hardly more important. Its principal printer was Francesco dei Rossi, who during the six years from 1646 to 1652 with the assistance of a number of Jewish editors and proof-readers printed about ten books.† Before his

---

* Ersch & Gruber 46. He printed the first book at Este near Padua in 1643 and was probably the founder of the press at Bassano in 1657. Fumagalli 114. In 1739 a Hebrew grammar was printed there.

† "Thrones of the House of David" printed 1646, contains the following license:

Faccio fede io Sebastian Venier Avvocato à ci` deputo dal santissimo officio dell' Inquisitione d'haver veduto un libro hebreo in quarto intitolato Chisod lebeth David ciòe sedia della casa di David auttor Leon di David del Bene comincia ialzù e ciòe s'essalteranno le misericordia finisce uva lezion goel ciòe venira Sion recuperatore di tutti num 200.   Seb. Veron. qui sup. mari prop.

Commissarius sancti officii Venet.   Provicarius sancti officii Verona vidit has litteras.

Title page of "Thrones of the House of David"
Rossi, Verona, 1646

day there had been no Hebrew printing at Verona except in the years 1594–5 when Francesco delle Donne assisted by a member of the Bak family of printers at Prague published two books * at the press established by Sebastiano delle Donne in 1570.† A few Biblical books were followed in 1650 by the first part of an edition of the Mishnah which was finished in Leghorn, 1656. Notwithstanding this meagre record of Hebrew books, the Jews of Verona in all other respects were not behind other communities in their contributions to the history of their people. Their activities like their sufferings were those common to the times. Like the Jews of Padua they entered the ghetto as a result of priestly agitation in 1604, and like all other cities they added their quota to the list of martyrs faithful unto death.

In the cemetery of Verona there lies Rabbi Abraham Saba a Castilian scholar and the author of half a dozen widely read books. In 1497 he was exiled from Portugal, and his stirring words present a thrilling picture of what life meant to the Jews in Catholic countries.

"Then the anger of the Lord burnt against his people, so that all the Jews who were in Portugal were ordered by King Emanuel, God blot out his name and memory! to leave the land within a certain time. Nor was this enough; but after the King had commanded that boys and girls should

---

* Minhah Belulah, Midrash Tanhuma. Ersch & Gruber 62.
† Fumagalli 515.

be torn from their parents for baptism and Christian education, and then that we should be deprived of our synagogues, he ordered that all our books should be seized. So I brought all my books into the city of Porto (Oporto) in obedience to the royal decree; but yet I took my life in my hands by carrying with me to Lisbon the 'Commentary on the Law' which I had composed, as well as a commentary to the treatise 'Ethics of the Fathers' and one to the 'Five Scrolls.'

"But when I reached Lisbon all the Jews came to me and told me that it had been proclaimed to the community that every Jew who might be found with a book or with phylacteries in his possession would be put to death. So straightway before I entered the quarter outside the city I took these books in my hand; two brothers went with me and dug a grave among the roots of a blossoming olive tree; there we buried them. And although a tree flourishing with lovely fruit stood there yet because of the Law which was within it did I call it 'Tree of Sorrow'; for I had buried there all that was pleasant in my sight— the commentary on the Laws and the Commandments, more precious than gold, yea, than much fine gold. For in them I had found consolation for the loss of my two little ones torn from me by force to become unwilling converts. And I had said, 'These (books) are the inheritance of those who worship God; therefore must they be better for me than even sons and daughters.'"

A century of such persecution so debased the taste of Jewish booklovers that in the seventeenth century we find the presses of Italy putting out books that at an earlier day would have been thrown aside as waste paper and buried in the Genizah of some synagogue. Compare the poor battered types and the tasteless title borders of the "Thrones of the House of David," printed at Verona in 1646 at the press of Francesco dei Rossi by three Polish printers from Cracow or "A Token for Good," printed at Chieri in 1627 by the author, with the noble works of the presses of Soncino, Bomberg, Di Gara and the early Bragadini. The "Token for Good" appears to have been the work of the press of one Joseph ben Gerson Conzio, who also printed at Asti,* and whose son deserves mention. Angelo Brofferio an Italian student of typography notes that the press was established by Abraham Conzio the son of Joseph Conzio as a pious tribute to the memory of his father in order to print the works that he had left in manuscript.†

Chieri is in Piedmont ruled by the Dukes of Savoy, who had gradually absorbed most of the principal cities of Northern Italy and who even-

* Conzio printed at Chieri:—

1627	Ot letobah, Maagal tob
1628	Dibre Esther
1629	Mareh Hayim
1630	Mekom binah

At Asti: 1628   Shir Yehudith (J. E. 4 : 203).

At Asti he printed at the press of Virgilio and Francesco Giangrandi. Fumagalli 83.

† H. B. 17 : 14.

אות לטובה

ייטיכפנים לת:ידה ולתעודה בסדר הא׳פא כיתא
ואותיותיו כאותיותיה במניין אשר סיכנן טובה
וזרעויכון ושיחו יככן גלטוןכוטריקון

ותעמוהבה אגל האותות שתים אמרות ביומר
מסק למחוברות להורות ⊕ הס ימן יפה
למביכים

נס זה לטובה יתנא בו קול מירים ב חירות
להבין סודות בדבכי אנרות

נתין כיתן לחתן מהקטן יוסף בן האלוף
כמהיר גרטום קונטיוונגל

ועל ידו כרסם פה קיירי אשר במרינת
פיימונטי ירוס לההור לטובה
בשנת השנה הטובח

In Chieri con Licenza de 'Superio.

Title page of "A token for Good"
Concio, Chieri, 1627

tually mounted the throne of a united Italy. They seem to have been comparatively free from prejudice and were lenient in the enforcement of ecclesiastical decrees against Hebrew books. An old decree of the Duke, promulgated in 1572 at the instance of Messer Vitale di Sacerdoti whose Italian name probably hides the Hebrew name Hayyim Cohen, provided that the Jews might print keep in their houses and carry abroad all sorts of Hebrew books except those prohibited by the Apostolic Index of Pope Pius IV.* As the presses declined and the general condition of the people grew worse, it seems as though the heart were taken out of the erstwhile proud scions of the ancient House of Israel. Humility bred by the necessity for avoiding the constantly uplifted heavy hand of oppression breathes throughout their lives and colors their every act. Even within their own walls they hardly dared stand erect and their self abasement is reflected in peculiar oriental form of politeness in speaking of themselves. No man speaks of himself other than the "Katon," the "little one," and bursts into glowing eulogium of the person addressed. In the printed books this expression of self abasement became more and more extravagantly exaggerated until we have men of distinction speaking of themselves as "the old man who has not gained wisdom," † "the fox, son of the lion,"‡ "dust of the ground, like unto nothing-

* R. E. J. 5 : 227–236.

† Meshullam b. Abraham Pinkerli in Hilkhot Ketannot 1704.

‡ Jacob b. Samuel Hagiz, ibid.

ness," * "a worm, not a man," † "the little one and poorest among the poor,"‡"a tail of the lions,"¶ "the lowly one who has no knowledge of books but gropes among them like a blind man."** The books themselves bear traces of the degeneration of the taste of the publisher and readers. To what other cause can be ascribed their uncritical blindness than to the general depression of spirit and wretchedness of life that accompanied and followed the wars pestilence and religious oppression under which the Jew suffered much more than any other element of the people.

The struggle for mere existence absorbed all active energy; their little leisure was devoted to charity and prayer; there was no time for things of beauty. When David b. Rafael Hayim Bueno printed a prayer book in 1706 at the Bragadini press, he proudly speaks of its beautiful type; in fact the type is anything but beautiful. So at a later date Benjamin b. Aaron Polacco prints a manual for the night service of Hoshaanah Rabbah and Shabuot with the poorest types. The publication in 1712 of the "Daughter of the King" and the "Holy Seed" at the Bragadini press illustrates one aspect of this general condition of depression. Solomon b. David Altaras the corrector records

* Abraham b. Solomon Haber Tob in Responsa of Meir Lublin 1618.
† Judah b. Moses Naftali in Pentateuch 1560.
‡ Jacob b. Josefa Sorsina of Castellaz in Tanna debe Eliyahu 1598.
¶ Leon Modena in Hahinukh, 1601.
** Mordecai b. Benzion Ghirondi.

that the printing of the book began at Frankfurt but before it was finished the Frankfurt Judengasse was burned* and the people barely escaped. The unfinished books in the house of the Christian printer were saved and were taken to Venice there to be finished at the Bragadini press by Menahem Polacco.

The Polacco family of printers whose names appear in many books during this century were as the name indicates Polish Jews. Menahem and his brother Benjamin sons of Aaron Polacco † and Menahem b. Isaac Polacco printed a number of books until the sixth decade.

The family of Foa of Sabbioneta threw out branches that flourished in Venice and Pisa. Dr. Isaac Foa of Venice had books especially printed for his little five year old son Gad for his pleasure and instruction in 1735 and for some years thereafter ‡ and Dr. Samuel Foa who likewise had a son Gad did the same for him.¶ Gad son of Isaac Foa who printed for the Bragadini-Vendramin presses, in turn had books printed for his son Isaac in 1760** and in 1762†† and seems to have had a

* Jany 14–15, 1711. See Kracauer, Die Gesch. d. Judengasse in Frankf. a M. p. 334.

† "Stampator Ebraico in Cà Bragadini." See license printed in "Parts of Mishneh Torah" 1740.

‡ 1735 Selihot. 1739 Bible.

¶ 1736 Arba Taaniyot, ornamented with the Foa arms, a palm tree with Magen David and two lions rampant similar to the printer's mark of Tobia Foa of Sabbioneta.

** Ozar Nehmad.

†† Sekhiyot hahemda.

press of his own as late as 1795.* Gad son of Samuel Foa preserved the tradition of the family by publishing school books printed at both Vendramin and Bragadini presses,† published in 1778 Rashi's commentary on portions of the Bible. In 1785 he had established a press of his own at Pisa known as the Stamperia Fua or Foa.‡ He was followed at Pisa by members of the Molcho family, Samuel & Joseph who printed several books aided by Jacob Tobiana and Jacob Nunez Vais.¶ At Mantua the d'Italia family resumed printing about the end of the second decade of the Eighteenth century assisted by Benjamin Polacco of Venice.**

* Maamadot veshir hayihud.

† See Hemed Elohim 1720.

‡ Meil Zedaka, Bigda Kodesh. Partial list of Jewish printers, compositors and correctors at Bragadini press:—

1700	Simha Calimani
	Zalkaman b. Yekutiel Richetti
1700–46	Meir di Zara
1707	Moses Hai b. Joseph Venturin
1712–19	Solomon b. David Altaras
1712–60	Menahem b. Aaron Ashkenazi Polacco
	Benjamin b. Aaron Ashkenazi Polacco
1720	Hananiah Marun
	David b. Rafael Hayim Bueno
1720–78	Gad b. Samuel Foa
1720–60	Mordecai b. Solomon Civita
1741	Isaac Foa
1760	Menahem b. Isaac Polacco
1760–2	Isaac b. Gad Foa
1795	Gad b. Isaac Foa

¶ 1810   Amer naki

      Mahzor (Tunis rite)

   1818   Mazref Lasekhel

Sine dato   Oheb Mishpat

      Mishpat Zedek

** 1724–27.

Dr. Rafael Hayim d'Italia conducted the press for about fifty years and was succeeded by his son Eliezer Solomon d'Italia likewise a physician who printed until near the beginning of the 19th century.   Perhaps the most important work of this press was the Minhat Shai 1742–44 a grammatical work by Jedidiah Solomon Norzi.*

The press at Leghorn, however, which began about the middle of the seventeenth century was to play a more important part because it became the only Italian source of supply for the peninsula and the Orient.   Its productions, nearly all liturgical and Kabbalistic, had neither beauty nor intrinsic value and were intended to satisfy the simple tastes of a people living for the time far beyond the cultural influence of the best in their own literature.

Under the enlightened policy of the Duke of Tuscany Leghorn received a great influx of Jews

* Partial list of Mantua publications:—

1723	Shulhan Arukh
1724	Kelale hadikduk
1737	Seliha Yafah
1740	Seder Nahon
1742–44	Minhat Shai
1744	Pene Yizhak
1777	Seder hehaarakhah
1778	Shir Yedidut
1781	Psalms
1785	Rashe habekhain
1785	Kerobot for Simhat Torah
1788	Prayers for victory of Joseph II's Army

Steinschneider mentions Emunat Hahamim printed by Alb. Panzoni the archducal printer at the press of San Benedetto. Cat. Bodl. 2286.

Title page of Zophenat Paaneah
Martinelli, Venice, 1661

who had contributed largely towards its importance
as a commercial centre.   From about 1650 to 1660
Jedidiah b. Isaac Gabbai author of the work entitled Kaf Nahat maintained a press known as the
press "del Kaf Nahat". * His books bore a
shield with six flowers and the arms of the Duke
and his printer's mark, three crowns and the motto
"These are three crowns but the crown of a good
name is above all of them", testifies to the proper
pride of the man of good fame.

For nearly a century, no Hebrew books appeared at Leghorn.   In 1740 Rafael Meldola and
a partner named Ricci established a press† and since
then up to the present Leghorn has continued to

* He published among other books the following:—
        1650   Asharot
        1656   Ez Hayim
                 Responsa of David Simra
                 Dabar beitto
                 Tur Pitda
                 Toldot Adam
        1658   Keneset Hagedolah
        1660   Yalkut Shimeoni
† 1740   Kinat Soferim
           Seder Tikkun Shobebim
           Kontres Hok leyisrael
  1742   Hose Zion
  1743   Seder Hamizmorim
           Seder Arba Taaniyot
  1745   Shiba Enayim
Correctors and printers:—
         Isaac b. Moses di Paz
         David Hayim b. Samuel Bazi Cohen
         Moses b. Rafael Meldola
         David b. Solomon Hassan
         Zebi b. Joseph Hacohen of Hamburg

supply Cabbalistic books and liturgical works for the African, Asiatic as well as Italian Jews. At the same time another press was established by Eliezer Saadon which seems to have lasted for about fifty years during a portion of which he had as partner Abraham Isaac Castello.* Among other printers were Abraham Meldola,† Moses Athias,‡ Carlo Giorgi,¶ Giovanni Vincenzo Fal-

* 1743   LeDavid Emet
  1780   Letters of Moses Zacut
  1787   Veshob Hakohen
  1788   Derekh Yeshara
  1796   Shomer Mussar
The following approbation appears in the letters of Moses Zacut:
Os Muy ill. S. S. Parnassim, Sed.
Ulst (Vist) a Escanià feita e establesida pelos S. S. Hahamim nella firmados em ordem aò Decr. de S. S. do dià 3 Jullio 1780 do theor a qual.
Vist e consid. quanto.
Decretarao e Decretando aprovarao e aprovao ditta Escania tal qual em ella e a Mesma permetterao imprimirse respectivamente nos libros de que se tratta juntamente com esta approvacao de S. S. Muy Ill. affirm. e tudo ec. omni ec.
                        Isaac Vita Recanati P. P.
                        Paltiel Semah
                        Isaque Vais Villa Real
                        Moisè Correa Belmonte
                        Liorne em 16 Jullio 1780
    Foy Leido e publicado presente Decr. por mi abaixo assignado Cancell. presentes os S. S. Reuben Isurun Lopeo e Mordohai Marache. Test.   Manuel Nunes Cancell.
  † 1743   Shibhe Todah
  ‡ 1762   Hemdat Yamim   1766   Siah Yizhak
    Compositors:—
                        Moses b. Jona Ashkenazi of Constantinople
                        Joseph b. Abraham Ashkenazi of Furth
                        Moses Hai b. Jacob Rafael Milol.
  ¶ 1772   Hokhmat hamisken   1776   Korban Hagigah
    1773   Yefe Nof   1779   Hamakhria
    Printer, Moses Hai b. Rafael Milol
    Publisher, Jacob b. Isaac Nunez Vais.

erno,* and Jacob Nunez Vais, who after having published at the presses of the others entered into partnership with the founder of the Livornese press the aged Rafael Meldola.†

In the nineteenth century the press at Leghorn prospered steadily and is today the most important Hebrew press in Italy. Moses Joshua b. Jacob Tobianna was the first of the new printers of this century; and his press after a long career ‡ was bought and continued by Israel Costa & Co.¶ whose business was in turn bought by the son of Rabbi Abraham Baruch Piperno and continued under the old firm name.**

Eliezer b. Menahem Ottolenghi who called himself "printer and bookseller," a designation adopted by all the Livornese printers, established a press which had a successful career of about twenty

* 1777   Mahne Reuben
  1789   Tikkun Soferim
  1790   Shaar haheshek
  1797   Derekh Yesharah
  Publisher, Jacob Nunez Vais.

† 1784   Abodat Hatamid
  1791   Likute tehillim

‡ 1822   Mesillat Yesharim
  1840   Hadar Zekenim

¶ 1867   Letters of Azulai
  1868   Maase Shaashuim
  1878   Petah enayim
  1891   Rokheb Arabot
  1892   Shibhe Pesah

** H. B. 6 : 109.

years,* and was continued by his heirs.† Solomon Belforte & Co.,‡ and Elijah Benamozegh ¶ are two important printers of our times, and with a mere mention of two of the earlier printers Sanson Gentilomo ** and Jacob b. Judah Ashkenazi & Brother,†† we may close our list of printers of Leghorn.

Here and there attempts were made under varying conditions to print Hebrew with but little

* 1824　Pirke Abot
　1830　Mibhar hamaamarim
　1831　Pene hamayim
　1834　Bible with Italian marginal translation of difficult words. A copy of a similar work published by the Bragadini press in 1739
　1836　Tikkune Shabbat
　1839　Maor veshemesh
† 1858　Sheber bath Ammi
‡ 1836　Moade Adonai
　1841　Kerie Moed
　1846　Aseret hadebarim
　1858　Maskil lemosheh
　1864　Nora Tehillot
　1873　Hanokh lanaar
　1878　Megalle Amukot mini hoshekh
　1879　Letters of Saadya
　1884　Sabua tob
　1891　Haggadar (Tunis rite)
　1892　Canticles
¶ 1852　Sas anokhi
　1858　Sebahim Shelamim
　　　　Psalms
　1861　Hamebasser
　1864　Beer Yizhak
　　　　Zikhron Yerushalayim
　1866　Hesed veemet
　1890　Masat Benjamin
** 1838　Psalms.
†† 1857　Seder Bene Yisrael.

success. To Ferrara one time famous for its Hebrew press came Girolamo Filoni from Ficarolo in 1693.* After printing one Hebrew book,† a prayer book compiled by two Mantuan Jews, he melted his Hebrew letters and made Latin letters of them,‡ an act that tells its own tale without need of further comment. In Montefiascone a town lying a few miles north of Viterbo the press of the Episcopal Seminary printed a Hebrew grammar in 1706 dedicated to the founder of the seminary library, the Cardinal Marcantonio Barbadico. In Florence the court printer Francesco Moücke a litterateur and scholar ¶ printed a Hebrew prayer book with new type for Joseph Gabbai Villareal and his brother in 1715 by special permission and favor of the Duke Giovanni Gasto di Medici. Witness the long Latin privilegium which is printed in the book.**

* Fumagalli 129.
† Siddur Miberakhah.
‡ Ersch & Gruber 45.
¶ Fumagalli 147.
** Privilegium to Seder Tefillot Firenze 475. Press of Francesco Moücke.

JOANNES GASTO
Dei Gratia
Magnus Dux Etruriae, etc.

Cum Franciscus Moücke Typographus Florentinus, necnon in hac Civitate Librorum Negociator Nobis humiliter exposuerit se Libros Hebraicos, & Rascenses summa cum impensa typis editurum, & timens ne ab aliorum Typographorum arte aliquid detrimenti huic novo Operi inferatur; inde preces Nobis porrexerit, ut lege ad decennium valitura sub certae poenae sanctione interdiceremus, ne in ullis nostrarum Ditionum Civitatibus, vel locis praedicti Libri tam editi, quam interum per dictum Moucke edendi, imprimerentur; Nos animo

In the 19th century Florence again saw a Hebrew press established by Rabbi Hananya Elhanan Cohen or as his Italian name runs Graziadio Vita Anania Coën at which he the "pastor of the holy flock" printed a special prayer on the rededication of the synagogue in 1828.*   In his native Reggio where he established a Rabbinical school, he printed school books on religion and ethics † at the press of Davolio.

versantes hoc in perenne decus Etruriae nostrae fore cessurum, & laudabilem aequitatem, qua Summi Principes novorum Operum Auctoribus consulere solent, sequentes & justae supradicti Francisci Moücke petitioni clementer annuere volentes, universis, & singulis Impressoribus, Typographis, Bibliopolis, & hujusmodi Negociatoribus Ditiones nostras habitantibus, seu frequentantibus, & ipsorum cuilibet mandamus, & prohibemus praedictos Libros jam editos, quam iterum per dictum Moucke edendos, sine speciali ejusdem Francisci Moückə consensu, & voluntate in omnibus, & quibuscumque Dominiis nostris, etiam in Civitate Pistorii, ejusque Comitatu & Montaneis, & in quocumque alio loco jurisdictioni nostrae subjecto licet de eo specifica, & expressa mentio fieri deberet, imprimere, aut imprimi facere, nec alibi impressor venales habere, & tenere audeat per Annos decem enumerandos ab infrascripta die sub poena Scutorum quinquaginta de Libris septem pro Scuto pro quolibet Opere suto, sive non suto, & pro qualibet vice, & amissionis eorundem, cuius poenae quarta pars Fisco nostro, & magnae nostrae Ducali Camerae, altera Magistratui, seu Judici condemnanti, seu exigenti, altera Privilegiato supradicto, altera vero pars Accusatori, seu Denuntiatori publico, seu secreto applicetur, & acquiratur, contrariis quibuscumque non obstantibus.

In quorum sidem praesens Diploma per infrascriptum Secretarium Senatoremque nostrum expediri, & plumbei Sigilli appensione muniri jussimus, & Nostra etiam manu firmavimus.

Datum Florentiae in Nostro majori Palatio anno Salutiferae Incarnationis millesimo septingentesimo trigesimo quarto, die prima Mensis Decembris, Magni vero Nostri Ducatus Anno XII.

JO. GASTO,
Carolus Ginori a Secretis & Senator

* Nepi & Ghirondi 104.
† Lekah tob, Shebilè Emunah.

[405]

Padua also saw a revival of its ancient press in the 19th century by Antonio Bianchi * and by Francesco Sacchetto.†

So no doubt other towns might be named that printed Hebrew during the 19th and the present century, for my researches in the history of the recent presses has been quite superficial and many data may have escaped my notice.

Enough however has been said to indicate the revival of interest and activity in Hebrew typography in the beautiful land which saw the beginning of the art and saw its destruction through the pitiless hand of the demon of religious fanaticism and racial antipathy. With the Risorgimento came the uplifting of the long down-trodden Jew, and with his renascence came a renewed interest in his literature and history, though it must be said by no means in the measure that might have been expected. For the Italian Jew seems to be first an Italian and his intense patriotism and the absence of any of the ancient barriers to free intercourse with his fellows and participation in their common activities have in a measure made him indifferent to his peculiar history and literature. We find him obliged to begin again as though he were a child, this ancient trouble-worn and gray-haired Israel, and his presses print prayer books and school books in Hebrew and essays in the

* 1855 Isaiah with translation & commentary by Samuel David Luzzatto.
  1862 Pirke-Abot with translation by Lelio della Torre.
† 1872 Pentateuch with Italian Trans. by Sam. David Luzzatto.

vernacular. He has forgotten much, nearly all of his ancient store of knowledge. For during that period of his history following the Renaissance he was beaten and starved and hunted like an animal and his memory of the things once dear to him was almost obliterated. His printers made books for him without beauty or taste and he knew it not. Their poor type and inartistic devices far removed from the ancient sources of technical excellence did not displease him. No one apparently knew enough to cut new types or cut them well and no one cared for fine paper, clear ink, correct texts or even press work. The era of the cowled inquisitor had followed the days of the rebirth of the white naked gods of Greece and all Italy was for the Christians one vast confessional, for the Jews a chain of poverty stricken terrorized ghettos. The period of mania has passed away, the incubus of clericalism is disappearing. A united and free Italy awaits its happy destiny. "She feels her ancient breath, and the old blood move in her immortal veins."

When Elijah Benamozegh, a preacher and rabbi, established a printing press and began the publication of Hebrew books in the middle of the 19th century, Steinschneider, that unenthusiastic temperate critic and scholar said of him "It is well known that the first printers like the first copyists were scribes and scholars. Portuguese brethren have always kept the praiseworthy combination of arts or industry with letters and it is a pleasure to see a Rabbino-predicatore and author not disdaining to work with voice, pen and press. Would that Germany's presses came into such competent hands!" *

In these days the voice of the Renaissance printers again is heard in the very accents of old. Says the printer Israel Costa in 1878 † "May there be many in Israel to publish good books now hidden and buried in manuscript in the world's libraries. Thank God that in Austria and Prussia they have done valiant work and have saved them and if Italian Jews of means would do something, let them emulate Davide Frizzi.‡ How good is our position" he adds in a burst of enthusiastic patriotism, "and pleasant our lot for there is nothing lacking in the Kingdom of Italy, may its glory be exalted and may it attain the greatness of the most exalted Kingdom in the world."

Here ends the story of the Hebrew press in Italy. At its very beginning more than four hundred years ago it attained its highest perfection. After more than four centuries through bitter vicissitudes and heartbreaking discouragement it strives anew, now feebly now more vigorously, to realize the ideal and aim of the old printer, in response to an immemorial desire of the people of the Book, "to make books, many and without ceasing."

* H. B. 2 : 12.

† In colophon of Petah Enayim.

‡ The author of the book, a philosophical, physical and mathematical elucidation of many matters contained in the Talmud,—the author is a Royal Engineer and a Dr. of Phil. and Med.

BIBLIOGRAPHY

Principal works consulted in the preparation of this book. Other authorities are cited in the footnotes.

ASULAI, H. J. D.
"Shem Hagedolim" Frankfurt-am-Main, 1847.

BACHER, W.
"Die Hebräische Sprachwissenschaft vom 10 bis zum 16. Jahrhundert." Trier, 1892.

BENJACOB, I. A.
"Ozar Hasefarim" Wilna, 1880.

BERLINER, A.
"Aus meiner Bibliothek." Frankfurt-am-Main, 1889.
"Censur and Confiscation Hebräischer Bücher im Kirchenstaate." Berlin, 1891.
"Geschichte der Juden in Rom" Frankfurt-am-Main, 1893.
"Gutachten Ganganelli's-Clemens XIV-in Angelegenheit der Blutbeschuldigung der Juden." Berlin, 1888.
"Ueber den Einfluss des ersten hebräischen Buchdrucks auf den Cultus und die Cultur der Juden." Frankfurt-am-Main, 1896.

BIALLOBLOTSKY, C. H. F.
"The Chronicles of Rabbi Joseph ben Joshua ben Meir the Sphardi." London, 1836.

BLAU, L.
"Studien zum althebräischen Buchwesen." Budapest, 1902.

BROWN, H. F.
"Studies in the History of Venice." New York, 1907.

"The Venetian Printing Press." New York & London, 1891.

CARMOLY, E.

"Annalen der hebräischen Typographie von Riva di Trento." Frankfurt-am-Main, 1868.

CHWOLSON, D.

"Reshith Maase Hadefus Beyisrael." Warsaw, 1897.

CONFORTE, D.

"Kore Ha-Dorot" (ed. Cassel) Berlin, 1846.

DEPPING, G. B.

"Die Juden in Mittelalter" Stuttgart, 1843.

DE ROSSI, G. B.

"Annales Hebraeo-Typographici Sec. XV." Parma, 1795.

"Annales Hebraeo-Typographici ab an. MDI ad MDXL" Parma, 1790.

"Annali Ebreo-Typografici di Cremona." Parma, 1808.

"Annali Ebreo-Tipografici di Sabbioneta sotto Vespasiano Gonzaga." Parma, 1780.

"De Typographia Hebraeo-Ferrariensi Commentarius Historicus" Parma, 1780.

FREIMANN, A.

"Daniel Bomberg und seine hebräische Druckerei in Venedig." Z. H. B. 10 : 32.

"Ueber Hebräische Inkunabeln." Leipzig, 1902.

FUMAGALLI, G.

"Lexicon Tpographicum Italiae; Dictionnaire Geographique d'Italie pour servir a l'histoire de l'imprimerie dans ce pays." Florence, 1905.

FÜRST, J.

"Bibliotheca Judaica." Leipzig, 1863.

GANS, D.

"Zemah David." Warsaw, 1859.

GRAETZ, H.
"Geschichte der Juden." Leipzig.

GUICCIARDINI
"History of the Wars of Italy" London 1756.

GUBERNATIS, A. DE
"Materiaux pour servir a l'histoire des etudes orientales en Italie." Paris, 1876.

GÜDEMANN, M.
"Geschichte des Erziehungswesen und der Cultur der Juden in Italien während des Mittelalters" Vienna, 1884.

HEILPRIN, J.
"Seder Hadorot." Warsaw, 1897.

HEBRÄISCHE BIBLIOGRAPHIE (ED. STEINSCHNEIDER)

JEWISH ENCYCLOPEDIA

JEWISH QUARTERLY REVIEW.

JOST, I. M.
"Geschichte des Judenthums und seiner Sekten" Leipzig, 1859.

JOSEPH, HA COHEN,
"Emek Habaca" (ed. Letteris) Vienna, 1852.

KRISTELLER, P.
"Die Italienischen Buchdrucker und Verlegerzeichen bis 1525." Strassburg, 1893.

LOEW, L.
"Graphische Requisiten und Erzeugnisse bei den Juden." Leipzig, 1870.

MANZONI, G.
"Annali Tipografici dei Soncino." Bologna, 1883–1886.

MICHAEL, H. J.
"Or Ha-Hayim." Frankfurt-am-Main, 1891.

NEPI & GHIRONDI
"Toledot gedole Yisrael" Trieste, 1853

BIBLIOGRAPHY

Omont, H.
"Specimens de charactères Hébreux gravés a Venise et a Paris par Guillaume le Bé (1546–1574)" Paris, 1887.

Perles, J.
"Beiträge zur Geschichte der Hebräischen und Armäischen Studien," München, 1884.

Putnam, G. H.
"Books and their Makers during the Middle Ages." New York and London, 1897.

Popper, W.
"The Censorship of Hebrew Books." New York, 1899.

Rabbinovicz, R. N.
"Maamar al hadfasat ha-Talmud." Munich, 1877.

Reusch, F. H.
"Die Indices Librorum Prohibitorum des sechzehnten Jahrhunderts." Tübingen, 1886.

Revue des Etudes Juives.

Sacchi, F.
"I Tipografi Ebrei di Soncino." Cremona 1877.

Schwab, M.
"Les Incunables orientaux et les impressions orientales au commencement du XVI siecle." Paris, 1883.

Soave, M.
"Dei Soncino celebri tipografi italiani nei secoli XV, XVI." Venezia, 1878.

Steinschneider, J.
"Einiges über R. Samuel Usque's Trost Israel's in seinen Trübsalen." Berlin, 1893.

Steinschneider, M.
"Catalogus Librorum Hebraeorum in Bibliotheca Bodleiana." Berlin, 1852-60.

"Jüdische Typographie und Jüdischer Buchhandel."
in Ersch und Gruber's Encyclopedia vol. 28 pp.21–94.

VOGELSTEIN UND RIEGER.
"Geschichte der Juden in Rom."   Berlin, 1896.

WIENER, S.
"Bibliographie der Oster-Haggadah. 1500–1900"
St. Petersburg, 1902.

WOLF, J. C.
"Bibliotheca Hebrea."   Hamburg & Leipzig, 1715–
1733.

ZEITSCHRIFT FÜR HEBRÄISCHE BIBLIOGRAPHIE.

ZUNZ, L.
"Zur Geschichte und Literatur."   Berlin, 1845.

INDEX

INDEX

INDEX